THE NEW LAWS OF OUTER SPACE

This book maps out the moral, legal and societal issues brought forth by the use of autonomous systems such as AI and smart robots in outer space.

Humanity is on the brink of a new space era in which projects for permanent human colonies on the Moon and space missions with autonomous AI systems will soon become a reality. Principles and provisions of international space law fall increasingly short in tackling this scenario. Experts and institutions have recommended improvements to the legal framework, such as new international agreements, or policies that would not require any amendment to conventional law. Most of the time, such proposals and recommendations overlook the challenges posed by technology and how autonomous and intelligent systems in outer space require moral and legal standards of their own.

This book argues that the traditional focus on satellite communications, space-related services, and the appropriability of celestial resources needs to be integrated by new laws of outer space regulating cybersecurity law and environmental law, data governance and consumer protection. The new laws of outer space will increasingly concern the development of new standards for the behaviour and decision-making of AI systems and smart robots, with and without humans aboard deep space missions and in next-generation colonies.

What laws shall govern us out there, in a new terra incognita? This is the question that the book sets out to answer.

The New Laws of Outer Space

Ethics, Legislation, and Governance in the Age of Artificial Intelligence

Ugo Pagallo

•HART•
OXFORD • LONDON • NEW YORK • NEW DELHI • SYDNEY

HART PUBLISHING

Bloomsbury Publishing Plc

Kemp House, Chawley Park, Cumnor Hill, Oxford, OX2 9PH, UK

1385 Broadway, New York, NY 10018, USA

29 Earlsfort Terrace, Dublin 2, Ireland

HART PUBLISHING, the Hart/Stag logo, BLOOMSBURY and the Diana logo are trademarks of Bloomsbury Publishing Plc

First published in Great Britain 2024

A catalogue record for this book is available from the British Library.

A catalogue record for this book is available from the Library of Congress.

Library of Congress Control Number: 2024944050

ISBN: HB: 978-1-50997-618-8
ePDF: 978-1-50997-620-1
ePub: 978-1-50997-619-5

Typeset by Compuscript Ltd, Shannon

To Eleonora,
Sun of my life

ACKNOWLEDGEMENTS

This book can be traced back to 2017. By then, I had become (and still am) a proud member of the Scientific Committee of Turin's Planetarium in Pino Torinese, a small town 30 minutes from downtown Turin, in the hills towards East and the Po Valley. The concept of planetariums was developed throughout the centuries through the goodwill of amateur astrologers and, in the early 1910s, was refined by Oskar von Miller's project on 'rotating star spheres'. Theatres were built for educational and entertainment purposes to introduce everyday people to the marvels of astronomy. A hundred years later, this introduction has also related to the technological impact of our species in outer space. Shows include the basics of celestial navigation and the 'night sky' put at risk by myriad satellites. Infini.to – the Planetarium of Pino Torinese – has represented the ideal environment in which the ideas of this book on astronomy and technology have matured. A special thanks to all members of the Scientific Committee and the staff. We all miss our founder president, Attilio Ferrari.

Over the past five years, I have been also discussing different elements of this book with several colleagues and friends around the world, including eight scholars in four continents: Gianmaria Ajani, Woody Barfield, Pompeu Casanovas, Cristina Dalle Ore, Massimo Durante, Patrick Lin, Marco Ricolfi and Fumio Shimpo. A special thanks to my wife Eleonora Bassi who started reading the first draft of this book in the summer of 2023. This final version is the result of two waves of amendments in December 2023 and March 2024, as occurred with the consolidated text of the Artificial Intelligence Act in EU law in roughly the same months or weeks. Eleonora's comments, suggestions and vision helped me to strike a more proper balance between the new challenges of outer space and the old wisdom of classic thinkers: Aristotle, Plutarch and Seneca. I admit that the aesthetics of outer space still remain between the lines of this book.

Also, thanks to the 'law and technology' think tank of young scholars at the University of Turin. Our discussions on environmental sustainability (Jacopo Ciani), data governance (Ludovica Paseri) and strict space law (Giovanni Tricco) have been source of inspiration. Also, thanks to the English check by Beatrice Balzola and the team at Hart Publishing, in particular, Roberta Bassi and Verity Stuart. Finally, thanks to the curiosity of students on my courses and at my lectures around the world. These students will be my age, approximately, in 2060. This is the long-term view of this book. Since my guess about what we should normatively expect in outer space covers the 2030s and some aspects of the 2040s, I entrust such students with the legacy of tackling the problems of this book in the 2050s and 2060s, when they are 'our age'.

Despite the number of inputs by reviewers, colleagues and friends, I am conscious that the book may still contain imprecisions, ambiguities or mistakes. This eventuality reminds me of the old joke of professors congratulating students for the errors made in their PhD theses. The joke spread in early 2023 due to the first use of large language models and what EU law dubs 'general purpose AI models' passing routinely bar exams on a monthly basis. The law professor thanks a student because all mistakes demonstrate that the student did not use the magical powers of generative AI to write the thesis. Some inaccuracies prove that no ChatGPT was at work. Any imprecisions, ambiguities or mistakes in this book are similarly mine.

Martiniana Po
Easter 2024

CONTENTS

ACRONYMS

ACT	Automated Cooperative Trajectories
AI	Artificial Intelligence
A/IS	Autonomous and Intelligent Systems
AIA	Artificial Intelligence Act
AIDA	Special Committee on Artificial Intelligence in a Digital Age
ASAT	Anti-Satellite Weapons
AV	Autonomous Vehicle
CCW	Certain Conventional Weapons
CER	Critical Entities Resilience Directive
CIA	US Central Intelligence Agency
CIMON	Crew Interactive Mobile Companion
CFR	Charter of Fundamental Rights of the European Union
CNN	Cable News Network
CNSA	China National Space Administration
COMSAT	Communications Satellite Corporation
COPUOS	UN Committee on the Peaceful Uses of Outer Space
COTS	Commercial off the Shelf (cheap space components)
CSA	Canadian Space Agency
CJEU	Court of Justice of the European Union
DARPA	US Defense Advanced Research Projects Agency
DORA	Digital Operational Resilience Act
DRACO	Demonstration Rocket for Agile Cislunar Operations
DRM	Digital Rights Management
DSDG	UNDESA Division for Sustainable Development Goals

EASA	European Aviation Security Agency
ECSS	European Cooperation for Space Standardization
EGNOS	European Geostationary Navigation Overlay Service
ENISA	European Union Agency for Cybersecurity
ENMOD	Convention on the Prohibition of Military or Any Other Hostile Use of Environmental Modification Techniques
ESA	European Space Agency
ESA/SCC	System for the specification, qualification, and procurement of the electrical, electronic, and electro-mechanical components for use in space programmes
ESPI	European Space Policy Institute
EUMETSAT	European Organisation for the Exploitation of Meteorological Satellites
EuroQCI	European Quantum Communication Infrastructure
EUSPA	European Union Agency for the Space Programme
EUTELSAT	European Telecommunications Satellite Organization
FAA	US Federal Aviation Administration
FCC	US Federal Communications Commission
GDPR	General Data Protection Regulation
GEDACS	Global Elevation Data Adaptive Compression Systems
GEO	Geosynchronous Orbit
GEOSS	Global Earth Observation System of Systems
GGE	Group of Governmental Experts
GIS	Geographic Information System
GLEX	Global Space Exploration Conference
GNSS	Global Navigation Satellite System
GOVSATCOM	EU Governmental Satellite Communications
GPS	Global Positioning System
HLEG	High-Level Expert Group
HRI	Human–Robot Interaction

IADC	Inter-Agency Space Debris Coordination Committee
IAU	International Astronomical Union
ICANN	Internet Corporation for Assigned Names and Numbers
ICAO	International Civil Aviation Organization
ICT	Information and Communication Technology
IEEE	Institute of Electrical and Electronics Engineers
IGA	ISS Intergovernmental Agreement
iGCAS	Improved Ground Collision Avoidance Systems
IHL	International Humanitarian Law
ILRS	International Lunar Research Station
IMSO	International Mobile Satellite Organisation
INMARSAT	International Maritime Satellite Organization
INTELSAT	International Telecommunication Satellite Organization
IoE	Internet of Everything
IoT	Internet of Things
IRIS	EU Infrastructure for Resilience Interconnectivity Security by Satellite
ISO	International Standardization Organization
ISR	Intelligence, Surveillance and Reconnaissance missions
ISRO	Indian Space Research Organization
ISS	International Space Station
ITU	International Communication Union
JAXA	Japan Aerospace Exploration Agency
KA-SAT	Viasat's satellite network
LAWS	Lethal Autonomous Weapons Systems
LEO	Low Earth Orbit
LMGT	Lockheed Martin Global Telecommunications
MAPS	Multi-level Autonomous Piloting Systems
MHC	Meaningful Human Control

MIFR	Master International Frequency Register
ML	Machine Learning
NAS	National Airspace System
NASA	US National Aeronautics and Space Administration
NATO	North Atlantic Treaty Organization
NIS	Network and Information Systems
NOM4D	Novel Orbital and Moon Manufacturing, Materials and Mass-Efficient Design
Non-GSO	Non-Geosynchronous Satellite System
OCSE	Organization for Economic Co-operation and Development
ODMSP	Orbital Debris Mitigation Standard Practices
PAROS	Prevention of an Arms Race in Outer Space
PCA	Permanent Court of Arbitration
PLD	Product Liability Directive
QKD	Quantum Cryptographic Keys of Distribution
ROS	Russian Orbital Segment
Roscosmos	Russian Federal Space Agency
SASTIND	State Administration of Science, Technology and Industry for National Defense in China
SAW	Surface Acoustic Wave
SDG	Sustainable Development Goals
SEA	Single European Act
SESAR	Single European Sky Air Traffic Management Research
SNP	Space Notification and Plans Division
SPR	Space Publication and Registration Division
SSA	Space Situational Awareness
SSC	Space Systems Coordination Division
SSD	Space Services Department
SSN	Space Surveillance Network

SST	Space Surveillance and Tracking
STM	Space Traffic Management
TFEU	Treaty on the Functioning of the European Union
UAE	United Arab Emirates
UAS	Unmanned Aircraft Systems
UDHR	Universal Declaration on Human Rights
UNCLOS	UN Convention on the Law of the Sea
UNCOPUOS	UN Committee on Peaceful Use of Outer Space
UNDESA	UN Department of Economic and Social Affairs
UNIDIR	UN Institute for Disarmament Research
UNOOSA	UN Office for Outer Space Affairs
UN-SPIDER	UN Space-Based Information for Disaster Management and Emergency Response
USC	United States Code
USOS	ISS US Orbital Segment
VLOS	Visual Line-Of-Sight
VPN	Virtual Private Network
VSD	Value Sensitive Design
WCIT	World Conference on International Telecommunications
WIA	Well-Being Impact Assessment
WIPO	World Intellectual Property Organization

TABLE OF CASES

TABLE OF EU MATERIALS

TABLE OF INTERNATIONAL CONVENTIONS AND TREATIES

TABLE OF NATIONAL LEGISLATION

UNITED STATES

TABLE OF UNITED NATIONS MATERIAL

UN COPUOS – Committee on the Peaceful Uses of Outer Space

TABLE OF OTHER MATERIALS

Introduction

From time to time, human societies must address the classic question of how to govern a new space or territory. This book starts from the assumption that, with regard to the field of space law, we are currently facing one of these moments. This conjecture rests on: (i) the multiplication of space activities and the myriad satellites in orbit; (ii) new permanent stations around the Earth and the Moon by the mid-2030s; (iii) the interception of asteroids with their precious metals; down to (iv) the integration of the space and Earth environments, on the one hand, and space and cyberspace on the other hand. Autonomous spacecrafts equipped with artificial intelligence (AI) systems and smart robots – that can replicate themselves in deep space missions, even beyond the solar system – fulfil what, only a few years ago, looked like science fiction: the establishment of celestial colonies. For better or worse, a new generation of mass explorers and space tourists visiting the first hotels in lunar orbit may be expected soon.

Which laws should govern a new space or territory has often ignited extremely divisive controversies throughout the centuries. In the Western tradition, for example, the bittersweet relationship between Aristotle and his great disciple Alexander is particularly instructive in this respect. Aristotle had to take care of the laws of the 'new territories' that Alexander planned to annex. While Aristotle idealised the middle- or small-sized dimension of the political community (*polis*), Alexander built an amazing kingdom that extended from Greece to Egypt, Persia, Babylon and beyond. Whilst Aristotle sharply divided Greeks and Barbarians, Alexander aimed to integrate them. In *Parallel Lives*, Plutarch reports Alexander's view on who, between the pupil and the master, was the greatest.[1] What triggered the letter that Alexander sent to Aristotle when Alexander was already in Asia was the publication of some Aristotelian treatises:

> Alexander to Aristotle, greeting. You have not done well to publish your books of oral doctrine … For my part, I assure you, I had rather excel others in the knowledge of what is excellent, than in the extent of my power and dominion. Farewell.[2]

Scholars have wondered what Aristotle may have taught Alexander, and to what extent his teachings may have influenced the pupil: in the early 1800s, the German philosopher G.W.F. Hegel claimed that the political greatness of Alexander was the material transposition, so to speak, of the philosophical greatness of his Master. By contrast, more than a century later, Bertrand Russell declared that Aristotle's role

[1] Plutarch, *Plutarch's Lives*, translated by P Perrin (Cambridge, MA, Harvard University Press, 1967).
[2] ibid 7.4.

was irrelevant.[3] Although we may concede that, overall, Russell might have been right in claiming that Aristotle's teachings had little or no influence on Alexander's grand political and military plans, some of his publications suggest he might have taught and explained things which Alexander might have ignored. The rapid disaggregation of Alexander's kingdom soon after his death in 323 BCE – that is, the year before Aristotle's – draws attention to a crucial part of Aristotle's reflection, ie, the principles and rules that, according to him, should have been established in the political community, and moreover, the ways in which such principles and rules should have been preserved. As claimed in the sixth book of *Politics*:

> We must therefore employ the results obtained in the inquiries that we have made already [ie, in the fifth book of the *Politics*] into the causes of the preservation and the destruction of constitutions, and attempt in the light of those results to establish the safety of the state, carefully avoiding the things that cause destruction, and enacting such laws both written and unwritten.[4]

Drawing on the warnings of Aristotle, the inquiry of this book regarding the 'new laws of outer space' should not be understood in strictly legal terms. Instead, the analysis adopts a multidisciplinary approach to tackle the practical challenges of the field. In addition to legal expertise, the analysis comprehends ethics and psychology, philosophy of technology and computer science, the history of ideas and ethnology, politics and economics. The focus on the new laws of outer space must be grasped in accordance with the broader Aristotelian meaning of the word 'law', which includes the constitution, regulation and moral grounds of every political community, namely, the *politeia*, *nomos* and *ethos* of outer space activities.

In particular, as regards the first meaning of the new laws of outer space – ie, their *politeia* – the focus is on the basic norms and principles of the law. They regard the ways in which policies, procedures or standards are established and implemented in the public arena. In ancient times, this role was carried out by the founders of the political community. Among others, some of these legendary statesmen have been the Spartan Lycurgus (circa 820 BCE) and the Athenian Solon (638–558 BCE). In the modern ages, this was the endeavour of Jefferson and the other Founding Fathers who created the federal Constitution during the so-called 'second' American Revolution in the 1780s.[5] In the case of space-related activities, the constitutional tenets of the field must be traced back to the 1960s and 1970s with the first agreements of the international community: the Outer Space Treaty of 1967 and the Liability Convention of 1972, amongst others.

The second meaning of the laws of outer space has to do with enforceable statutes and legislation. The norms of national or regional law makers complement treaties and conventions of international space law. Multiple regulations related

[3] B Russell, *The Philosophy of Logical Atomism* (New York, Routledge, 1972).

[4] Aristotle, *Politics*, edited and translated by J Barnes (Princeton, Princeton University Press, 2017) 1319 B.

[5] JJ Ellis, *The Quartet: Orchestrating the Second American Revolution* (New York, Vintage, 2016).

to outer space activities have been adopted in the field of scientific research and national defence, as well as satellites and Earth remote sensing. Over the past few years, national and regional legislators, such as the European Union (EU), have strengthened such provisions with a new array of norms on cybersecurity and environmental protection, data privacy and machine safety, consumer law and product liability, up to the use of celestial resources. One of the thorniest issues raised by such national or regional legislation is whether and to what extent such *nomos* aligns with the general legal framework established at the international level.

The third meaning of the laws of outer space concerns the Aristotelian notion of *ethos* – that is, the moral grounds of the political community that hinge on what, according to the claims of meta-ethics and discussions of moral theories on notions of obligation, prohibition, or permission, is right or wrong. The *ethos* of space law also refers to the role of social customs and the agreements in political communities on values and principles that are at stake with the norms of legislators. The *ethos* of the community is essential in order to grasp not only the principles and rules that will govern human behaviour but also the ways in which such principles and rules can be preserved in accordance with Aristotle's warnings to Alexander.

The *ethos* of space law is arguably one of the most overlooked topics in the current debates on the new laws of outer space. This lack of attention is critical – especially among legal experts – because the resilience of the legal system largely depends on the moral grounds on which both the constitution and legal regulations lie. This book examines the manifold features of this side of the law with samples of sound international collaboration, soft law and customary law, and the emotions that the adventures of astronauts still evoke among their human fellows on Earth. The more the challenges caused by the commercialisation of space resources, the dual uses of technology with their military implications, or the crisis of authority in international space law suggest to scholars that we should amend the laws of outer space, the less its *ethos* can be underestimated. This is a lesson learned from ancient ages and modern times. The principles of international space treaties and conventions from the 1960s and 1970s drew on this very tradition when establishing space as the 'province of mankind' and astronauts as the 'envoys' of our species.

However, in addition to ethics, legislation and governance, attention must be drawn to another critical ingredient of the analysis: technology. Arguably, there would be no space law without the corresponding technologies. In addition to supporting infrastructure equipment and deep-space communication networks, in-space propulsion engines, satellites and spacecrafts, the increasing use of AI systems and other emerging technologies – for example, anthropomorphic robots – has disrupted the field since the mid-2010s. There are AI systems for orbit adjustments and collision avoidance, maintenance procedures and removal of space junk, manoeuvrability and optimisation of on-orbit services, space data processing and space-based services, and the support of human activities (for example, humanoid robots and other artificial companions for healthcare and the well-being of astronauts). The regulation of the behaviour and decision-making of this new kind of agent (for example, autonomous and intelligent systems) complements the regulation and governance of the traditional actors in the field, such as public organisations, governments and sovereign states in international space law, as well as private corporations and individuals in national space law. The unique features of AI systems – for example, autonomy and a certain degree of unpredictability – trigger new types of risk that affect both the *nomos* and *ethos* of space law. Such AI systems and smart robots represent the 'new Argonauts' of this book.

Space law experts must be attentive to the branches of the tree on which they sit. This is why the first chapter of this book is devoted to technology – namely, its requirements (what technology is supposed to be) and functions (what technology is called to do). Just as occurs with ethics and the forces of the market, and social customs and the law, we should not underestimate the power of technology as a regulatory system of its own. Furthermore, technology sets up the environment where further technologies interact, from information and communication technologies to barcodes, high-frequency trading systems, or myriad applications on the Internet of Things. By supplementing humans as users of products and services, we are no longer needed in the loop. This is not a problem per se. Civilian applications of autonomous systems – for example, rovers built to improvise their own ways across unspecified fields and obstacles on the Moon or Mars – suggest that autonomy is essential for space missions. However, increasingly autonomous artificial agents and systems require meaningful human control, especially in the military sector. How to strike a balance between the behaviour of autonomous and intelligent systems and meaningful human control over them is another of the thornier issues regarding the new laws of outer space.

Since the late 1950s, technology has raised the classic question of what laws should be adopted in a new domain of human activity and interaction. After land, sea and air, it is time for outer space. The book scrutinises 65 years of space law in order to understand the obsolescence of the international legal framework and the impact of technological innovation on this field. It is still an open issue as to what laws should be adopted in next-generation colonies and interplanetary missions populated by autonomous and intelligent systems by the mid-2030s. In the quest for the laws of new spaces, this book, which is divided into 10 chapters, is organised as follows. In addition to elements of philosophy of technology, Chapter 1 inspects the ancestors of space law, ie, aviation law and the rise of information technology. These fields are the strict predecessors of this enquiry over the laws of new spaces. Chapter 2 illustrates the law makers' response, namely the tenets of international space law laid down in the 1960s and 1970s, the deadlock in the field caused by the failure of the Moon Agreement in the 1980s, and the activation of national and regional law makers with their own regulations and intergovernmental conventions. Chapter 3 further examines this legal framework in connection with the privatisation trends that started in the 1990s. Roughly three-quarters of space-related activities today are conducted by the private sector. The legal impact of this privatisation draws attention to the private – as opposed to the criminal or military – side of the law with issues of jurisdiction, cross-waivers of liability, and arbitration clauses. National and international provisions of space law have simply fallen short in terms of coping with the staggering increase of space-based services and space-related activities, also considering current promises on next-generation space tourists, mass explorers, scientists or settlers.

Chapters 4 and 5 complete the inquiry into public and private actors of space law with the new generation of artificial agents and AI systems that, over the past decade, have begun to shape the field. Chapter 4 defines technology and clarifies how some of its crucial features, such as the autonomy of AI systems, may trigger problems of security, social acceptability and trust. Chapter 5 focuses on the legal impact of AI and smart robots in the fields of the laws of war – for example, international humanitarian law and civil liability. The aim of this part of the book is to explain its subtitle. Issues of ethics, legislation and governance of space activities and missions – ie, their *ethos*, *nomos* and *politeia* – must be grasped 'in the age of AI'. Most next-generation colonies and Mars missions will be undertaken by a panoply of such AI systems and robots by the 2030s and 2040s.

To further corroborate this claim, Chapter 6 considers both the US-led Artemis Accords from 2020 and the China-led International Lunar Research Station programme from 2021. These crucially depend on technological advancements that raise troublesome questions of morality, legality and geopolitics in outer space. The occupation of lunar places, the appropriation of meteorite resources and the protection of safety zones through military outposts on the Moon may sound futuristic, but they are not. Smart rovers, AI systems and self-assembling 3D bio-printers building artificial colonies on the Earth's natural satellite are not so distant – despite actually being 239,000 million miles away from the nearest government office. Chapters 7 and 8 illustrate why the bell has tolled here on Earth. We should be attentive to the twofold integration of space and Earth environments on the one hand, and of space and cyberspace on the other hand.

Chapter 7 illustrates this integration with the fair organisation, assignment and coordination of satellite activities upset by the breathtaking advancements of technology. From the launch of massive single satellites in the Golden Age of space law, trends are such that experts predict there will be around 100,000 satellites in low Earth orbit by 2030. The staggering number of satellites literally enveloping our world clarifies old and new issues of space law. Old issues concern the regulatory powers of international authorities, such as the International Telecommunications Union in satellite law. The new issues of space law regard the twofold challenge under scrutiny in Chapter 8. On the one hand, it is all about the overall sustainability of space-related activities with the increasing interdependence between space and Earth environments. On the other hand, the cybersecurity issues posed by space-based services will be understood in connection with the protection of critical digital infrastructures on our planet. The Russian aggression to Ukraine made this connection crystal clear in February 2022.

Chapter 9 insists on the open issues of the field and its growing intricacy with the crisis of authority in international space law. This crisis concerns traditional regulatory powers, the overall rationality of the normative system, and its moral grounds. Some propose re-engineering the international space law agreements and institutions; others recommend strategies and policies for the formal and effective institutional management of space activities that do not require amendments to conventional law. In the best possible light, such proposals only cover a part of the troubles of space law. Further problems include issues of cybersecurity and data governance, environmental protection and consumer law that fall outside of the traditional regulatory framework of the field. As stressed in the final chapter of this book, we can assume an ideal scenario in which both public and private actors abide by all provisions and principles of the field, and yet the uniqueness of the environment and technologies making next-generation missions and colonies feasible still pose a further set of questions on thresholds of moral and legal evaluation. The problem concerns a new generation of *sui generis* standards for space law, as much as stricter or more flexible standards for AI in outer space, which include norms and rules for human–robot interaction. The development of these standards will shape the new laws of outer space, especially considering that the new Argonauts of this book will populate most deep space missions and celestial colonies. Both the US-led Artemis Accords and China's International Lunar Research Station aim to be operating at full speed by the late 2030s.

The overall aim of the analysis is to stress three different kinds of novelty that we should expect as a result of current trends in space law regarding the principles, regulations and moral grounds in the field. New laws for outer space will be necessary because of: (i) the obsolescence of the previous legal framework; (ii) the unique challenges of technology in the age of AI; or (iii) the growing complexity of the field with new sectors of expertise that complement the traditional focus of specialists in space law. The classic question of how to govern a new space or territory revolves around moral values, economic interests and legal principles that the regulatory claims of technology will complement. The interdependence between Earth and space environments, the increasing dependence of our planet on space-related activities and a new partnership between human actors and artificial agents are the novelties of our age. The book addresses such novelties in the spirit of that which Aristotle may have taught Alexander. The laws of new territories comprise the establishment of new rules (*nomos*) and principles (*politeia*), as much as their preservation (*ethos*), 'for it is not difficult for any form of Constitution to last for one or two or three days'.[6] We should prevent this risk in current discussions on the new laws of outer space.

[6] Aristotle (n 4) 1319 B.

1

Technology

This chapter examines the ways in which technology affects our values, principles and goals by opening up new spaces for human activities and interaction. Two case studies are particularly instructive as they concern the current debate on space law, space ethics and the amazing speed of technological innovation. The first case study concerns the ancestor of space law and what happened from a legal viewpoint when technology made an old human dream possible: flying. The second case study refers to the creation of a brand-new space, the so-called cyberspace. These two case studies intend to put the birth of space activities and missions in the proper perspective because, rather than a simple means to attain whatsoever end, technology should be considered a regulatory system of its own. All dimensions of human ingenuity, from land to sea, from air to space, up to the creation of cyberspace, have been affected by the enveloping effect of technology. As occurs with ethics and the law, economy and social customs, technology also aims to govern human behaviour by its means.

I. Between Means and Ends

In the past century, the vibrant philosophical debate on the development of technology has revolved around two main issues: what is technology and what is it supposed to do?[1] One of the lessons learned from this debate on the requirements and functions of technology has to do with the idea that technology is something neutral, ie, a simple means to attain whatsoever end. This idea can be traced back to the philosophy of Aristotle. In *The Nicomachean Ethics*, Aristotle distinguishes three kinds of rationality or *dianoia*. He refers to theoretical rationality, which includes physics, metaphysics and mathematics, as parts of the philosophical reflection that does not depend on human action. Practical rationality is, conversely, linked to that part of the world which is doable, feasible and operable by human beings. Finally, *dianoia* denotes the art of producing things with the

[1] See D Ihde, 'Philosophy of Technology' in P Kemp (ed), *Philosophical Problems Today*, vol 3 (Dordrecht, Springer, 2004) 91–108; M Franssen, G-J Lokhorst and I van de Poel, 'Philosophy of Technology' in EN Zalta and U Nodelman (eds), *The Stanford Encyclopedia of Philosophy*, 2023, available at https://plato.stanford.edu/archives/spr2023/entries/technology.

corresponding know-how that Aristotle used to call *poiesis*. Aristotle differentiated this kind of technological rationality, or *poiesis*, from the previous ones on the basis of whether or not such forms of rationality have a virtue of their own.[2]

In the opinion of Aristotle, both natural and practical virtues of theoreticians, statesmen and philosophers depend on the fact that their 'actions' have an end unto themselves. For example, it is the virtue of legislators to make their citizens good by forming habits in them.[3] On the contrary, Aristotle claimed that artists and those who make or produce things have no virtue of their own. There is no virtue in *poiesis* because the art of producing, or making things, does not have to be evaluated in accordance with the ends to be attained through such technological know-how. Instead, the assessment regards whether this know-how is good enough to accomplish a particular goal, such as building a house or a weapon. In the Aristotelian sense, in pronouncing that an artist or artisan is 'good' or 'bad' – for example, today we might call someone working in the field of ethical design a 'good designer' – one is qualifying that artist's or artisan's behaviours or actions rather than what they are making or doing. In the wording of *The Nichomachean Ethics*:

> Since there are many actions, skills, and sciences, it happens that there are many ends as well: the end of medicine is health, that of shipbuilding, a ship, that of military science, victory, and that of domestic economy, wealth. But when any of these actions, skills, or sciences comes under some single faculty … then in all these cases the end of the master science is more worthy of choice that the ends of the subordinate science, since these latter ends are pursued also for the sake of the former. And it makes no difference whether the ends of the actions are the activities themselves, or something else additional to them, as in the sciences just mentioned.[4]

There are two reasons why this distinction between theoretical rationality, practical rationality and *poiesis* appears to be odd or even counterintuitive in our times. On the one hand, the ways in which humans produce things and know how to make them may affect the ends to be attained through the means of technology. Some scholars claim, for example, that we should add a new principle to the traditional framework of bioethics – ie, the principle of explicability to adequately address the new challenges posed by artificial intelligence (AI).[5] On the other hand, technology should be understood as a regulatory system of its own. As also occurs with Aristotle's practical sciences of ethics and the law, economy and social customs, the aim of technology is to govern human behaviour by its own means. Readers of electronic books know it well: the use of digital rights management (DRM)

[2] See Aristotle, *The Nichomachean Ethics*, translated and edited by Robert Crisp (Cambridge, Cambridge University Press, 2000).

[3] ibid II.1, 1103 B.

[4] ibid 1094 A.

[5] See L Floridi et al, 'AI4People – An Ethical Framework for a Good AI Society: Opportunities, Risks, Principles, and Recommendations' (2018) 28(4) *Minds and Machines* 689.

prevents users from sharing and copying the books they are reading for personal purposes. Technology is not neutral simply because it can reinforce or contradict the normative instances of the law, ethics or society.

An example of how social regulatory systems can reinforce each other is given by the 1996 Treaties of the World Intellectual Property Organization (WIPO) on the use of DRM, where such techniques illustrate the convergence between powerful economic interests, the provisions of the law, and technology. However, the claims of such regulatory systems may also clash and even cause the normative claim of another regulatory system to become irrelevant. The EU Electronic Money Directive 46/2000 reminds us of how the regulatory claims of the law may fail vis-a-vis technological innovation. Soon after the implementation of the Directive, which aimed at expanding traditional forms of centralisation to online interaction, new forms of payment, such as PayPal, made the legal regulation obsolete: the EU legislators in Brussels had to amend themselves with a new directive, Directive 2009/110/EC, from 2009.

Some later chapters of this book are devoted to analysing this interplay between ends and means of technology interacting with further regulatory systems in society. In this context, attention is drawn to two case studies on the interaction between technology and the law that are especially instructive for the current debate on space law, space ethics and the amazing speed of technological innovation. The first case study concerns civil aviation and the second case study relates to cyberspace. These two case studies put the birth of space activities and missions into the proper perspective: the first US and Soviet space missions – and, moreover, the corresponding legal regulations in the late 1960s and 1970s – drew on the two decades of experience of both civil aviation law and the development of information and communication technology (ICT). The computing power of the first human landing on the Moon (the 1969 Apollo 11 mission) was that of an iPhone 5. Advancements in technology often force humans to clarify their goals and values, and, perhaps, even question them. The following section inspects the legal ancestor of our field – that is, international aviation law.

II. The Birth of Aviation

The development of aviation technologies between the late 1800s and early 1900s made Leonardo da Vinci's dream come true: humans could fly. Since it is fair to concede that airspace, par excellence, has no natural boundaries, scholars and institutions had to invent new rules to govern this new space for both military purposes and civilian transport. This was not, of course, the first time law makers, courts or scholars had to address the issue; after land and sea, airspace soon became the 'third order' of the legal domain. However, what kind of rules and principles should apply was not so obvious. For a while, analogy helped: in the early 1940s, the rules of maritime law, or admiralty law, were extended to the regulation of the first civil aviation transportation rules, such as in Italy with the Code of Navigation from 1942. It was soon apparent that the uniqueness of aviation technologies would require some rules of their own – for example, standards on safety, security and the airworthiness of the aircraft. In addition, by opening airspace to human activities, it was clear that aviation technologies would dramatically reduce geographical distances, thus raising international concerns.

After a toothless attempt to govern, via the Paris Convention from 1919, this new domain of law on an international level, a new wave of regulations was discussed during the Second World War, culminating in 1944 with the Chicago Convention on Civil Aviation. The Chicago Convention provided a remarkable example of subordination of national acts and regulations to principles and provisions of international law, although, admittedly, not covering the military uses of aviation technologies. Military uses were therefore later regulated with the creation of the United Nations (UN) and its Charter governing the use of force in 1946. The UN Charter was soon complemented by the 1948 Universal Declaration on Human Rights (UDHR) and the four Geneva Conventions on the laws of war from 1949, which aimed to complement the 1907 Hague Convention on 'the Laws and Customs of War on Land' and its annex. Decades later, in 1977, two additional Protocols were inserted concerning the protection of victims of both international and non-international armed conflicts. These normative acts represent the core of 'international humanitarian law' (IHL).

Today, the boundaries between military and non-military uses of aviation technologies are still those defined by the Chicago Convention on Civil Aviation. Article 3, for example, distinguishes 'civil aircraft' from 'state aircraft', stating that it only covers the set of civil aircraft and clarifying that 'aircraft used in military, customs and police services shall be deemed to be state aircraft'. On these bases, the 1944 Convention has provided a set of common principles, rules and standards on air services and civil aviation operations for the international community. All UN state members, except Lichtenstein, have ratified the 1944 Convention. In legal theory, the model is often summed up with the formula of 'legal monism', that is, the idea first developed by Immanuel Kant and then refined by the Austrian scholar Hans Kelsen, according to which provisions of national law should be subordinated to international law.[6] The rules of international civil aviation law – notably the Chicago Convention from 1944 – indeed illustrate a centralised legal governance and regulation model that may resemble some assumptions of legal monism.[7]

The regulatory powers of an ad hoc organisation support this quasi-federal legal framework. The Chicago Convention established the International Civil Aviation Organization (ICAO), equipped with a Council and an Assembly so that,

[6] H Kelsen, *General Theory of the Law and the State*, translated by A Wedberg (Cambridge, MA, Harvard University Press, 1945).

[7] P Gragl, *Legal Monism: Law, Philosophy, and Politics* (Oxford, Oxford University Press, 2018).

according to Article 37 of the Convention, the ICAO 'shall adopt and amend from time to time, as may be necessary, international standards and recommended practices and procedures'.

Later, attention will be given to the progressive integration of principles, rules and standards of the international aviation community with those of space law, such as security traffic management. In this context, the focus should be on the regulatory powers of the ICAO and a lesson learned from such regulatory powers. The laws of physics often support legal monism. The ICAO's powers include communication systems and air navigation aids, characteristics of airports and landing areas, rules of the air and air traffic control, licensing for operating and mechanical personnel, airworthiness of aircraft, their registration and identification, meteorological information and logbooks, aeronautical maps and charts, customs and immigration procedures, down to aircraft in distress and investigation of accidents. Article 54 of the Convention further defines the 'mandatory functions' of the Council, which include the power to 'adopt, in accordance with the provisions of Chapter VI of this Convention, international standards and recommended practices; for convenience, designate them as Annexes to this Convention; and notify all contracting States of the action taken'.

Soft law tools complement such powers of the ICAO: the aim is to clarify specific issues of current law, propose a solution or suggest a framework for a fruitful debate on possible solutions. Pursuant to Article 54(m) of the Convention, the ICAO can 'consider recommendations of the Air Navigation Commission for amendment of the Annexes and take action in accordance with the provisions of Chapter XX' of the Convention. These authoritative powers of the ICAO can hardly be overestimated. They regard the ethos rather than the legal rules of civil aviation. The soft law of the ICAO does not have the same binding force of the 1944 Convention, yet all UN states (ie, the Contracting States of the Convention) should collaborate in securing that their national regulations are aligned with the standards and recommended practices of the ICAO. This form of international cooperation is critical for two reasons: (i) the challenges of technological innovation, such as today's autonomous aircraft systems and the development of new legal standards; and (ii) the balance between national and international law. Several regulatory powers in civil aviation law are up to national or regional law makers, as occurs, for example, with the regulations of the US or the EU in the civil aviation sector. Thus, a certain amount of coherence between the legal framework provided by international law with the powers of the ICAO and the legal framework set up by national and regional authorities will be expected. In accordance with the tenets of legal monism, such coherence entails that the regulatory powers of national and regional authorities should never contradict international law, or at least not overly and not necessarily. In the words of Kelsen:

> The basic norm of international law, then, and thus of state legal systems, too, whose powers are delegated to them by international law, must be a norm that establishes

> customs – the reciprocal behaviour of the states – as a law-creating material fact. Although general international customary law is more recent in origin than the state legal systems, this does not stand in the way of its serving as the basis of their validity.[8]

After 80 years in the making, I may dare to say that international civil aviation law is the closest approximation of Kelsen's ideas on top-down norms and the central role of international law in shaping the regulation of all members of the international community. In the mid-1940s, law makers established a set of rules and principles for a brand-new territory, such as airspace, that binds all nations and is still valid law today. The framework comprehends all three pillars of every legal order: (i) a constitution, ie, the 1944 Convention; (ii) regulations, such as the rules of the ICAO and national aviation authorities; and (iii) a well-defined ethos on safety and security, trustworthiness and integrity. The robustness of these three essential components in civil aviation governance explains the regulatory success of international law. The constraints of the physical environment also recommended the adoption of a Kelsen-like monistic model. Time and again, throughout this volume, the lack of a similar international space organisation – such as the ICAO in civil aviation – will be used as evidence to highlight some flaws in current space law.

However, legal monism has its limits. These limits depend not only on power and enforceability but also on the complexity of that which should be governed and regulated. Such intricacy can be illustrated with the novelty of a brand-new environment created by technology (ie, cyberspace), as well as the competition among regulatory systems, such as law, ethics and technology in the governance of cyberspace. The second case study in this chapter clarifies why traditional tenets of the law fell short in terms of coping with the normative challenges of this new environment.

III. The Birth of Cyberspace

Aviation is not the only example of new natural spaces opened up to human activities by technology. Since the early 1950s, ICT has progressively created a new space of its own. Decades later, the growing social interaction on the internet, through the services of the World Wide Web and other networks (such as peer-to-peer systems), ultimately raised the pivotal question about what laws, if any, had to be established in this brand-new territory, namely, the cyberspace of the mid-1990s. The set-up of both the infrastructure and logical levels of the 'network of networks' (that is, the internet) not only

[8] See B Litschewski Paulson and SL Paulson (eds), *Introduction to the Problems of Legal Theory: A Translation of the First Edition of the Reine Rechtslehre or Pure Theory of Law* (Oxford, Oxford University Press, 1997), para 49(a)–(b), at 108.

posed tricky engineering problems of communication and information flow but also challenging issues regarding jurisdiction, law enforcement and the extra-territorial effects of legislation. These cyber-problems soon reverberated throughout the fields of all legal systems, including space law: the functioning and regulation of today's networks and information systems for satellites and mega-constellations, for example, will be integrated into the cybersecurity network of critical sectors that drive human societies, for example, the EU NIS2 Directive 2022/2555.

Admittedly, human societies have been bound by the use of ICT since the very beginning of their history and by the most basic form of ICT: writing. Over the centuries, however, human societies have mainly depended on energy and essential resource-related technologies. Therefore, what is new in today's societies is the fact that for the first time ever, human societies depend on ICT and, furthermore, on information and data as their vital resources.[9] By the end of the 1990s and into the 2000s, this dependency was not so obvious. The first generation of internet surfers still had the impression that cyberspace was a space of its own, a 'virtual reality' that had popped up beside their old natural world. This first-glance impression favoured early misrepresentations of the new space. The manifesto of John Perry Barlow, *A Declaration of Independence of Cyberspace* from 1996, illustrates the ethos of that era:

> Governments of the Industrial World, you weary giants of flesh and steel, I come from Cyberspace, the new home of Mind. On behalf of the future, I ask you of the past to leave us alone. You are not welcome among us. You have no sovereignty where we gather. We have no elected government, nor are we likely to have one, so I address you with no greater authority than that with which liberty itself always speaks. I declare the global social space we are building to be naturally independent of the tyrannies you seek to impose on us. You have no moral right to rule us nor do you possess any methods of enforcement we have true reason to fear.[10]

A generation later, this vision is simply naïve. In certain jurisdictions, such as EU law, cyberspace is one of the most regulated fields of the legal domain. This trend of legal regulation – and even over-regulation – started with the first wave of normative acts in the mid-1990s in the fields of computer crime, personal data protection and intellectual property, among others. New techniques were adopted to abide by legal provisions, embedding some of them into technology. As was noted in the first section of this chapter, in 1996, the WIPO, under the auspices of the UN, adopted two treaties, the Copyright Treaty and the Performances and Phonograms Treaty, which provided the legal umbrella for the adoption of technological measures such

[9] U Pagallo, 'Good Onlife Governance: On Law, Spontaneous Orders, and Design' in L Floridi (ed). *The Onlife Manifesto: Being Human in a Hyperconnected Era* (Springer, Dordrecht, 2015) 161–77.

[10] JP Barlow, 'A Declaration of the Independence of Cyberspace', 1996, available at https://www.eff.org/it/cyberspace-independence.

as the use of DRM techniques to protect intellectual property rights in cyberspace. In the words of Article 11 of the WIPO's Copyright Treaty:

> Contracting Parties shall provide adequate legal protection and effective legal remedies against the circumvention of effective technological measures that are used by authors in connection with the exercise of their rights.

In addition to the civilian and commercial sector, further issues of internet governance and regulation addressed the criminal side of the law. In 2001, a landmark agreement – the Cybercrime Convention – was opened for signature in Budapest, after having been negotiated by the member states of the Council of Europe along with Canada, Japan, South Africa and the US. The Convention benefited from the national experience of several countries that, since the early 1990s, amended their own rules on criminal law, both substantial and procedural, with a new generation of cybercrimes. The Budapest Convention represents a milestone in the laws of cyberspace and has been complemented with further intergovernmental and regional agreements, such as the EU NIS2 Directive from 2022, which integrates space activities in the functioning of networks and information systems that drive today's human societies. Such agreements often go hand in hand with cooperation protocols signed together with the private sector and the gatekeepers of the internet. However, it is striking that the definitions of several crucial notions, such as cyberattacks, remain open to discussion. Although the Tallinn Manual, under the auspices of the North Atlantic Treaty Organization (NATO) alliance, has provided some authoritative definitions and 95 rules of international law in cyberspace – first in 2013 and then, in 2017, with its version 2.0 – it is fair to concede that we are some distance from achieving binding notions.[11]

The lack of agreements within the international community is, of course, nothing new. However, the subordinate role of international law in the regulation and governance of cyberspace is striking. Indeed, most powers are conferred upon states and private companies. In support of this assumption, it is worth illustrating the case of the Internet Corporation for Assigned Names and Numbers (ICANN). Founded in 1998 and located in Los Angeles, ICANN is the non-profit organisation responsible for the namespaces and numerical spaces of the internet. In a nutshell, ICANN is the regulatory mail carrier of cyberspace, thus exerting considerable powers on namespaces and numerical spaces. So far, ICANN has been more than effective in ensuring the stable functioning of the entire system. However, several states have attempted to regain or strengthen their control over the internet by devolving the powers, originally conferred upon ICANN, back to a UN agency, the International Communication Union (ITU). The idea is that an international agency is more likely to be effectively controlled and directed than an American multi-stakeholder group. Over the past decade, the lack of international

[11] M Schmitt, *Tallinn Manual 2.0 on the International Law Applicable to Cyber Operations* (NATO Cooperative Cyber Defence Centre of Excellence, 2017).

agreement has become an open clash, as shown by the World Conference on International Telecommunications (WCIT-12) held in Dubai in 2012 and the ITU's Plenipotentiary Conference held in Bucharest, Romania in 2022. On the one hand, the sponsors of the ITU solution are countries such as China, Russia, Saudi Arabia, Algeria, Sudan and Egypt. On the other hand, defending – so far successfully – ICANN and its powers are the US, the EU and Canada, which support the Western viewpoint of a decentralised and free cyberspace where UN agencies are kept at bay. Indeed, according to this view, crucial aspects of the governance and functioning of the internet will remain in the hands of a non-profit organisation, such as ICANN.

For better or worse, there is no such thing as a constitution of the internet, a UN convention or a coherent international legal framework. It would be questionable to even claim that cyberspace has some form of *nomos* since the choices of national regulators are often hard to understand, not only for their citizens but also for those citizens of other jurisdictions where rules are applied extra-territorially. These open problems are exacerbated by the way in which cyberspace is disciplined. Rather than a sort of Kelsen's legal monism, as illustrated in the previous section through the tenets of international civil aviation law, internet governance looks like a labyrinthine patchwork of regulatory systems, both public and private, in which international law plays a limited role. This extraordinary circumstance may depend on how cyberspace spontaneously evolved over its first years since a master plan to set up such a 'network of networks' never existed. Rather than a coordinated intervention at the international level under the auspices of the UN, the spontaneous evolution and growth of cyberspace concerned the engagement of professional associations, non-governmental organisations and private companies vis-a-vis a few national or regional regulators. Scholars and institutions have often referred to this new space of regulation as the fourth domain of the law, after land, sea and air. We noted that by the early 2000s, most people – and law makers – still represented the emergence of this new digital world with a series of dualities: online versus offline, virtual reality versus real world, digital versus analogue. In a few years, these dualities will have evaporated.[12]

In 2015, a group of experts set up by the European Commission summed up the challenges of this new world with the formula of 'onlife' and *The Onlife Manifesto*.[13] The formula suggests that cyberspace and the internet should not be grasped as a new space which simply adds to land, sea or air, as was Barlow's misguided understanding in the mid-1990s, or as may be the case for those billionaires who aim to build an artificial island in the middle of nowhere simply to rule over this new territory as a founding father. The digital transformation of human societies suggests, on the contrary, that all previous dimensions of human interaction on

[12] U Pagallo, *La tutela della privacy negli Stati Uniti d'America e in Europa: modelli giuridici a confronto* (Milan, Giuffrè, 2008).

[13] Floridi (n 9).

land or sea, in air or space, have been affected by the internet and cyberspace. The reason depends on technologies that 'envelop' the world, as occurs with the functioning and regulation of networks and information systems of satellites integrated with the critical sectors that drive today's human societies, such as energy and digital infrastructures. The following section explores this technological 'envelopment of the world' that transforms who we are as well as what we know and what we do onlife. Notwithstanding the teachings of Aristotle, technology is a regulatory system of its own.

IV. Enveloping the World

The role that technology plays in human evolution can be illustrated with Stanley Kubrick's famous match cut in his film *2001: A Space Odyssey*. Ape-like tribes of early humans were contending for control over water resources thousands of hundreds of years ago. The triumph of the ancestor who understood how a bone could be used as a weapon is cut with the images of a spacecraft travelling to Clavius Base, a US lunar outpost, to the sounds of Richard Strauss' 'The Blue Danube'. Kubrick wisely left the interpretation of this match cut up to his viewers and aficionados. However, it seems fair to concede that what links the ape-like hero to the engine of the spacecraft and its discomforting AI commander, HAL 9000, is technology. In general terms, we can accept the opinion of the Spanish philosopher José Ortega y Gasset, according to whom, as a species, humans should be grasped as *homo technologicus*.[14]

By referring to a bone, an engine or the AI wicked intelligence of HAL 9000, *2001: A Space Odyssey* invites us to reflect on three different orders of technology.[15] First-order technologies are those between humans and Mother Nature, such as the axe. Humans share this ability to make and employ first-order technologies with many species – for example, beaver dams. Still, only humans came up with the idea of making tools to interact with other tools, namely, technological artefacts that are no longer related to the interaction with humans and the natural environment, but rather to other technologies. Second-order technologies that are in-between humans and other technologies abound in our everyday life, like keys and lockers, screwdrivers and screws, and so on. 'The engine, understood as any technology that provides energy to other technologies, is probably the most important, second-order technology.'[16]

Third-order technologies were already mentioned in the previous section, along with cyberspace and the advent and proliferation of ICTs since the 1960s.

[14] U Pagallo, *The Laws of Robots: Crimes, Contracts, and Torts* (Dordrecht, Springer, 2013).

[15] See L Floridi, 'Technology's In-betweenness' (2013) 26 *Philosophy and Technology* 111; and M Durante, *Computational Power: The Impact of ICT on Law, Society and Knowledge* (Abingdon, Routledge, 2021).

[16] Floridi (n 15) 112.

Third-order technologies work in-between other technologies that set up the environment of the system. By providing an environment where further technologies interact, humans are no longer needed in the loop. Barcodes, high-frequency trading systems and the myriad applications of the Internet of Things (IoT) – or the Internet of Everything (IoE) with autonomous spacecrafts and satellites – exemplify this order of technology that functions in-between other technologies, supplementing humans as users of products and services.

Since the mid-1980s, scholars have debated the uniqueness of the challenges brought about by third-order technologies in connection with the tenets of a new field, namely 'computer ethics'.[17] A decade later, it was the turn of legal experts to discuss whether and to what extent the challenges of cyberspace would have merited a field of their own. In 1996, the same year as Barlow's manifesto, Judge Frank H Easterbrook famously argued against cyberlaw as a unique field of legal studies and litigation. His arguments have gone down in history as the Law of the Horse:

> Lots of cases deal with sale of horses; others deal with people kicked by horses; still more deal with the licensing and racing of horses, or with the care veterinarians give to horses, or with prizes at horse shows. Any effort to collect these strands into a course on 'The Law of the Horse' is doomed to be shallow and to miss unifying principles.[18]

Much as with Barlow's declaration of cyber-independence, it seems evident that the set of legal issues posed by ICTs and computer-related technologies would not have been solved through the use of analogy in the traditional legal fields of governance and regulation.[19] The uniqueness of cyberlaw issues triggered by the use of third-order technologies and their 'enveloping effect' became crystal clear with the extra-territorial effects of human interaction, the growing use of self-enforcing technologies (for example, DRMs) and other forms of legal automation in this new space of human interaction.[20] What, up until the mid-1990s, was considered the exception – such as the regulation of the extra-territorial effects of legislation through ad hoc conventions or provisions of international private law – progressively turned out to become the rule. Re-arrangements in the legal enforcement system through the regulatory tools of technology raised a whole new set of thorny issues. Most depended on how the law was increasingly transformed into a matter of access to and control over information in digital environments. As Lawrence Lessig cautioned, the threat is that 'controls over access to content will not be controls that are ratified by courts; the controls over access to content will be controls that are coded by programmers'.[21]

[17] H Moor, 'What is Computer Ethics?' (1985) 16 *Metaphilosophy* 266.

[18] FH Easterbrook, 'Cyberspace and the Law of the Horse' (1996) 207 *University of Chicago Legal Forum* Article 7.

[19] L Lessig, *Code and Other Laws of Cyberspace* (New York, Basic Books, 1999).

[20] Pagallo (n 9).

[21] L Lessig, *Free Culture: The Nature and Future of Creativity* (New York, Penguin, 2004) 152.

The troubles of cyberlaw in relation to the regulation of third-order technologies have reverberated throughout the entire fabric of the law. Technology is a regulatory system of its own that may render the regulatory means of the law and ethics, economics and society superfluous or ineffective. Over the past few years, the disruption of AI systems has made this threat clear, mainly because of the impact of technology in the fields of human rights law,[22] criminal law,[23] constitutional law,[24] business and contract law,[25] tort law[26] and administrative law,[27] amongst others.[28] Arguably, one of the features of AI that has primarily attracted the attention of scholars and the public at large is the 'autonomy' of such systems and how humans may attain 'meaningful control' over them. Space law experts have increasingly been considering these problems of artificial agency.[29] However, these issues should not lead to overlooking the uniqueness of such an environment, just like outer space with its own problems of scale and astrophysical laws. In other words, in addition to the unique problems that technology may pose in the normative domains of law and ethics, we should not underestimate the unique problems that technology may pose when displayed in outer space.[30]

The challenges of technological regulation have been illustrated so far with activities in natural spaces that are transitioning from the use of second-order to third-order technologies and their legal regulation (for example, drones in aviation law), and digital spaces that have hinged on third-order technologies since their inception (for example, the IoE). Outer space adds to the problems relating to activities in a natural space that nonetheless hinge on using third-order technologies as their condition. Spacecraft and space stations, in-space propulsion engines and deep-space communication networks, and support infrastructure equipment and satellites, are all forms of third-order technology. On 12 April 1961, these technologies realised another ancient human dream when Yuri Gagarin became the first man in space. This extraordinary event once again triggered the question of

[22] W Barfield and U Pagallo, *Advanced Introduction to the Law and Artificial Intelligence* (Cheltenham, Edward Elgar, 2020).

[23] G Hallevy, *Liability for Crimes Involving Artificial Intelligence Systems* (Dordrecht, Springer, 2015).

[24] M Hildebrandt, *Smart Technologies and the End(s) of Law: Novel Entanglements of Law and Technology* (Cheltenham, Edward Elgar, 2015).

[25] G Sartor, 'Cognitive Automata and the Law: Electronic Contracting and the Intentionality of Software Agents' (2009) 17(4) *Artificial Intelligence and Law* 253.

[26] Pagallo (n 14).

[27] R Calo and DK Citron, 'The Automated Administrative State: A Crisis of Legitimacy' (2020) 70 *Emory Law Journal* 797; and, DE Engstrom, DE Ho, CM Sharkey and MF Cuéllar, 'Government by Algorithm: AI in Federal Administrative Agencies', *NYU School of Law, Public Law Research Paper No 20-54*, 2020.

[28] S Chesterman, *We, the Robots? Regulating Artificial Intelligence and the Limits of the Law* (Cambridge, Cambridge University Press, 2021).

[29] I Bratu, AR Lodder and T van der Linden, 'Autonomous Space Objects and International Space Law: Navigating the Liability Gap' (2021) 18(3) *Indonesian Journal of International Law* 423; and A-S Martin and S Freeland, 'The Advent of Artificial Intelligence in Space Activities: New Legal Challenges' (2021) 55 *Space Policy* 101408.

[30] U Pagallo, E Bassi and M Durante, 'The Normative Challenges of AI in Outer Space: Law, Ethics, and the Realignment of Terrestrial Standards' (2023) 36 *Philosophy & Technology* 23.

what principles and regulations should govern a new domain of human activities that a sample of third-order technology made possible. Under the auspices of the UN, sovereign states addressed these questions throughout the 1960s and 1970s. The final section of this chapter introduces the international regulatory framework set up in those decades.

V. The Birth of Space Activities

Human activities in airspace were originally related to the use of second-order technologies, such as engines and the overall airworthiness of the aircraft. Eighty years later, civil aviation law is still tackling the transition from second-order to third-order technologies with the regulation of remotely piloted aircraft and drones. The legal technique has been to add annexes to the 1944 Chicago Convention, such as standards and recommended practices on definitions of 'accident' (ie, the 13th amendment to Annex 13 from 2011), aircraft taxonomies and marks (the 6th amendment to Annex 7 from 2012), the procedure of 'special authorisation' in the case of 'unmanned' aircraft systems (the 43rd amendment to Annex 2 from 2012) and so on. At the regional and national levels, the laws of several jurisdictions, such as the EU and the US, have complemented the ICAO's recommendations with their own provisions.[31]

Other fields of legal regulation have not needed to address such problems of technological transformation that occur in civil aviation or road transportation, such as autonomous vehicles.[32] Spacecrafts, satellites and deep-space communication networks are all samples of third-order technologies that fit neatly into the most recent generation of AI systems and smart robots for outer-space activities. Remarkably, the international community addressed the regulatory challenges posed by the advancement of space technologies since the late 1950s and 1960s in a reasonable amount of time under the auspices of the UN. Law makers once again had to address the set of moral principles and legal rules that should govern a new space or territory. In the hottest years of the Cold War, the result was noteworthy. Agreements and conventions of space law from 1967 to the mid-1970s can be regarded as the Golden Age of the field. Such agreements and conventions still provide the tenets of today's legal framework with the establishment of a new domain of international law with its own principles and rules.

The next chapter is devoted to this Golden Age of space law. Retrospectively, a general consensus exists among scholars and historians. The international law makers of the 1960s and 1970s could be compared with the most outstanding

[31] U Pagallo and E Bassi, 'The Governance of Unmanned Aircraft Systems (UAS): Aviation Law, Human Rights, and the Free Movement of Data in the EU' (2020) 30 *Minds & Machines* 439.

[32] R Jenkins, D Cerný and T. Hríbek (eds), *Autonomous Vehicle Ethics: The Trolley Problem and Beyond* (Oxford, Oxford University Press, 2022).

legislators of all times – such as the Spartan Lycurgus or the Athenian Draco in Ancient Greece – and yet, such merits should not overlook the fact that pillars of 'their' normative framework are increasingly under stress.[33] The reasons are multiple and include trends of privatisation and militarisation that fall within the loopholes of the legal system as much as the disruption of AI and smart robots that supplement further advancements of technology, such as connectivity networks for mega-constellations of satellites on the internet of everything. To appreciate the challenges of this scenario – and which tenets of today's space law are correspondingly under stress – it is thus necessary to flesh out, first, the set of rules and principles that the UN General Assembly adopted in the 1960s and 1970s. The aim is to appreciate on this basis which principles and provisions of the Golden Age are in trouble 60 years later.

[33] See D Tan, 'Towards a New Regime for the Protection of Outer Space as the Province of All Mankind' (2000) 25(1) *Yale Journal of International Law* 145; LL Manzione, 'Multinational Investment in the Space Station: An Outer Space Model for International Cooperation' (2002) 18(2) *American University International Law Review* 507; F Lyall and PB Larsen, *Space Law: A Treatise* (Abingdon, Routledge, 2018); and AN Pečujlić, *The Space Law Stalemate: Legal Mechanisms for Developing New Norms* (New York, Routledge, 2023).

2

Launching States

Technology is at the heart of space law and its regulations. When space technologies made an old human dream come true, ie, humans could fly in outer space, the UN responded with a full array of conventions, declarations, and agreements starting from the early 1960s. This chapter sums up such normative acts that still provide the pillars of today's legal framework. Rights, duties and obligations of international law concern the responsibilities of sovereign states launching 'things' and humans into outer space. The international provisions of space law are complemented by a set of intergovernmental agreements on cooperation, such as the set-up of the International Space Station in 1998. Against the background of this differentiation between international and intergovernmental sources of space law, the chapter further assesses multiple national regulatory frameworks on space-related activities that have been piling up in recent years. The overall aim is to illustrate the intricacy of the field between international space law and national space law, between legal monism and legal dualism.

I. The Labour of a New Legal Space

By the mid-1950s, the 'space race' was about to begin, once again raising the question of the principles and rules that had to be established in this novel dimension of the legal domain. Previous international agreements from the 1940s offered little help to address the development and challenges of space technologies, such as spacecrafts and satellites that were largely, if not exclusively, under the control of the two world superpowers: the US and the Soviet Union. It was noted in Chapter 1 that the 1944 Chicago Convention – namely, Article 3 – does not cover the activities of 'state aircraft'. Similarly, the activities of the states in the exploration and use of outer space resources fell outside the scope and purposes of the 1949 Geneva Conventions on the laws of war: either such activities could entail peaceful, legitimate scientific purposes, or the provisions of such conventions on the use of force could hardly prevent or govern all activities related to the potential militarisation of outer space.[1]

[1] U Pagallo, 'Robots of Just War: A Legal Perspective' (2011) 24 *Philosophy and Technology* 307.

However, the difficult task of envisioning principles and rules for a brand-new legal space not only concerned the limits of international regulations and the unfeasibility of drawing some sort of analogy just relying upon them; the difficulty of the task was exacerbated by the constraints of the Cold War between the US and the USSR with their corresponding blocs. The North Atlantic Treaty Organization (NATO) was created in 1949 and the Warsaw Pact was created in 1955. Technology would have once again played a major role in the realisation of a new legal field. The great polymath John von Neumann argued that the only defendable policy for the US–USSR deadlock was an immediate nuclear attack, an opinion that was rather common at the time.[2] In retrospect, we may concede that the advent of any significant technological advance in weapons and tactics can lower the thresholds of entry into war; yet, when technology is in the hands of a few states – as occurred throughout the Cold War era with the development of thermonuclear weapons and satellites – it is likely that reaching a consensus on treaties may be easier. The permanent members of the UN Security Council could indeed have a shared interest, such as controlling the spread of technology. At the end of the day, the labour of space law as a new legal field lasted a decade.

In 1957, the US and its Western allies submitted, for the first time, their proposals to limit space activities for 'peaceful and scientific purposes' before the UN. The USSR rejected such proposals. A good explanation is that the Soviet Union was ready to launch the world's first satellite and, above all, to test its first intercontinental ballistic missile. Western proposals could, in other words, be interpreted as the offer of the party to lose the space race. On 4 October 1957, the US was caught completely off guard when the USSR successfully launched Sputnik 1, the first artificial Earth satellite, into an elliptical low Earth orbit.

In 1958, the US Congress passed the National Aeronautics and Space Act, which established the National Aeronautics and Space Administration (NASA). By the end of that year, a first compromise was attained at the international level. In December, with UN Resolution 1348 (XIII), the General Assembly established the ad hoc Committee on the Peaceful Uses of Outer Space (COPUOS), which was complemented with the creation of a small expert unit, ie, the Office for Outer Space Affairs (UNOOSA). The aim of the international resolution was to set up an expert unit within the UN Secretariat to promote space peace. A year later, in 1959, the General Assembly established COPUOUS as a permanent body, restating its mandate with Resolution 1472 (XIV). The mandate included the promotion of international cooperation and close contacts with governmental and non-governmental organisations, together with the exchange of information on outer space activities.

However, it was soon apparent that COPUOS and UNOOSA – still representing two tenets of today's international space governance – would have fallen short in terms of coping with the threats of the Cold War. The same year in which Yuri

[2] AJ Field, 'Schelling, von Neumann, and the Event That Didn't Occur' (2014) 5(1) *Games* 53.

Gagarin and Alan Shepard became the first men in outer space, things turned particularly ugly on Earth. On 17 April 1961 – that is, five days after Gagarin completed his one-orbit journey around the Earth – about 1,300 Cuban exiles armed with US weapons and sponsored by the CIA landed at the Bay of Pigs in an unsuccessful attempt to overthrow Fidel Castro's regime. Four months later, on 17 August, East Germany (DDR) started to erect the Berlin Wall. A few weeks later, at 11:32 am on 30 October, the USSR detonated the Tsar Bomb (a 50-megaton hydrogen bomb) over the Novaya Zemlya archipelago, causing the largest human-made explosion in history. A year later, in October 1962, the Cuban missile crisis marked the moment in which the US and the USSR came closest to conflict.

On the brink of a nuclear precipice, humankind was spared another catastrophe. In 1963, the UN General Assembly approved one more resolution and the first declaration on outer space. Resolution 1884 (XVIII) of 17 October welcomed the declarations of both the US and the USSR 'not to station in outer space any objects carrying nuclear weapons or other kinds of weapons of mass destruction', therefore calling upon all UN member states to similarly refrain from such activities. Declaration 1962 (XVIII) of 13 December 1963 approved a list of eight legal principles to govern all state activities in outer space. Such principles paved the way for the ethos of the space race. They included freedom and equality of states in the exploration and use of outer space and the celestial bodies so that any national attempt of appropriation by claim of sovereignty would have been illegitimate. In particular, pursuant to the fourth principle of the Declaration:

> The activities of States in the exploration and use of outer space shall be carried on in accordance with international law, including the Charter of the United Nations, in the interest of maintaining international peace and security and promoting international co-operation and understanding.

Notwithstanding the merits of the 1963 Declaration, most of the work still had to be done. The act was nothing more than a non-binding declaration that had to be complemented with the enforceable provisions of a treaty or a convention. It is noteworthy that, after the 1963 Resolution and Declaration, negotiations required two further years of heated discussions to flesh out a common ground: the devil was in the legal details. In June 1966, the US and the USSR submitted separate drafts of an outer space treaty to the UN General Assembly. The text for a mutually agreed treaty was discussed over the rest of that year and was finally adopted in Resolution 2222 (XXI).

On 19 December 1966, the UN General Assembly approved the definitive version of the 'Treaty on Principles Governing the Activities of States in the Exploration and Use of Outer Space, including the Moon and Other Celestial Bodies' – in short, the Outer Space Treaty. The agreement was opened for signature in Washington DC, Moscow, and London on 27 January 1967, entering into force on 10 October 1967. It still represents the pillar of today's space law. The next section illustrates the principles and clauses of the hard-won compromise between the world superpowers and their blocs.

II. The 1967 Outer Space Treaty

The 1967 Treaty has 17 articles. These can be divided into two sets. The first set of provisions refers to the principles already endorsed by the UN member states with the 1963 Declaration on outer space. These articles sum up what could be dubbed the ethos of this new legal field. Article I establishes the principle of freedom and space as the 'province of mankind': the exploration and use of outer space should benefit all countries. Article II repudiates every claim of sovereignty and national appropriation over outer space. Article III copies and pastes the fourth principle of the 1963 Declaration, which was quoted in the previous section. Article IV bans the use and test of nuclear weapons and other kinds of weapons of outer space mass destruction. Article V sets up the safeguards for the new explorers of outer space, namely, 'astronauts as envoys of mankind'. Articles VI and VII represent the backbone of the agreement on responsibilities and duties for the enforcement of the new legal principles of outer space.

In particular, Article VI covers the legal responsibility that States Parties bear. All states are internationally responsible for the national activities of both their governmental agencies and non-governmental entities. Since states bear responsibility for what such private actors may do in outer space, private actors shall act under the 'authorization and continuing supervision by the appropriate State Party'.

On the other hand, Article VII concerns liability and damages. If something goes wrong, States Parties are liable either because they launched the object that caused damage or because they authorised the mission of a private actor and, hence, 'procured' the launching of the object. In addition, a State Party is liable when the object was launched in their territory or facilities. In all these cases, states are thus 'internationally liable' for damages to another state. This liability includes damages to individuals and legal persons, such as corporations, that fall under the jurisdiction of that State Party.

Three generations of scholars and experts in space law have dissected the provisions of the 1967 Treaty. It is noteworthy that the international lawgivers acknowledged the limits of the text they adopted. For example, regarding the provisions of Article V on the 'envoys of mankind', such norms were soon complemented with the Rescue Agreement from 1968, ie, the UN agreement on the rescue of astronauts and their return to Earth, as well as the return of objects launched into outer space. Some other problems refer to the vagueness of some legal formulas, such as that of 'damages' in Article VII. Experts of tortious liability know that damage – as a prerequisite of liability – is a flexible concept that hinges on the different human interests that can be at stake, and on the extent to which a certain form of behaviour or chain of events can impact that interest. Therefore, the 1967 Treaty left several questions on the kind of damages that would finally be covered by the general principle of Article VII open. If this was not enough, international law makers had to clarify the kind of liability that should be established for such damages: strict liability, liability that depends on fault and negligence, or both?

Another critical aspect of the international agreement had to do with its overall architecture. Although the first articles of the 1967 Treaty look like a model of international legal monism – as was noted in the previous chapter regarding the 1944 Chicago Convention – they are not. The Outer Space Treaty firmly rests on the sovereignty of the States Parties and a corresponding dualistic approach to international law. Contrary to Kelsen's assumptions, there is no delegation of legal powers by international law to state legal systems.[3] While Article VIII establishes that jurisdiction and control over and ownership of objects launched into outer space are up to the States Parties in accordance with their 'registries', the second part of the Treaty is mostly devoted to international cooperation rather than procedures on how to enforce the clauses of the agreement. Article IX refers to 'appropriate international consultations' that states should undertake when they believe they – or other States Parties – can harmfully interfere with the activities of other states. Articles X, XI and XII essentially deal with international cooperation, whilst Article XIII settles problems of implementation pursuant to an intergovernmental approach. We will soon be dealing with this difference between the international versus intergovernmental approach, but, in the phrasing of Article XIII of the Outer Space Treaty:

> Any practical questions arising in connection with activities carried on by international intergovernmental organizations in the exploration and use of outer space, including the Moon and other celestial bodies, shall be resolved by the States Parties to the Treaty either with the appropriate international organization or with one or more States members of that international organization, which are Parties to this Treaty.

As a product of the Cold War, the 1967 Treaty was thus designed according to a sovereign-centric approach. This does not mean that we should overlook the ethos of the Treaty with its noble principles, such as the statement of Article II that no national appropriation of outer space by claims of sovereignty shall be deemed admissible. However, the fact that the sovereign states of the international community agreed to limit their powers must be understood in connection with the tenets of dualism in international law that shape both the rules and principles of this legal domain.[4] Such tenets can be grasped in accordance with three main points. First, the role that international agencies and institutions play in space law regards the functioning of governmental powers and intergovernmental cooperation rather than the top-down enforcement of rules and principles of international law; it is noteworthy that the Treaty sets up no new organisations – as the international community did with the Chicago Convention on Civil Aviation – and does not even mention COPUOS or UNOOSA. Second, the interplay between national and international legal sources necessarily leaves much leeway to national

[3] H Kelsen, *General Theory of the Law and the State*, translated by A Wedberg (Cambridge, MA, Harvard University Press, 1945).

[4] JG Starke, 'Monism and Dualism in the Theory of International Law' in SL Paulson (ed), *Normativity and Norms: Critical Perspectives on Kelsenian Themes* (Oxford, Oxford University Press, 1999).

decisions, even in the case of such international conventions as the 1944 Chicago Convention.[5] In the case of the 1967 Outer Space Treaty, national discretion includes how to interpret key notions underpinning the Treaty, such as the appropriation and militarisation of space. The general or vague nature of several legal formulas in the Treaty, which has been the bane of generations of experts, arguably represents the fruit of a hard-won political settlement. Third, as a corollary of legal dualism, the duties and obligations of sovereign states hinge on their own will. By ratifying treaties and conventions, states can always opt out of such agreements, as shown by Article XVI of the Outer Space Treaty on withdrawal.

Subsequent provisions of space law then have to be assessed in light of this overall architecture of Cold War international law that rests largely on the sovereign powers of the UN member states. It was noted above that States Parties of the 1967 Treaty were well aware of the limits of their compromise. Clauses had to be improved shortly afterwards. After the UN agreement on the rescue of astronauts in 1968, the next step of this work in progress concerned the elucidation of Articles VI and VII of the Outer Space Treaty on the international responsibility and liability of the launching states. Thanks to the work of the Legal Subcommittee of COPUOS – and the 'goodwill' of the global superpowers with their blocs – the complex set of issues related to the liability and responsibility of the launching states was drafted in three dozen articles, but that required three years of negotiations until consensus was attained before the UN General Assembly.

The Convention on International Liability for Damage Caused by Space Objects was finally adopted by Resolution 2777 (XXVI) of 29 November 1971. The Convention was opened for signature on 29 March 1972, entering into force on 1 September of that year. Although the provisions of the Convention should be grasped in accordance with the pillars of legal dualism, as previously introduced in this section, clauses of this new international agreement may have looked like a form of legal monism. This ambiguity provides a guide as to how we should interpret duties and obligations that the states have had, throughout the 1970s and onwards, in the international arena in relation to their launching efforts and outer space activities.

III. The 1972 Liability Convention

The 27 articles of the 1972 Convention represent the apex of the international efforts to govern this new domain of the law, ie, outer space. Relying on the ethos of the 1967 Treaty, the aim was to set the rules, or *nomos*, regarding the liability and accountability of sovereign states. Whilst Article I defines the meaning of the three key terms of the Convention – that is, 'damage', 'space object' and 'launching

[5] U Pagallo and E Bassi, 'The Governance of Unmanned Aircraft Systems (UAS): Aviation Law, Human Rights, and the Free Movement of Data in the EU' (2020) 30 *Minds & Machines* 439.

state' – Article II provides the foundation of the whole agreement by adopting the principle of strict liability for damages caused by the launching states. The principle is justified by the uniqueness of the legal space that had to be regulated and the corresponding level of risk related to outer space activities. In the words of Article II:

> A launching State shall be absolutely liable to pay compensation for damage caused by its space object on the surface of the Earth or to aircraft in flight.

Article III further specifies the liability regime for damages that do not affect flying aircraft or the surface of the Earth. This differentiation is critical because launching states bear two different kinds of liability based on their activities in outer space. Liability of Article II is strict: it is up to the launching state to demonstrate its lack of responsibility, for example, due to gross negligence of the claimant state under Article VI of the Convention. Liability of Article III, on the other hand, depends on the fault of the launching state or the persons for whom such a state is internationally responsible. This differentiation represents the backbone of the 'primary rules' of the law for outer space, namely, the rules that aim to directly govern the behaviour of launching states.

Articles IX–XX of the Convention aim to complement such international rules on the liability of launching states with the 'secondary rules' of the law, such as the procedural rules on compensation claims. Whereas the 'diplomatic channels' of Articles IX and XIV should be prioritised, the Convention also aims to regulate the cases in which no settlement of the claim is feasible through such channels. Should, perhaps, the latter be the case, the parties to the lawsuit – that is, two or more launching states – shall resort to the international arbitration of the Claims Commission. Under Article XV of the 1972 Convention, such a commission is composed of three members: two members individually chosen by each party, and the chairman chosen by both parties jointly. Yet, at the time of writing, it is striking that these provisions have been invoked only once, in 1978, when a Soviet satellite, Cosmos 954, accidentally re-entered the Earth's atmosphere. Cosmos dispersed some 50 kg of radioactive uranium-235 over northern Canada. Though luckily underpopulated, the USSR finally paid Canada for just compensation of damages and costs for the multi-year clean-up operation.[6]

In addition, several crucial notions and key terms that refer to the 'primary rules' of the 1972 Convention were – and admittedly still are – open to multiple and even opposing interpretations. It can be hard to determine, for example, whether a state incurs in fault or whether the damages covered include indirect damages.[7] Doctrinal efforts of jurisprudence – for example, the ruling of the International Court of Justice on due diligence duties and fault standards in the Corfu Channel

[6] M Benkö, *Space Law in the United Nations* (The Hague, Martinus Nijhoff Publishers, 1985).

[7] CQ Christol, 'International Liability for Damage Caused by Space Objects' (1980) 74(2) *American Journal of International Law* 346.

case – partially solve problems of negligence and foreseeability in outer space.[8] As was stressed in the previous chapter – dealing with the implementation of rules and principles of the law of the sea to civil aviation law – analogy has its limits. These limits were exacerbated by the unique challenges that outer space triggers with its extremely hazardous environment.

The troubles of the Liability Convention, both as law in the books and as law in the making, should not overlook the merits of this agreement. The ethos of the 1967 Outer Space Treaty as the 'province of mankind' and astronauts as the 'envoys' of our species was backed up by a liability regime. The Convention represented a necessary but insufficient condition for the establishment of a new legal framework. The international law makers did not consider the 1972 Convention – or the 1967 Treaty for that matter – as the arrival point of their regulatory efforts, but rather as a work in progress. The conjecture hinges on the fact that, soon after the agreement on the liability regime for outer space activities, negotiations continued to add another central piece of the regulatory framework. A couple of years later, the General Assembly adopted the Convention on Registration of Objects Launched into Outer Space under Resolution 3235 (XXIX) from 1974.

In light of this legal crescendo, the benefits of seeing the evolution of international space law since the 1960s clarify a crucial difference in retrospect. Whilst the Liability Convention represents the apex of international efforts to govern the new legal domain of outer space through the means of a binding agreement, the Registration Convention represents the Golden Age of these regulatory efforts, but also their end. The paradox can be summed up with a popular metaphor of ancient Greek culture, according to which swans sing only when they die. The next section aims to shed light on this crucial moment in the mid-1970s, focusing on the Registration Convention as the rise and fall of the top-down efforts of the international legal community.

IV. The Swan Song

The Registration Convention entered into force on 15 September 1976, complementing key provisions of the Rescue Agreement and the Liability Convention by establishing that launching states must maintain a registry of their own space objects and that they should provide the UN with information on the objects they launch into outer space. Previously, no launching state would have been held accountable if there was no way to specify which state's object was involved in an accident or which outer space object caused it. The 1976 Convention therefore provided a mechanism to assist in the identification of space objects. By expanding the scope of the UN Register of Objects Launched into Outer Space set up under

[8] JA Dennerley, 'State Liability for Space Object Collisions: The Proper Interpretation of "Fault" for the Purposes of International Space Law' (2018) 29(1) *European Journal of International Law* 281.

Resolution 1721B (XVI) of 1961, the aim was to address further issues of responsibility for launching states relating to their space objects, such as burdens of proof regarding their identification, therefore strengthening, on this basis, the provisions of the previous international agreements.

Traditionally, scholars supplement the four normative acts we have seen so far – namely, the 1967 Treaty, the 1968 Rescue Agreement, the 1972 Liability Convention and the 1976 Registration Convention – with a further international agreement, the Agreement Governing the Activities of States on the Moon and Other Celestial Bodies, known as the Moon Agreement. Elaborated by the Legal Subcommittee of COPUOS since 1972, the Agreement was adopted by the General Assembly in 1979 through Resolution 34/68. The practice of referring to these agreements as the five international pillars of outer space developed when the Moon Agreement entered into force in 1984, when a fifth country, Austria, finally ratified it.[9]

However, the Moon Agreement should be understood as the fifth legal pillar of outer space with some reservations. The 1979 Agreement is the pact related to outer space activities with the least support among UN member states, namely, only 11 signatories. It reaffirms and elaborates on many of the provisions of the previous space treaties and conventions as applied to the Moon and other celestial bodies. Among its principles, the Moon and its natural resources are conceived of as the common heritage of humankind, whereas such resources should be used exclusively for peaceful purposes. Moreover, the UN shall be informed of the location and purpose of every station established on those bodies. In addition, the Agreement establishes that all activities of launching states should not disrupt the environment of the Moon and other celestial bodies. Still, it was precisely the exploitability and appropriability of the natural resources of the Moon and other celestial bodies that represented an insurmountable hurdle to reaching a consensus. A new international regime would have had to establish conditions and procedures for such exploitation of celestial resources. Article 11(3) of the 1979 (dis)Agreement illustrates this impasse:

> Neither the surface nor the subsurface of the Moon, nor any part thereof or natural resources in place, shall become property of any State, international intergovernmental or non-governmental organization, national organization or nongovernmental entity or of any natural person.

As a result of the political deadlock in the 1980s, the international regime that had to be established – to govern the exploitation of celestial resources when such exploitation would become feasible, according to the wishes of the Agreement – never saw the light of day. Although most UN member states, whether communist, capitalist or non-aligned, abandoned the project, this does not mean that further

[9] S Goguichvili, A Linenberger, A Gillette and A Novak, 'The Global Legal Landscape of Space: Who Writes the Rules on the Final Frontier?', *Wilson Center*, October 2021, https://www.wilsoncenter.org/article/global-legal-landscape-space-who-writes-rules-final-frontier.

relevant agreements may not be signed. Despite the risks of fragmentation that had to be expected as a consequence of the Moon Agreement impasse, the deadlock of the 1980s, following the 1972 Liability Convention and the 1976 Registration Convention, recommended further ways to attain consensus in the international arena. Such ways included the means of the soft side of the law as well as new intergovernmental agreements for cooperation in outer space. As regards soft law, the General Assembly adopted two further declarations on principles in the 1980s and two in the 1990s: the 'broadcasting principles' (1982); the 'remote sensing principles' (1986); the 'nuclear sources power principles' (1992); and the 'benefits declaration' (1996). The forms of intergovernmental agreements include the Civil International Space Station agreement under the coordination efforts of the US and its agency, NASA, in 1998.

The swan song of this section thus concerned the regulatory efforts of international legislators on the hard side of the law rather than resolutions of soft law or agreements at the intergovernmental level. The cumulative work in progress of international space law – which ended abruptly with the failure of the Moon Agreement – will be supplemented by the scrutiny of new developments in the governance of outer space and the shaping of its constitution through further sources of international law. After all, the *nomos* of this domain of legal regulation has continued to evolve.

V. A World of Agreements

The binding outer space treaties covered in the previous sections have been accompanied by several UN declarations and agreements that, although not binding, often have considerable authoritative power. As was already noted in the previous chapter, such authoritative powers can be as effective as the role of the soft powers of the ICAO in developing standards, clarifying issues of civil aviation law or suggesting a framework for a fruitful debate on possible solutions for those issues. We should never underestimate the strength of soft law.

In the field of space law, some UN agreements have had a similar effect. The previous section mentioned agreements on the activities of states related to the use of satellites for international direct television broadcasting, or Earth remote sensing from outer space. Some of these agreements have effectively set up the international framework for the activities of launching states and their national legislations, paving the way for a global top-down regulatory effort. It was noted in Chapter 1 that another set of laws – ie, the laws of physics – often play a crucial role in supporting the approach of legal monism: considering the use of satellites, one of the most urgent issues for the governance of outer space had to do with the regulatory framework for the radio-frequency spectrum and corresponding satellite orbits that should have prevented physical and electromagnetic interferences since the very beginning of outer space activities. Furthermore, both radio-frequency spectrum and geosynchronous orbits (GEOs) must be used in an efficient, equitable and economically sustainable way.

These constraints had recommended the adoption of a strict top-down regulatory approach, as had occurred with the powers of the ICAO in the field of civil aviation, since the 1960s. The agency charged with the governance of such activities is the ITU. We encountered the ITU in the previous chapter when dealing with the regulatory issues of cyberspace. There it was noted that some UN member states, such as China and Russia, intended – and still aim – to reshape the governance of the internet in accordance with a traditional approach of international law, according to which the regulatory powers of ICANN, the non-profit organisation based in California, should be devolved to a UN agency, such as the ITU. Whilst these attempts to divest ICANN of its powers have so far failed in the field of cyberspace governance, things developed in an entirely different way with regard to the governance of outer space. Many understandable reasons lie behind this outcome. The first of these is the historical context in which decisions had to be made to establish the new legal rules for outer space in the hottest years of the Cold War back in the early 1960s.

By then, it was evident that both the public and private use of the Earth's orbits for telecommunications and other services would dramatically increase, therefore creating the need for an effective regulatory system at the international level. The most natural candidate was the ITU since it offered both the know-how in creating international communication standards and the political safeguards of an agency under the control of sovereign stakeholders. Established in 1865 as the International Telegraph Union – namely, the first international organisation in the world – it is worth emphasizing that the ITU is still a pillar of the international governance of outer space, together with COPUOS and UNOOSA. A special ITU department – the Space Services Department (SSD) – was appointed to tackle crucial issues relating to the organisation, assignment and coordination of activities in outer space.

In particular, the SSD is responsible for capturing, processing and publishing data, as well as for coordinating and recording procedures for space systems and Earth stations, including recording in the Master International Frequency Register (MIFR). One of the most critical powers of the SSD is the scrutiny of the frequency assignment notices that are submitted by the launching states and their administrations, to be included in the coordination procedures of the international authority. In addition, the SSD is responsible for managing the procedures for space-related assignments or allotment plans of the ITU. The SSD assigns orbital slots to the UN member states so that they can license the use of such slots through national regulation. The parameters of the assignment concern the region involved, the type of frequencies used in the outer space activities of the launching state, and the longitudinal parameters of the orbit. The SSD provides assistance to each state on all of the above issues through three divisions: the Space Publication and Registration Division (SPR); the Space Systems Coordination Division (SSC); and the Space Notification and Plans Division (SNP).

The international agreement on the powers of the ITU and the SSD – with its three divisions – does not mean, of course, that all problems are solved, even considering the part of outer space governance which is under the direct control of the ITU. Later chapters in this book will stress time and again the persisting problems of overpopulated orbits, radio frequency interferences and the allocation of spectra.

Yet, in addition to the powers of the ITU, the survey of the international sources of space law that aim to govern the activities of the launching states would not be completed without a reference to other kinds of agreements. This is the case for the International Space Station Intergovernmental Agreement (IGA) of 1998. The Agreement is not only interesting because it complements the traditional hard and soft tools of international law examined in the previous sections; it is also noteworthy because it illustrates how advancements in technology and impasses in the international community recommended an intergovernmental rather than UN form of agreement and cooperation. Although both approaches should be deemed compatible – according to the sovereign-centred view of international law discussed earlier in this chapter – this compatibility does not entail that the clauses of every intergovernmental agreement can simply be deduced from the norms and principles of the international framework. Rather, the clauses of such agreements between national governments add another layer of complexity to the sources of international space law. Such intergovernmental agreements either fill the gaps of international law or complement its provisions with, at times, highly controversial measures.

VI. From International to Intergovernmental Agreements

From a legal viewpoint, the IGA is an intergovernmental rather than an international agreement. It involves 15 sovereign states. From a scientific viewpoint, the International Space Station (ISS) represents today's largest modular station in low Earth orbit that functions as a research laboratory for physics and astronomy, astrobiology and meteorology etc. The ISS also tests the resilience of spacecraft systems and the equipment that will be required in deep space missions. According to Article 1 of the IGA, the aim is to create:

> A long term international cooperative framework on the basis of genuine partnership, for the detailed design, development, operation, and utilization of a permanently inhabited civil Space Station for peaceful purposes, in accordance with international law.

The four Memoranda of Understandings concern NASA and four cooperating space agencies: the European Space Agency (ESA), the Canadian Space Agency (CSA), the Russian Federal Space Agency (Roscosmos) and the Japan Aerospace Exploration Agency (JAXA). Such agencies shall determine their role and responsibilities concerning the design, development operation and effective use of the space station. The ISS is divided into two areas: the Russian Orbital Segment (ROS) with six modules, and the eight modules of the US Orbital Segment (USOS). USOS supports roughly three-quarters of the services for NASA, around one-tenth for JAXA and one-tenth for the ESA, and around two to three per cent for the CSA.

The regulation of this new space of human interaction – ie, a permanently inhabited civil space station – rests on the principle of national sovereignty. This means that the main partners of the project – the US, Russia, Japan, Canada and the European partners[10] on the space station – are not only liable for what they provide for in the project but also, under Article 5 of the IGA, 'each partner shall retain jurisdiction and control over the elements it registers and over personnel in or on the Space Station who are its nationals'. As a corollary of sovereignty, the new legal space of permanently inhabited space stations is defined by the principle of extra-territoriality, according to which it is possible to determine the laws that are applicable for activities occurring in or on the station. Each project partner applies its own national laws of intellectual rights protection, tortious liability or criminal responsibility depending on the nationality of the personnel and the elements registered by the launching state. Although the EU is not to be considered a sovereign entity, or even some sort of federal state, EU Member States wisely chose to be considered in the IGA as one entity as regards the applicability of EU law to the activities in and on the ISS.

The extension of national jurisdictions over activities in or on space stations should be strictly understood in accordance with the general principles and rules of the UN space treaties. The IGA, after all, concerns activities in the space station rather than how astronauts and spacecrafts reach that place. Tortious liability for damages caused by space objects, whether or not on the Earth's surface or to aircraft in flight, is covered by the 1972 Liability Convention; damage (and damages) caused by national personnel or by the elements registered by the partners of the ISS project have to be assessed in accordance with the extra-territorial effects of a certain jurisdiction – for example, EU law in the case of the European Columbus Laboratory.

This twofold level of legal safeguards and space regulations fits hand in glove with the dualistic model of international law, as discussed in the previous sections. Either UN space agreements have left much leeway to further decisions of its member states or such agreements do not apply to the new scenarios of outer space with its rules and norms. The IGA embraces this latter view of international space law by complementing its provisions, for example, as concerns matters of liability. Article 16 of the IGA sets up a 'cross-waiver of liability' which prohibits all launching states and their related entities – that is, contractors and sub-contractors, users or customers – from claiming damages against each other. Moreover, all ISS partners should implement this clause in their contracts with users, customers and contractors. It is then up to each partner and jurisdiction how to apportion

[10] The 10 Member States of the ESA are Belgium, Denmark, France, Germany, Italy, the Netherlands, Norway, Spain, Sweden and Switzerland; the UK joined in 2012, with Hungary and Luxembourg committing to the Space Station programme in 2019 as well as ESA cooperating state Slovenia.

responsibility within their own legal boundaries. For example, claims arising between the ESA and one of its partners or users can be covered by contractors or sub-contractors that do not concern other international partners. As the ESA website is keen to inform us:

> Space Station users will be asked to agree to an interparty waiver of liability as part of their contract with the European Space Agency, stating that each party will not bring claims in arbitration or sue the other party as a result of International Space Station activities. The applicable law for disputes and the detailed procedures in case of arbitration will be decided mutually by the Space Station users and European Space Agency. The contract will specify the country where the Arbitration Tribunal shall sit, normally in the country where the user has his legal seat.[11]

The increasing role that sovereign states directly play in shaping the laws of outer space – in addition to the treaties and declarations of the UN General Assembly and the governance of the ITU, COPUOS or UNOOSA – is confirmed by the panoply of national regulations and space agencies that have been building up in recent decades. However, this increasing role of sovereign states is a double-edged sword, since it reminds us of how space law was born with an 'original sin', such as the militarisation of space in the Cold War era.[12] The creation of the ISS with the corresponding intergovernmental agreement confirms this conjecture. The agreement establishes that conflicts of jurisdiction among partners must be resolved through the application of already developed national and international rules and procedures. Still, the 2022 Russian aggression in Ukraine, and the subsequent international sanctions on Russia, have had obvious repercussions on the ISS project.

At the time of writing,[13] it is an open question how much or whether Russia will lower, redirect or cut funding from its side, or whether it will abandon the project before 2028, setting up a new space station of its own or with China by the mid-2030s. Whatever the timing, these are not simple condominium problems. These problems cast a light on a fundamental drawback of legal dualism in international law. What is at stake not only concerns the regulations of space law with its peculiar constitution, but also the ethos of space activities.

[11] The document is available at https://www.esa.int/Science_Exploration/Human_and_Robotic_Exploration/International_Space_Station/International_Space_Station_legal_framework.

[12] BE Bowen, *Original Sin: Power, Technology and War in Outer Space* (London, Hurst, 2022).

[13] As CNN was keen to inform us on 2 March 2023, the Russian cosmonaut Andrey Fedyaev was a member of the Crew-6 team in the seventh astronaut flight SpaceX has carried out on NASA's behalf since 2020. In 2022, NASA and Roscosmos adopted a ride-sharing agreement that aims to guarantee continued access to the ISS. Notwithstanding the invasion of Ukraine, 'Russia remains the United States' primary partner on the space station. Officials at NASA have repeatedly said the conflict has had no impact on cooperation between the countries' space agencies'. In a news briefing from 24 January, 2023, Fedyaev stressed that 'space cooperation has a very long history, and we are setting the example of how people should be living on Earth'. See https://edition.cnn.com/2023/03/01/world/spacex-nasa-crew-6-launch-thursday-scn/index.html.

VII. What Sovereign States Want

Almost every legal system has its own set of regulations related to outer space activities that span across a variety of legal fields, such as national defence and scientific research, satellites and Earth remote sensing, the use and appropriation of celestial resources, amongst others. At times, it is a matter of faith, rather than formal reasoning, in terms of finding logical coherence in this patchwork of national laws vis-a-vis the provisions of international law. More than 70 states have their own space agencies, whereas 14 are effectively orbital launching states. However, the lack of launching capabilities does not mean that some countries have not entered – or aim to be a part of – the big league. Luxembourg is a good example. Despite being one of the smallest countries in Europe, Luxembourg is one of the largest satellite operators in the world. It will come as no surprise that the Grand Duchy offers quite an interesting case study to assess current developments in space law.

The legal framework for space activities in Luxembourg includes three basic pieces of legislation: the Law on Electronic Media (1991), the Law on the Exploration and Use of Space Resources (2017) and the Law on Space Activities (2020). The overall aim of Luxembourg is to foster the growth and diversification of activities carried out by space actors, especially from private industry in its own territory. Luxembourg provides for the management of risks relating to space activities and state liability by assuming duties and obligations under the 1976 Registration Convention. On this basis, the authorisation and supervision of space activities are up to the Ministry of the Economy and the Luxembourg Space Agency, along with the registration of space objects launched into outer space. To attract business, the Law on Space Activities includes tax exemption for insurance contracts that cover the space objects registered by Luxembourg and tax credits for investments made by operators of space objects.

The rush by Luxembourg to involve itself in space activities and the use of space resources has been extensively debated in connection with Luxembourg's claim that space resources are appropriable pursuant to Article 1 of its 2017 law on the use of space resources. 'Asteroid mining' represents the most relevant space project in terms of Luxembourg's aim to develop niche economic platforms. This form of 'appropriation' may seem to be in direct conflict with the ethos of the UN treaties. Whilst Article I of the 1967 Agreement establishes that the exploration and use of outer space should benefit all countries – and Article II repudiates national appropriation over outer space – we noted time and again that such legal formulas on appropriation, damages or fault are open to multiple interpretations. Some think there is no incompatibility between international law – for example, Articles I and II of the Outer Space Treaty – and the national law of Luxembourg, since such appropriations, such as extracting golden nuggets from an asteroid, would still be in line with the wording of the UN treaties.[14] Others stress that this

[14] E Tepper, 'Structuring the Discourse on the Exploitation of Space Resources: Between Economic and Legal Commons' (2018) 49 *Space Policy* 1.

national regulation draws on a basic principle of old French property law regarding the separable legal nature of mines or the surface of the land.[15] Apart from business incentives with the promise of property rights, the appropriation of resources could, in addition, be deemed legitimate in accordance with the classic argument of John Locke developed in Chapter 16 of the *Second Treatise of Government*.[16] What humans own is because of their work, efforts and ingenuity. This proprietary approach spawns the critical distinction that Locke draws between the expansion of the states as territorial appropriation and the property rights that individuals have in relation to goods and things.

Locke's differentiation is relevant because this kind of argument is also at stake with the US Space Resource Exploration and Utilization Act from 2015, namely, Title IV of the Commercial Space Launch Competitiveness Act, which establishes the right of US citizens to all asteroid resources they can obtain.[17] Rather than an overt violation of Article II of the Outer Space Treaty, the US Space Law 'should be seen as a valid interpretation of Article II given the numerous ambiguities inherent in the article itself'.[18] By distinguishing between the territorial expansion of states and the rights of individuals to possess, own, transport, use and sell either asteroid resources or space resources, the claim is that the US Act does not assert any sort of sovereignty over celestial bodies. On the contrary, the distinction would shed light on how the legal status of outer space as a global commons does not preclude the commercial extraction of space resources, as occurs in other fields of international law, such as the law of the sea or Antarctica. The very fact that no specific clause of international space law prohibits this extraction of space resources can be interpreted as the basis for the legitimate extraction and appropriation of such resources. It is worth noting that the International Institute of Space Law supported this view.[19]

These trends of national space law on extraction and appropriation of space resources draw attention to traditional, well-known coordination problems and potential antinomies between public international law and national space law.[20] Such problems should be understood in accordance with the open issues of legal

[15] J Su, 'Legality of Unilateral Exploitation of Space Resources under International Law' (2017) 66(4) *International and Comparative Law Quarterly* 991.

[16] J Locke, *Two Treatises of Government*, edited by P Laslett (Cambridge, Cambridge University Press, 2013).

[17] C Foster, 'Excuse Me, You're Mining My Asteroid: Space Property Rights and the US Space Resource Exploration and Utilization Act of 2015' (2016) 2 *University of Illinois Journal of Law, Technology & Policy* 407.

[18] PP Blount and CJ Robison, 'One Small Step: The Impact of the US Commercial Space Launch Competitiveness Act of 2015 on the Exploitation of Resources in Outer Space' (2016) 18(2) *North Carolina Journal of Law & Technology* 160.

[19] M Smith, 'International Institute of Space Law OK with US Asteroid Mining Law', *Spacepolicyonline*, 24 December 2015, https://spacepolicyonline.com/news/international-institute-of-space-law-ok-with-u-s-asteroid-mining-law.

[20] JI Gabrynowicz, 'One Half Century and Counting: The Evolution of US National Space Law and Three Long-Term Emerging Issues' (2010) 4 *Harvard Law and Policy Review* 405.

dualism in international law. Although a certain degree of flexibility stems from the open clauses of international space law that may accommodate multiple diverse applications at the national or regional level, several scholars believe that legislation such as the US 2015 Space Act or the Luxembourg 2017 Law on Space Resources represents a breaking point in international space law.[21] The claim is that every form of appropriation infringes upon the principle of outer space as a province of humankind. Rather than a sort of infinite *res nullius*, space as a global commons entails that no property rights can be granted in outer space unless they are enshrined in an international act.[22] Countries such as Luxembourg or the US cannot give themselves the authority to promise property rights over space resources before they are extracted. The problem is not whether such appropriation is illegitimate, as the international regime for the exploitation of celestial resources envisioned by the 1979 Moon Agreement supports this view. The problem lies with the unilateral claim of property rights enshrined in the US Space Act, and the laws of Luxembourg on outer space, for that matter.

However, the drawbacks of current international space law do not entail any 'state of nature'. The formula is often used to depict the international arena as a state of conflict and chaos, as suggested by the philosophy of Thomas Hobbes. According to Chapter XIII of *Leviathan*, the state of nature is a 'war of all against all', in which nothing is unjust and human life is 'solitary, poor, nasty, brutish, and short'.[23] This condition not only illustrates the ordeal of every civil war or the lawless territories of North America before the advent of the European colonies; in the opinion of Hobbes, a potential conflict defines the interaction between sovereign states because of the lack of a superior government. This is an idea that even the cosmopolitan Kant would later accept in his critique of Hobbes.[24] In the words of the English philosopher:

> In all times, Kings, and persons of Soveraigne authority, because of their Independency, are in continuall jealousies, and in the state and posture of Gladiators; having their weapons pointing, and their eyes fixed on one another; that is, their Forts, Garrisons, and Guns upon the Frontiers of their Kingdomes; and continuall Spyes upon their neighbours; which is a posture of War. But because they uphold thereby, the Industry of their Subjects; there does not follow from it, that misery, which accompanies the Liberty of particular men.[25]

Over the past century and more, the international community has aimed to tackle this Hobbesian scenario and the very idea that, ultimately, the laws of international relations hinge on what sovereign states want. This chapter has summed up the

[21] F Tronchetti, 'The Space Resource Exploration and Utilization Act: A Move Forward or a Step Back?' (2015) 34 *Space Policy* 6.

[22] ibid. A general framework for this debate can be found in MN Shaw, *International Law*, 9th edn (Cambridge, Cambridge University Press, 2021).

[23] T Hobbes, *Leviathan* (Pacific Publishing Studio, 2011).

[24] I Kant, *Perpetual Peace: A Philosophical Essay*, translated by MC Smith (Crows Nest, Allen & Unwin, 1903).

[25] Hobbes (n 23).

efforts of the international community in accordance with the dualistic model of international law along with its pros and cons. We noted that the sovereign-centred approach is compatible with an effective regulatory system that has managed, for example, both the public and private uses of GEOs for telecommunications and other services under the responsibility of the ITU and the SSD in recent decades. However, this sovereign-centred approach is also the source of some critical issues in today's space law. These include the opinions of several scholars, according to whom national laws on the appropriability of space resources would clearly infringe on principles and rules of the UN space treaties, as well as the very idea of outer space as a legal commons.[26] Whether or not we agree with this claim, it seems fair to admit that the unilateral activism of sovereign states could ultimately dissolve the *nomos* of outer space and constrict its original ethos to a purely commercial dimension.

The frequent use of legal analogies and overt proposals on how to amend the legal framework confirms the troubles in the field. The limits of international space law can be illustrated with the alternative between the non-appropriation of celestial resources and the new property rights in outer space. Rather than a sharp alternative, some propose more nuanced solutions, such as excluding asteroids under a minimum diameter from the definition of 'celestial bodies'.[27] Likewise, environmental concerns for space activities – currently covered by the general principle enshrined in Article IX of the Outer Space Treaty – suggest strengthening such provisions on how to prevent harmful contamination of space, with the corresponding risks for space activities through an environmental impact assessment of space missions,[28] or establishing that space resources should be deemed as resources that should not be available to humans after all.[29]

The limits of analogy are also apparent vis-a-vis such parallelisms – for example, between the laws that shall govern activities in outer space and the governance model adopted by the Antarctic Treaty,[30] or the analogy with deep sea fishing.[31] Such limits of analogy work both ways – that is, not only to support the claim that space resources are not appropriable on the basis of, say, Part XI of the UN 1982 Convention on the Law of the Sea, but to contend, (as the Luxembourg government did) that fish in the high seas, as well as resources in outer space, are no one's

[26] G Oduntan, 'Imagine There are No Possessions: Legal and Moral Basis of the Common Heritage Principle in Space Law' in K de Feyter (ed), *Globalization and Common Responsibilities of States* (Abingdon, Routledge, 2017).

[27] M Hoffmann and F Bergamasco, 'Space Resources from the Perspective of Sustainability: Legal Aspects' (2020) 3 *Global Sustainability*,. doi:10.1017/sus.2019.27.

[28] L Viikari, *The Environmental Element in Space Law: Assessing the Present and Charting the Future* (The Hague, Martinus Nijhoff Publishers, 2008).

[29] RE Loder, 'Asteroid Mining: Ecological Jurisprudence beyond Earth' (2018) 36(3) *Virginia Environmental Law Journal* 275.

[30] C Collis, 'Territories beyond Possession? Antarctica and Outer Space' (2017) 7(2) *The Polar Journal* 287.

[31] I Feichtner, 'Mining for Humanity in the Deep Sea and Outer Space: The Role of Small States and International Law in the Extraterritorial Expansion of Extraction' (2019) 32(2) *Leiden Journal of International Law* 255.

property until caught, therefore becoming the property of both fishers and today's space companies.[32] Therefore, the fact that such analogies may either support or contradict opposing claims, particularly regarding the appropriability of space resources, indicates the shortcomings of a legal framework born to govern a set of human activities that have dramatically changed since then. To substantiate this claim, it is worth mentioning the disruption of new actors in the outer space arena, such as private companies backing the space activities of old traditional launching states. Such disruption adds a further layer of complexity to the intricate interplay between national and international law.

VIII. New Actors

In the 1960s and 1970s, when the bulk of today's space law was laid down, the only actors were sovereign states. The fact that international space law revolves around the rights and obligations of launching states is not only a homage to the philosophy of Thomas Hobbes, but instead mirrors the state of affairs in the 1960s and 1970s, when states had an oligopoly over space technologies. Nowadays, around three-quarters of space activities are carried out by the private sector. This new scenario entails a whole set of thorny legal issues and, once again, the question of the extent to which legal analogy can help to address them. Some legislation, such as the US Space Law and Luxembourg's Law on the Exploration and Use of Space Resources, clarify this shift in the role that the private sector has in backing space activities. The focus has accordingly been on whether the Outer Space Treaty prohibition on national appropriation applies to the private sector,[33] and to what extent the rights and duties of the private sector should not exceed those of the launching states.[34] This view on the rights and duties of public and private actors begs the question of the limits that space law imposes on the launching states through the principles and rules of the UN treaties. The problem is not solved by stressing that such treaties give responsibilities to the states for the activities that private companies carry out. Scholars and institutions alike (eg, UNOOSA) have stressed time and again the growing shortcomings of the law in tackling the activities of private companies.[35]

[32] J Steele, 'Luxembourg and the Exploitation of Outer Space' (2021) 29(1) *Nottingham Law Journal* 32.

[33] C Davis and M. J. Sundahl, 'The Hague Working Group on Space Resources: Creating the Legal Building Blocks for a New Industry', *Law Faculty Articles and Essays*, Cleveland State University, 2017, no 1044.

[34] G Oduntan, 'Aspects of the International Legal Regime concerning Privatization and Commercialization of Space Activities' (2016) 17(1) *Georgetown Journal of International Affairs* 79.

[35] See CL Deem, 'Liability of Private Space Transportation Companies to Their Customers' (1983) 51 *International In-House Counsel Journal* 340; VC Ernest, 'Third Party Liability of the Private Space Industry: To Pay What No One Has Paid Before' (1991) 41 *Case Western Reserve Law Review* 503; and B Ziemblicki and Y Oralova, 'Private Entities in Outer Space Activities: Liability Regime Reconsidered' (2021) 56 *Space Policy* 101427.

These shortcomings of space law in terms of coping with the disruption of private actors are critical for three reasons. Although the drivers of such legal disruption will be thoroughly examined later on in this book, they ideally conclude the survey of this chapter on the pillars of international space law and its current limits. The first limit concerns how the impact of private actors on pillars of international law adds a further layer of complexity to current debates on duties and obligations of launching states – ie, what scholars sum up as the 'privatisation of space' – by raising a new generation of private-to-private rights and obligations with the corresponding lawsuits. Waivers of liability, such as those illustrated with the contractual clauses of ESA for the use of the European Columbus Laboratory in the ISS, arguably fall short in terms of tackling many challenges of the privatisation of space. Second, the critical role of Elon Musk's satellites in the Ukrainian resistance against the 2022 Russian occupation poses new questions in the military domain, such as dual uses of outer space technology and the extent to which current international space law may properly tackle the militarisation of space.[36] Third, current promises of space tourism, space hotels, mass space exploration and so on raise a further class of issues that can be dubbed the democratisation of space.[37] The more everyday people will be involved in outer space missions and activities, the less current regulations of national and international space law will seem properly equipped to tackle the charge of a new generation of space tourists, explorers and even colonisers.

Against this backdrop, the next chapter aims to address such a disruption of private actors in outer space activities that triggers the question of what rules and principles will govern human activities in a new domain of the law. The quest for a new legal framework has so far related to public actors, from the pioneering principles and regulations of the 1960s to national legislation in the 2010s. The analysis of this chapter will be complemented by the manifold ways in which the new role of private actors in outer space may affect principles and regulations of this realm of human interaction, as well as the ethos of the space community.

[36] We will return to Musk's role in the 2022 Russian aggression to Ukraine in chs 7 and 8 below.

[37] E Bassi and U Pagallo, 'The Democratization of Outer Space: On Law, Ethics, and Technology' in M Arias Oliva et al (eds), *Smart Ethics in the Digital World – Ethicomp* (Madrid, Dialnet, 2024).

3

Leaving Earth, Privately

Scholars have stressed the drawbacks of today's space law, either regarding traditional limits of international law or vis-a-vis trends of 'privatisation'. The numbers are staggering. More than five years ago, around 70 per cent of space activity already involved the private sector, and these figures will realistically keep growing over the years. In its 2018 annual report, UNOOSA predicted the business will generate revenues of $1.1–2.7 trillion by 2040. Other reports confirm the magnitude of this business. This chapter draws attention to the manifold ways in which this scenario exacerbates the shortcomings of the regulatory framework, its governance and ethos. The challenges include compliance with international space law, thorny issues of jurisdiction, damages to be covered at both the national and international levels, and duties, rights and obligations that will increasingly concern not only public institutions and private companies (for example, Space X), but also litigation among private parties. It illustrates the changes in the field with the very idea of the 'astronaut' and how trends of privatisation and further advancements of technology – such as AI systems and smart robots – may affect the pillars of the law.

I. The Privatisation of Outer Space

Over the past three decades, the increasing role of private companies in space-related activities has been under the radar of scholars. The impact of space-focused corporations in the field can be appreciated in connection with three metrics: (i) the disruption of a market traditionally populated by military contractors such as Lockheed and Boeing; (ii) the dramatic decrease of costs relating to these private space-based activities; and (iii) the corresponding increase in the number of activities. For example, at the time of writing, the orbital delivery costs of NASA's Space Shuttle were around $20,000/kg, whilst the costs of SpaceX's Starship were $500/kg. The decrease in costs supports the increase in activities: in the 2010s, the average number of satellites launched per year was about 280. Current trends suggest that by 2030, the number will grow up to a hundred times more satellites launched per year.[1]

[1] M Byers and A Boley, *Who Owns Outer Space? International Law, Astrophysics, and the Sustainable Development of Space* (Cambridge, Cambridge University Press, 2023).

The same holds true for the number of astronauts: while in the first 60 years of space flights, around 600 astronauts were launched into outer space, by the next decade, it is reasonable to predict that the same number will represent the yearly standard.

These figures are only the tip of the iceberg. According to a report by SpaceTech Analytics in 2022, there were estimated to be over 10,000 space-focused companies globally.[2] More than half of them (5,582 space companies) had their headquarters in the US, almost 10 times more than the second country, the UK, with 615 firms. The activities of such private companies span across 20 different business sectors, including navigation and mapping, cloud solutions, space medicine and manufacturing. We have already noted that roughly three-quarters of all space-related activities are in the hands of corporations that have transformed a market traditionally dominated by heavyweight aerospace contractors. Scholars often refer to this scenario as the 'privatisation of space' or the 'New Space'.[3] The formulas have both a descriptive and a normative intent. The aim can either be to portray current trends of the space economy that should be traced back to the 1990s or to shed light on the legal effects of such space activities of private companies, such as liability issues that will eventually concern only private parties.[4] This section aims to illustrate the current state of the art with some of the most well-known space companies today, namely SpaceX, Blue Origin, Stratolaunch and Virgin Galactica. Launched by four billionaires – Elon Musk, Jeff Bezos, Paul Allen and Richard Branson, respectively – such corporations illustrate the profound transformation of principles and regulations of outer space and its ethos over the past two decades.

Elon Musk founded the Space Exploration Technologies Corp, or 'SpaceX', in 2002. SpaceX is by far one of the most important space companies globally. The original aim of the corporation was to reduce space transportation costs in order to enable the colonisation of Mars. The current core business regards spacecraft manufacturing, launching capacities, and, moreover, satellite communications, ie, Starlink. As of January 2023, after raising $750 million in a new funding round, the value of SpaceX was valued at $137 billion and growing. SpaceX has successfully completed all recent missions to the ISS, becoming one of the favourite partners of the US space administration NASA. In 2022, Benji Reed, the Director of this new powerful aerospace contractor, declared in a press briefing what the final purpose of the corporation is: 'We want to make life multi-planetary, and that means putting millions of people in space.'[5]

Another forceful aerospace contractor is Blue Origin. Jeff Bezos founded the company in 2000, with its headquarters in Kent, Washington. The core activities

[2] See SpaceTech Analytics, 'SpaceTech Industry Year 2021', January 2022, https://www.spacetech.global/spacetech-industry-year-overview-2021.

[3] A Vernile, *The Rise of Private Actors in the Space Sector* (Dordrecht, Springer, 2018).

[4] P Larsen, 'Commercial Operator Liability in the New Space Era' (2019) 113 *American Journal of International Law Unbound* 109.

[5] See Reed's announcement at https://www.space.com/spacex-launches-inspiration4-civilian-orbital-mission.

of Blue Origin are aerospace manufacturing and sub-orbital spaceflight services, whereas further projects concern the production of liquid rocket engines and orbital launch vehicles. Although Blue Origin is a leading company in such sectors of the space economy, competition is arguably tough. In 2020, the US government awarded a $579 million contract to develop a landing system for American astronauts on the Moon. Blue Origin presented its own offer to develop such a landing system. However, in 2021, NASA chose SpaceX as a partner for the upcoming missions of the Artemis project and, hence, the lander of the next-generation human spaceflights. Blue Origin filed a protest before the federal Government Accountability Office without success: the $2.9 billion contract to SpaceX from NASA was ratified. Blue Origin still has an esteemed revenue of $43 million annually and, on 20 July 2021, successfully completed its first crewed mission: the Blue Origin NS-16 with Jeff (and Mark) Bezos aboard. Because of the costs, for the moment, these crews are aimed at paying customers and celebrities eager to spend $50 million for a flight with the New Shepard launch vehicles. Further projects of the company include building space habitats. However, despite these vibrant activities – and drawing on the space missions that SpaceX has successfully completed, including all recent flights to the ISS – it seems fair to admit that Musk's company has gained a significant edge over Bezos'. The failure of an uncrewed mission of the New Shepard in September 2022 has not helped reduce the gap.

The case of Stratolaunch, the third company discussed in this section, sheds further light on the intricacy of the space economy and its current trends. The space race in the private sector is not only about heavyweight competitors but also about niche companies. Paul Allen, co-founder of Microsoft together with Bill Gates, created Stratolaunch in 2011 and headquartered it in Seattle, Washington. The company aims to specialise in air-launched transportation systems and, at the moment specifically, high-speed flight test services. Carrier aircraft should be grasped as launchpads for hypersonic and aerospace vehicles, such as the reusable Talon-A project for a vehicle that should reach Mach 6 speed – that is, six times the speed of the sound. Stratolaunch has several competitors, such as Arianespace and Vector Launch, whose estimated annual revenue is even bigger than that of Stratolaunch. Still, the company looks highly profitable in this specific segment of the space economy. The estimated annual revenue of Stratolaunch is almost $95 million per year. Since, at the time of writing, Stratolaunch 'only' had 305 employees, the estimated revenue for each company employee is a sound $ 307,500.

Finally, mention should be made of Richard Branson's Virgin Galactic, founded in 2004 and headquartered in the desert of Mojave, California. Here, the company also has one of its three operating bases. Virgin Galactic aims to be the first spaceflight company globally. The trips should last about an hour and a half. A promo of the company clarifies what to expect: 'Astronauts enjoy several minutes of out-of-seat weightlessness and breath-taking views of Earth from the spaceship's 17 windows.'[6]

[6] The promo is available at https://www.virgingalactic.com/news/virgin-galactic-launches-spaceflight-reservations-and-new-consumer-brand.

Later on in this chapter, we return to the very idea of 'astronaut'. How the notion is changing depends – also but not only – on the undertakings of Virgin Galactica. In 2021, the space tourism firm announced the success of its first test flight on the VSS Unity with humans aboard, including Branson, its boss. The business aims to organise 400 flights annually, with six passengers per flight paying $450,000 a ticket (with an initial deposit of $150,000, apparently largely refundable). The revenue should, accordingly, exceed $1 billion. The lengths to which these ideas go can be appreciated daily with the company's stock price and prediction. Meanwhile, in April 2023, after a significant mission failure, Virgin Orbit – the satellite launch company spin-off from Virgin Galactic in 2017 – filed for bankruptcy. Leaving aside the ups and downs of Branson's business, as well as the environmental concerns relating to all space tourism activities, the overall figures of the space economy remain impressive.

In addition to the four corporations of this section and the 10,000+ companies worldwide, there are more than 5,000 significant investors, 150 research and development hubs, and 130 state or governmental organisations involved in the business.[7] Navigation and mapping services (2,820 companies), cloud solutions (2,406), and manufacturing (1,048) are among the largest sectors of the space economy, with revenues predicted to be $1.1–2.7 trillion dollars by 2040.[8] Big money is also in communications. Rather than traditional broadcast communications, the business regards satellite services. By 2022, Space-X's Starlink had received more than half a million orders, which would translate to an annual revenue of $300 million at $50 per order. People struggling with poor terrestrial internet speed could smoothly multiply that number by 10. By the early 2020s, the satellite industry generated around $270 billion in revenue worldwide. However, such spectacular growth of the private sector has resulted in several tricky questions piling up in the legal domain.

In the previous chapter, we noted that the activities of private companies are traditionally disciplined under Article VII of the 1967 Outer Space Treaty on the 'international responsibility' of States Parties for the activities of their 'natural and juridical persons'. Therefore, most of the legal interplay between public authorities and private companies rests on the powers of national or regional regulators through, for example, licences, as well as contracts between public agencies and private companies.[9] While every national legal system has its specificities, all jurisdictions present provisions on procedural regularity, third-party liability, insurance premiums or law enforcement that provide the foundations for the bulk of national law regarding the activities of private companies in outer space.

[7] SpaceTech Analytics (n 2).

[8] UN Office for Outer Space Affairs (UNOOSA), *Annual Report 2018*, June 2019, available at https://www.unoosa.org/documents/pdf/annualreport/UNOOSA_Annual_Report_2018.pdf.

[9] S Freeland, 'Matching Detail with Practice: The Essential Elements of National Space Legislation' in CM Jorgensen (ed), *Proceedings of International Institute of Space Law* (Reston, VA, American Institute of Aeronautics and Astronautics, 2010).

Thus, it is against this backdrop that the next section will focus on such provisions of the law that define the liability of private companies for their outer space activities. The aim is to understand how the 'privatisation of space' may have affected the traditional legal framework laid down in the 1960s and 1970s, drawing attention to the interpretation of some crucial notions of this framework and the distribution of powers between national law authorities and the principles of international law. National regulators, for better or worse, complement the principles and provisions discussed in the previous chapter.

II. Business as Usual

The activities of space-focused private companies are mostly disciplined by provisions of national law, such as licences and authorisations, as well as the laws relating to contracts and insurance policies. The dispute between Blue Origin and NASA mentioned in the previous section stresses that contractual agreements and industrial or commercial offers hinge on the adjudicatory powers and procedures of what civil lawyers dub 'national administrative law'. Such norms include provisions on licensing and registration of private companies, safety and environmental obligations, indemnification and law enforcement provisions. Since national governments are responsible at the international level for the space-related activities of their 'own' private companies, it is comprehensible that governments have aimed to reduce their liability burdens by establishing a set of duties and conditions on private companies, which includes financial responsibility of the private company and compulsory insurance policies. In their best possible light, the purpose of all these provisions is to trigger a virtuous circle, namely fostering technological innovation by reinforcing the protection of individual and collective rights.[10]

A key ingredient of every technological regulation concerns insurance. An insurance premium is the factor through which the sum to be charged for a certain amount of insurance coverage is determined. The problem concerns collecting enough data on the probability of events, their consequences and costs, to determine the levels of risk and therefore the amount of insurance premiums on which the accountability for outer space activities may hinge. Several jurisdictions expect nongovernmental operators to obtain insurance before authorising their launches. For example, US federal law requires launch insurance limited to $500 million for each launch, although a lower amount of insurance can be set based on an ad hoc risk assessment by the US Federal Aviation Administration. Insurance must cover every probable loss from claims by third parties regarding death, bodily injury, property damages or loss resulting from activities carried out under the licence

[10] U Pagallo, 'From Automation to Autonomous Systems: A Legal Phenomenology with Problems of Accountability' (2017) *IJCAI International Joint Conference on Artificial Intelligence* 17.

of the US government.[11] However, to promote commercial development of space activities, law makers often complement such insurance policies with further forms of regulation, such as liability caps or waivers of liability.

Liability caps concern limited compensation schemes for incidents and pecuniary limits to the strict liability policies adopted in the field.[12] The Rome Convention of 7 October 1952 on damages caused by foreign aircraft to third parties on the surface illustrates how this approach works in practice. On the one hand, private companies, as well as their insurance providers, should know the exposure of their risk in advance. On the other hand, liability caps should counterbalance the dangers of liability for those benefiting from the technology, thus making risks insurable. The idea is to back technological advancements through the financial resources of a national or international treasury. The aim may present no issues in times of economic abundance and prosperity, and yet, as shown by the intergovernmental agreements underpinning the creation of the space station – ie, the ISS IGA from 1998 covered in the previous chapter of this book – advances in technology and outer space programmes may also recommend the adoption of more drastic solutions. In addition to liability caps shielding private companies and technological innovators in relation to space-related activities, legislators can also endorse liability waivers such as those inserted into the contractual clauses for activities carried out in and on the ISS.

The US Congress inaugurated this trend by placing a moratorium on the protection of the health and safety of crew and space flight participants in 2004. Except in cases of severe or fatal injuries, or contributing to a close call, US law establishes that space flight passengers and related crew assume all mission risks. The approach of 51 USC § 50914(b)(1) consists of a reciprocal cross-waiver of claims according to which each party agrees to be responsible for losses or property damages that it sustains. After public agencies, many private companies have followed suit by contracting around liability issues to resolve disputes extrajudicially. Blue Origin, SpaceX and Virgin Galactica may well impose cross-waivers of liability into their contracts so that each astronaut agrees to bear its own risks. Drawing on these trends, some scholars claim that contractual clauses and terms of services by private companies may help build up some certainty about the rules governing space law.[13] However, contractual clauses and waivers of liability have their limits; in particular, they cannot prevent obligations towards third parties to compensate for damage done by wrongdoing.

Tortious liability or – in the jargon of civil lawyers – non-contractual responsibility falls upon parties that are negligent, strictly accountable for the behaviour

[11] F Lyall and PB Larsen, *Space Law: A Treatise* (Abingdon, Routledge, 2018) 440.

[12] M Schaefer, 'The Need for Federal Preemption and International Negotiations Regarding Liability Caps and Waivers of Liability in the US Commercial Space Industry' (2015) 33(1) *Berkeley Journal of International Law* 223.

[13] D St John, 'The Trouble with Westphalia in Space: The State-Centric Liability Regime' (2012) 40 *Denver Journal of International Law & Policy*, 686.

of others, or responsible for damages that depend on their own intentional acts. Some argue that in certain jurisdictions, such as US law, most potential tortious claims relating to space activities could be adequately tackled.[14] This assumption rests on both quantitative and qualitative reasons. On the one hand, we noted that most space companies are headquartered in the US and therefore most third-party claims would likely involve US citizens and corporations. On the other hand, US law appears 'more favourable' than other national laws in terms of compensating damages done by wrongdoing, such as punitive damages. This is because US tort law is harmonised to a great extent by the common law tradition adopted by the 49 states (Louisiana being the exception). Considering, for example, the 27 different tortious liability regimes of the EU Member States, the rules of US tort law provide a more straightforward legal framework for technological regulation.[15] In the event of a satellite collision of an operator with another authorised space object, US tort law would allow better compensation for wrongful actions against property and persons: First, because – so goes the argument – every commercial satellite operator could be liable for lack of due care; and, second, because space mining operators could file claims against other US operators on celestial bodies.[16]

However, even US law has its limits. Although the national provisions of US space law with administrative licenses, insurance policies, or tortious liability issues are paramount, any jurisdiction falls short in terms of coping with the overall risks of uncertainty and fragmentation. Such risks depend on three aspects: (i) the distribution of powers between national, regional (such as EU law) and international law; (ii) the interpretation of some tricky formulas, such as the duties of launching states enshrined in international conventions; and (iii) issues of jurisdiction relating to the nationality of private companies. After all, we noted that 130 state or governmental organisations are involved in space activities with 10,000+ companies, 5,000 significant investors and 150 research and development hubs worldwide. This complex scenario may well trigger issues of legal uncertainty and even the lowering of legal standards. The following section examines how national law makers intend to tackle these risks, not only regarding 'what' should be decided, but also 'who' shall decide in some instances of space law.

III. Searching for a Jurisdiction

Sovereign states are free to specify the content of their laws on space activities as long as their acts are consistent with international duties and obligations.

[14] P Larsen, 'Commercial Operator Liability in the New Space Era' (2019) 113 *American Journal of International Law* 109.

[15] W Barfield and U Pagallo, *Advanced Introduction to the Law and Artificial Intelligence* (Cheltenham, Edward Elgar, 2020).

[16] PS Dempsey, 'National Laws Governing Commercial Space Activities: Legislation, Regulation, & Enforcement' (2016) 36(1) *Northwestern Journal of International Law & Business* 1.

However, this freedom entails that domestic legislations on licensing, insurance or indemnificatory regimes for space companies operating within their jurisdiction are often quite different from one another and may entail a lowering of legal safeguards regarding the evaluation of the technical and financial robustness of the applicant with its facilities, or the ability of victims to be compensated for the damage. Governments should determine that private companies will not endanger safety and public health, property and security, nor will they impose economic burdens on the national treasury. Yet, the discretionary powers of such authorities may nurture the creation of flag states, that is, more lenient states that set their requirements for space activities on the basis of mere economic purposes.[17] Since licences, as a prerequisite to space activities, are often defined in accordance with national and territorial principles,[18] a first step would be to establish a more appropriate registration mechanism for space-related activities.[19]

However, because the amendment of international agreements and national laws is notoriously time-consuming, most jurisdictions have tackled the potential fragmentation of the system through the extra-territoriality effects of their own rules. The regulation of 'private launching companies' makes this point clear. Some states regulate the launch site, and others the launch provider. A third approach has been endorsed by the US Commercial Space Launch Act of 1984, which applies regardless of whether the launch site is within or without the US. According to the Space Launch Act, the Federal Aviation Administration (FAA) has the power to license the launch and re-entry of expendable and reusable vehicles and operate a launch or re-entry site by every US citizen.[20] Nonetheless, this approach has not prevented thorny issues of liability involving US space-focused private companies. Consider the satellite collision that occurred on 10 February 2009. Iridium 33 – an active communication satellite of the US corporation, provider of data information coverage and band voice-to-messenger communication devices, phones and integrated transceivers – accidentally collided with another satellite, the derelict Russian military Kosmos 2251, at an altitude of about 500 miles above the Taymyr Peninsula in Siberia.

From a legal viewpoint, the tricky detail of the accident is that Iridium 33 was launched from a Russian-owned spaceport. This means that, after the collision, Iridium could have filed a claim for compensation under the 1972 Liability Convention, and yet, had it done so, it would have had to enlist the US State Department to negotiate on its behalf with the Russian Ministry of Foreign Affairs. Russia could have contended that it was up to itself to decide how to assign liability

[17] C Albert, 'Liability in International Law and the Ramifications on Commercial Space Launches and Space Tourism' (2014) 36 *Loyola of Los Angeles International & Comparative Law Review* 233.

[18] Freeland (n 9).

[19] A Taghdiri, 'Flags of Convenience and the Commercial Space Flight Industry: The Inadequacy of Current International Law to Address the Opportune Registration of Space Vehicles in Flag States' (2014) 19 *Boston University Journal of Science & Technology Law* 405.

[20] JI Gabrynowicz, 'One Half Century and Counting: The Evolution of US National Space Law and Three Long-Term Emerging Issues' (2010) 4 *Harvard Law & Policy Review* 405.

for the collision internally. After all, Article VII of the Liability Convention prohibits two parties from the same country from invoking the terms of the Convention against each other. In the wording of Article VII:

> The provisions of this Convention shall not apply to damage caused by a space object of a launching State to: (a) nationals of that launching State; (b) foreign nationals during such time as they are participating in the operation of that space object from the time of its launching or at any stage thereafter until its descent, or during such time as they are in the immediate vicinity of a planned launching or recovery area as the result of an invitation by that launching State.

In general terms, how to proceed when multiple states have a reasonable claim to being the claimant state and one of them is also the launching state of a company's space object can entail a vicious circle. It is worth noting that Iridium and Russia could not solve their dispute on the basis of the redress mechanisms set up with the Liability Convention. This loophole in the law soon prompted the international community – particularly the Permanent Court of Arbitration (PCA) – to address the troubles with dispute settlement of outer space-related activities. Some logical and practical puzzles of space law had quickly to be amended. On 6 December 2011, the Administrative Council of the PCA adopted the Optional Rules for Arbitration of Disputes Relating to Outer Space Activities (hereinafter 'the Outer Space Rules').[21] Such rules have been welcomed in the business community and among experts, since they provide 'a voluntary and binding means for the resolution of space-related disputes which is open to all space actors and specifically structured to meet the peculiar features of economic space activities'.[22]

However, another problem of space law relates to companies' nationality. All in all, there are no internationally consistent rules for establishing the nationality of a corporation.[23] The same corporation may claim different nationalities according to the jurisdiction under scrutiny, therefore triggering potential confusion about which domestic legal regime should apply. In common law jurisdictions, such as US law, the golden rule is that corporations are granted the nationality of the state under whose law it has been incorporated; in civil law jurisdictions, such as France or Germany, the nationality of the corporate entity is based on its principal centre of business. Therefore, it can be challenging to determine the proper jurisdiction between common law and civil law jurisdictions, and, moreover, additional problems of jurisdiction are generated by the group of flag states that sell citizenship by investment.[24] These legal problems are not unique

[21] F Pocar, 'An Introduction to the PCA's Optional Rules for Arbitration of Disputes Relating to Outer Space Activities' (2012) 38 *Journal of Space Law* 171.

[22] F Tronchetti, 'The PCA Rules for Dispute Settlement in Outer Space: A Significant Step Forward' (2013) 29(3) *Space Policy* 181.

[23] D Ireland-Piper, 'Extraterritoriality in East Asia: Jurisdiction and Criminal Law in China, Japan, and South Korea' in D Ireland-Piper (ed), *Recapping Principles of Jurisdiction at International Law* (Cheltenham, Edward Elgar, 2021) 13–47.

[24] MB Krakat, 'Genuine Links beyond State and Market Control: The Sale of Citizenship by Investment in International and Supranational Legal Perspective' (2018) 30(1) *Bond Law Review* 145.

to international space law,[25] but still, issues of dispute settlement, nationality of private companies, and jurisdiction add to the complexity of the field in terms of the distribution of powers between national and international law as well as the meaning of certain principles, or provisions of international conventions.

We noted that international space law is silent on the merits of contractual clauses and open issues of third-party claims that go together with the growing activities of private companies: 'In the absence of an established body with jurisdiction to adjudicate on the conduct of private companies in outer space, domestic legislation is likely the more effective option at present.'[26] Indeed, states are not only bearers of international duties and obligations, but are also regulators of private interactions between space companies and individuals. Both roles do not exclude each other because states are 'game players' and 'game designers' of today's space law. So far, the focus of this chapter has been on the latter role of governments in establishing the norms that corporations will follow in outer space. The insulation of spacefaring companies from liability – set up by their national governments with the international agreements from the 1960s and the 1970s – is not only complemented by national regulations on licensing and registration, insurance and jurisdiction, but domestic legislation also covers private-to-private interaction relating to outer space activities; that is, between private companies and individuals. How such interplay is governed by the law adds a further layer of complexity to the challenges posed by the privatisation of space.

IV. Parties to Private Lawsuits

Two pillars of private-to-private interaction relating to outer space activities are examined in this chapter, namely waivers of liability and arbitration clauses. On the one hand, US law (ie, 51 USC § 50914(b)(1) and Article 5 of the ISS IGA) grants waivers of liability for contractors and sub-contractors of space activities so that each part to a contract (including private astronauts) assumes its risks. On the other hand, the Outer Space Rules adopted by the PCA in 2011 have improved mechanisms of dispute resolution that are 'open to all space actors' and should consider 'the peculiar features of economic space activities'.[27] Although arguably expensive, commercial and investment arbitration in space-related activities shows that this mechanism is often effective in terms of addressing the troubles with dispute settlement among private companies.[28] The international community of PCA arbitrators must guarantee the skills and expertise of those

[25] G Stessens, *Money-Laundering: A New International Law Enforcement Model* (Cambridge, Cambridge University Press, 2000).
[26] S Freeland and D Ireland-Piper, 'Space Law, Human Rights and Corporate Accountability' (2022) 26(1) *UCLA Journal of International Law and Foreign Affairs* 1.
[27] Tronchetti (n 22).
[28] J Frohloff, 'Arbitration in Space Disputes' (2019) 35(3) *Arbitration International* 309.

who have to decide a case in a reasonable amount of time. In any event, space law contracts and licenses can always adjudicate the dispute as a matter of contract law in municipal courts.[29]

However, arbitration and contractual clauses hardly represent a one-size-fits-all solution for all the problems of the field. Note should be made of the protection of fundamental individual rights and principles of international law. All arbitration authorities should respect such rights and principles, and should not be overruled by waivers of liability. Some argue that space-related litigation falls outside the arbitration clauses of contracts because space companies should be internationally liable for their space objects.[30] Moreover, other scholars claim that the level of legal protection that private companies should guarantee in outer space must safeguard the basic rights of individuals.[31] Current trends of environmental law litigation show that some human rights obligations could be extended to space-focused corporations: oil and coal companies are increasingly under pressure from institutional investors and their stakeholders to be more transparent about risks associated with climate change regulation.[32] Considering the current standards of contractual clauses for outer space activities, such as space tourism, some think that 'it will not be legally or morally satisfactory that corporations providing such services require the individual participants to sign away their rights through contractual exclusion of liability clauses'.[33] Arguably, the more everyday people will be involved in outer space missions or activities that follow promises of space tourism, exploration or even settlements in celestial bodies, the less today's clauses of contracts and agreements among private parties will be able to tackle the legal challenges of space privatisation properly. The limits of arbitration clauses and cross-waivers of liability seem obvious once confronted with the SpaceX Director's vision of 'putting millions of people in space'.[34] In this case, arbitration clauses would be either too expensive or too ineffective.[35]

Further chapters of this book complement this 'individualistic approach' to the challenges created by the privatisation of outer space with the public interest at stake in the overall sustainability of the space industry. Such sustainability relates both to environmental and cybersecurity concerns, and the protection of human rights. However, by drawing attention to the different private actors potentially

[29] St John (n 13).

[30] AP Reinert, 'Updating the Liability Regime in Outer Space: Why Spacefaring Companies Should Be Internationally Liable for Their Space Objects' (2020) 62(1) *William & Mary Law Review* 324.

[31] J Lim, 'Charting a Human Rights Framework for Outer Space Settlements', *71st International Astronautical Congress (IAC) – The CyberSpace Edition*, October 2020, https://www.jusadastra.org/assets/files/IAC-20,E7,2,11,x60311(1).pdf.

[32] U Pagallo, J Ciani Sciolla and M Durante, 'The Environmental Challenges of AI in EU Law: Lessons Learned from the Artificial Intelligence Act (AIA) with its Drawbacks' (2022) 16(3) *Transforming Government: People, Process and Policy* 359.

[33] Freeland and Ireland-Piper (n 26).

[34] See Reed (n 5).

[35] E Bassi and U Pagallo, 'The Democratization of Outer Space: On Law, Ethics, and Technology' in M Arias Oliva et al (eds), *Smart Ethics in the Digital World – Ethicomp* (Madrid, Dialnet, 2024).

involved in any outer space lawsuit – from issues between 'juridical persons' to claims between corporations and individuals – we should not overlook how the decreasing costs and increasing activities of the space industry have reshaped the field, including the traditional meaning of some crucial space activities or actors. The regulatory efforts of national legislators in fleshing out conditions of legal certainty, or fair governance of space activities, must consider how such activities have been evolving. The status of astronauts is particularly instructive because the privatisation of space has affected this very status, forcing some national authorities to react.

In recent decades, astronauts have arguably represented 'the public face of the space program', returning to Earth 'with a smile and an inspiring word for the press'.[36] However, promises of space colonies or mass space tourism may impact the status of such individuals and their corresponding rights and duties, such as the 1968 Agreement on the rescue of astronauts and their return to Earth. The following section provides a concise story of this (private) actor. The aim is to cast further light on the privatisation of space and how such privatisation impacts not only the principles and regulations of space law but also its ethos. It is crucial to discuss some of the moral grounds on which all provisions of this chapter are based.

V. The Face of Space Programmes

The neologism 'astronaut' – from the Greek words *astron* (star) and *nautes* (sailor) – was popularised by J-H Rosny in 1925. Considered one of the founding fathers of modern science fiction, Rosny used the term 'astronautique' for the first time in his masterpiece *Les Navigateurs de l'Infini* (*The Navigators of Infinity*). The neologism was intended to ignite readers' imagination with the travel of some humans to Mars on the Stellarium, ie, the spaceship powered by 'artificial gravity' and made of an indestructible transparent material, 'argine'. A few years later, in 1930, the term 'astronaut' was used in a short story by Neil R Jones, *The Death's Head Meteor*. In 1934, the word appeared in the title of a poem by Eric Frank Russell published in the *Bulletin of the British Interplanetary Society*. The formulas 'astronaut' and 'astronautical' were finally institutionalised with the establishment of the annual International Astronautical Congress in 1950 and the foundation of the International Astronautical Federation in 1951.

The vicissitudes of the Cold War era soon made such formulas controversial. By the end of the 1950s, NASA's top executives were still undecided on what to call the crew members of the space missions. They could have been dubbed either sailors of the stars (astronauts) or sailors of space (cosmonauts), as proposed by Hugh Dryden, the Deputy Administrator of NASA. Eventually, the NASA Space

[36] MH Hersh, *Inventing the American Astronaut* (Basingstoke, Palgrave Macmillan, 2012).

Task Group and the Administrator of the Agency, T Keith Glennan, opted for the term 'astronaut', the common American and English term. The USSR chose the alternative: Yuri Gagarin, the first man to go into space, was referred to as the Soviet cosmonaut. The choice is often attributed to the pioneer of the Soviet aeronautics, and then cosmonautics, Mikhail Tikhonravov.[37] The distinction between American astronauts and Soviet cosmonauts soon became a further way to make the chasm of the Cold War and the opposite ethos of the two blocs clearer. Decades later, the People's Liberation Army Astronauts Corps of China started representing themselves and their foreign counterparts not as sailors of the stars or space, but, instead, as sailors of heaven: *hángtiānyuán*.

Leaving aside ideological conflicts, the term 'astronaut' refers to humans trained, equipped and deployed by a spaceflight programme either as a commander or as a crew member of the spacecraft. For about half a century, astronauts have been professional space travellers and military personnel. Current trends on the privatisation of outer space – as illustrated in this book through the promises of a new generation of space tourists, explorers, scientists or journalists – have stretched the meaning of the word: an astronaut is now often deemed to be anyone travelling into space. Such status may also include some billionaires, such as Bezos or Branson, flying aboard their own spacecrafts. However, this scenario – with the popularisation and democratisation of the term – may entail tricky problems of space law regarding, for example, the rescue of astronauts under the international agreement of 1968. Despite such an agreement not providing any definition of the term, national regulators, such as the US Federal Aviation Administration (FAA), distinguish different types of astronauts.[38] Although the list will likely keep growing, the current state of the art suggests distinguishing between five kinds of 'sailor': (i) traditional astronauts; (ii) spaceflight participants; (iii) commercial astronauts; (iv) private astronauts; and (v) space tourists.

Astronauts – with no further qualifications, in the words of the FAA – are those who fly in a vehicle above 50 miles high and are enrolled by the US agency NASA in its missions. Instead, a spaceflight participant is a human who flies to the ISS in a mission coordinated by NASA or Roscosmos. A commercial astronaut flies above 50 miles of altitude in a non-NASA vehicle: such an astronaut is a crew member who has to show, during the flight, that he or she is essential to public safety or can contribute to human space flight safety. A private astronaut is a human flying to the ISS to conduct commercial and marketing activities through a privately funded mission that includes the coverage of spaceflight on a commercial launch vehicle. Finally, a space tourist may be understood as a paying non-crew passenger flying private non-NASA or military vehicles above 50 miles high. As a reaction to the private sub-orbital spaceflights of Bezos and Branson, this differentiation among

[37] M Brzezinski, *Red Moon Rising: Sputnik and the Hidden Rivalries That Ignited the Space Age* (New York, Henry Holt & Co, 2007).

[38] Federal Aviation Administration (FAA), *Commercial Space Astronaut Wings Program*, order 8800.2, 20 July 2021, https://www.faa.gov/documentLibrary/media/Order/FAA_Order_8800.2.pdf.

different types of astronauts draws on the FAA's issue order on the eligibility criteria of 20 July 2021.[39] By conceiving a commercial astronaut as every human crew member who still has to prove expertise during the flight and is essential to public safety, or human space flight safety, an effect of the definition is to strip individuals such as Bezos and Branson of their status of astronauts.

The multiplication of different kinds of astronaut is, of course, the byproduct of the growing number of private flights, activities and missions. Whilst the space race has launched around 600 astronauts since the first cosmonaut Yuri Gagarin in 1961, it is likely that, in a few years, the figure will become the yearly standard, even leaving aside SpaceX's current promises of 'millions of people' in space. Current policies on waivers of liability and arbitration clauses will increasingly fall short in terms of coping with the normative challenges of this scenario populated by space explorers, scientists, tourists or settlers. The current privatisation and commercialisation of space missions not only regard sub-orbital trips that last about an hour and a half, as the 2021 promo of Virgin Galactic would have us believe by announcing the success of its first test flight with the VSS Unity; instead, the privatisation of space missions suggests celestial enclaves and deep space missions of everyday people interacting with AI systems, smart robots and further emerging technologies that should tackle both the technical issues of the flight and the mental and emotional challenges of long missions. This is one of the lessons learned from the experience of previous professional space travellers. As reported by CNN on 4 June 2022, astronauts such as Scott Kelly or Christina Koch, when returning to Earth after long space flights, 'couldn't wait to feel rain or ocean waves again', longing for the blue marble.[40]

Against this framework, we may wonder whether non-humans – ie, artificial agents such as smart robots and AI systems – could one day become crew members together with human scientists, explorers or settlers. The conjecture is supported by the increasing use of systems such as the Crew Interactive Mobile Companion (CIMON). This humanoid enables voice-controlled access to media and documents, navigation through operating and repair instructions, or planetary exploration, especially in conditions too dangerous or prohibitive for humans.[41] According to the strict definition of 'astronaut' provided by the FAA in 2021, it is arguable that some of these AI systems and smart robots are not only 'agents' but can also provide expertise during the flight and even be essential to public safety. This definition – which has stripped Bezos and Branson of their status as astronauts – may fit the new role that technology plays in outer space. The face of an astronaut can well turn out to be that of an anthropomorphic robot that induces humans to ascribe their own properties or characteristics to such an AI system.

[39] ibid.

[40] See the interviews at https://edition.cnn.com/2022/06/04/world/longterm-spaceflight-cognition-emotions-life-itself-scn/index.html.

[41] U Pagallo, E Bassi and M Durante, 'The Normative Challenges of AI in Outer Space: Law, Ethics, and the Realignment of Terrestrial Standards' (2023) 36 *Philosophy & Technology* 23.

A sound amount of work on human–robot interaction (HRI) illustrates how much the anthropomorphic features of these systems can also (but not only) be fruitful in outer space.[42]

VI. A New Kid in Space

The chapter has complemented the analysis of the public actors of international space law – as discussed in Chapter 2 – with an examination of the legal challenges posed by the privatisation of space and its actors. The legal challenges relating to the privatisation of space have included: (i) the interpretation of key provisions of the international legal framework, such as Article VII of the Liability Convention; (ii) the distribution of regulatory powers between international and national law regarding issues of licensing and registration; (iii) the further problems of jurisdiction with the nationality of private corporations; (iv) current practices on dispute resolution, waivers of liability and arbitration clauses that fall increasingly short in terms of tackling the international law duties of such corporations, such as the protection of fundamental rights; (v) the impact of private activities in outer space on the very meaning of such activities and actors, such as the notion of 'astronaut', with the corresponding issues of rescue and assistance under the provisions of the 1968 UN Agreement.

In addition to the complexity of this legal framework with its public and private actors, attention has been drawn to the impact that a further kind of actor – ie, AI systems and artificial agents – may pose in the field. The traditional view of scholars and experts often assumes that such technologies, like AI systems and smart robots, are simple tools of human interaction. This idea applies to AI systems and robots such as ESA's CIMON or NASA's Robonauts, together with the lunar programmes of the US, China, the EU, Japan or India, which hinge on further technological developments regarding smart robotic rovers and walkers, rappelers and rotorcrafts. The wrong assumption that such technologies represent a simple means or tool for human activities has affected most discussions on the new laws of outer space. The example of how the status of astronauts is changing confirms the view that most of the time, experts of space law either focus on the proliferation of legal statuses for human astronauts and how it may affect, for example, the Rescue Agreement clauses from 1968, or draw their attention to the substitution of the traditional human astronaut with robots.[43] How the interaction between human members and artificial agents of today's space missions and tomorrow's colonies is going to – and has to – be regulated is often overlooked.

[42] A Chandani, O Prakash, P Prakash, S Wagholikar and M Mehta, 'Robots and Artificial Intelligence: An Aid to Dependent People' in A Joshi et al (eds), *Information and Communication Technology for Competitive Strategies* (Singapore, Springer, 2022).

[43] D Goldsmith and M Rees, *The End of Astronauts: Why Robots are the Future of Exploration* (Cambridge, MA, Harvard University Press, 2022).

The problem of how the new actors of outer space – that is, AI systems and smart robots – will be governed complements the traditional issues of space law with a further set of moral and legal dilemmas that revolve around the autonomy of such artificial agents. Science fiction is once again the source of inspiration. In *Across the Zodiac*, a sci-fi book published in 1880, it is remarkable that Percy Greg does not use the term 'astronaut' as we do today, but rather just to refer to the narrator's own spacecraft:

> For the same reason which led me to start so long before the date of the opposition, I resolved, having regard to the action of the Earth's rotation on her axis to start some hours before midnight. Taking leave, then, of the two friends who had thus far assisted me, I entered the Astronaut on the 1st of August, about 4.30 P.M.[44]

Greg's 'Astronaut' reminds us of what the ESA has dubbed the 'disruption' of AI systems and smart robots in space activities and missions since the mid-2010s.[45] Such disruption regards how the rights of individuals interacting with AI systems in outer space must be protected, as well as how AI systems and robotic technologies may impact traditional notions of the field, in addition to the very idea of 'astronaut' and crews. The set of open problems in national and international space law that have been examined in Chapter 2 and this chapter is complemented in Chapter 4 with the analysis of a new technological disruption. The focus will not only be on public authorities or private actors, but also on the behaviour and decisions of artificial agents displayed in space activities and missions. A further layer of legal intricacy adds to the complexity in this field.

[44] P Greg, *Across the Zodiac* (London, Trübner, 1880) 32.

[45] European Space Agency (ESA), 'What is Space 4.0?', 2016, https://www.esa.int/About_Us/Ministerial_Council_2016/What_is_space_4.0.

4

The New Argonauts

In addition to next-generation space tourists, scientists, explorers and settlers, this chapter focuses on the activities, decisions and behaviour of AI systems, robots and other forms of autonomous and intelligent systems displayed in outer space. Drawing on the ESA's series of lunar missions dubbed the 'Argonaut Project', this bunch of AI technologies and robotic applications is summarised as the 'new Argonauts'. The first ESA Argonaut will be a spacecraft delivering cargo anywhere on the Moon by the end of this decade. Further Argonauts include next-generation astronaut assistants, such as the humanoid Crew Interactive Mobile Companion (CIMON) or NASA's Robonaut, a dexterous humanoid robot that uses its hands for construction and discovery in a way that far exceeds every suited astronaut. The aim of this chapter is to explain some basic properties of such AI systems and robots – for example, their autonomy, adaptability and intelligence – and how such engineering properties suggest some cautionary tales. These are illustrated by one of the most popular cycles of heroes and fantastic journeys in ancient Greek mythology, namely, the intrepid experiences of the Argonauts, a crew of sailors, and Jason, their leader, in his quest for the Golden Fleece.

I. Between Myths and Legends

Greek myths have traditionally been a source of inspiration for space missions. The US project to prepare the first humans for landing on the Moon in the late 1960s was known as the Apollo programme. Nowadays, NASA's plans to land the first woman and first person of colour on the Moon have been called the Artemis missions. In Greek mythology, Artemis is not only the twin sister of Apollo and goddess of the hunt and the wilderness, nature and care of children, but also one of the most relevant lunar deities often identified with Selene, the personification of the Moon. Even the ESA has followed this mythical suit. As the ESA website is keen to inform us: 'Argonaut is Europe's autonomous access to the Moon, allowing us to play a major role on the surface of our natural satellite.'[1] ESA's first Argonaut is planned to be a lunar lander that should allow versatile access to the Moon

[1] See https://www.esa.int/Science_Exploration/Human_and_Robotic_Exploration/Exploration/Argonaut.

through manifold options for its payloads – such as infrastructure delivery and power stations, cargo and rovers – up to scientific facilities.

The first reason for calling space missions after ancient Greek myths is thus apparent – that is, the series of thrilling trips and apparently impossible (or near-impossible) feats of both old and new Argonauts. However, in relation to ESA's Argonauts and NASA's Artemis project, the parallels with Greek myths not only suggest threats, risks, or problems that will have to be overcome, just as Jason and his crew did in legendary times; they also warn against 'the dramatic changes in faith, power and culture that Western civilisation has seen over the past three millennia'.[2] Myths and legends relating to the Argonauts cast light on some crucial problems of ethos and regulation – presented earlier in Chapter 1 – as the quest for the laws of such new territories as airspace and cyberspace. The first cautionary tale that the Greek myths propose through the fantastic trips of the Argonauts concerns human hubris. According to the interpretation of Seneca – the great Stoic philosopher of Ancient Rome – excessive pride, self-confidence, arrogance and insolence characterised the legendary adventures of the Argonauts.[3] Leaving aside any normative assessment of the ESA Argonaut Project, the hubris of the old Argonauts reminds us of the current troubles of space law, with the proliferation of space junk, overpopulated orbits, radio-frequency interference or the troubles of the privatisation and commercialisation of outer space, which were discussed in Chapter 3. In *Medea*, Seneca warns against the vanity and conceit of those who dared to go beyond the borders of the known world without paying due care to the consequences of their actions: 'The world so wisely severed by the seas / The pine of Thessaly united, bade / The distant waters bring us unknown fears.'[4]

From a legal viewpoint, the Argonauts opened up a Pandora's box. In the opinion of Seneca, their trips should make us wonder whether new laws are necessary,[5] whether 'the sacred federations of the world keep still inviolate'[6] and whether certain actions such as 'passing again with ravished foreign gold, atoned with fearful death upon the sea' must be deemed lawful, or should be punished.[7] A thousand years later, we noted a similar dilemma on the ethos of space law posed by national regulations, such as the US law and the Luxembourg law on the appropriability of space resources. The risk is that current space activities or lunar programmes such as NASA's Artemis may dissolve the ethos of space law by endorsing mere commercial purposes.[8] In the case of Seneca, all Argonauts had noble pedigree and leverage, but they primarily focused on their own business, or the business of lovers and families, paying little attention to the mess they contributed to creating.

[2] J Colavito, *Jason and the Argonauts through the Ages* (Jefferson, NC, MacFarland, 2014).
[3] Seneca, *Medea*, AJ Boyle (ed) (Oxford, Oxford University Press, 2014).
[4] ibid 301–04.
[5] ibid 351.
[6] ibid 602.
[7] ibid 611–12.
[8] A Boley and M Byers, 'US Policy Puts the Safe Development of Space at Risk' (2020) 370(6513) *Science* 174.

In space law today, it could be said that some of the problems that the Argonauts experienced in doing business illustrate old and new controversies on the notion of appropriation.[9]

Interestingly, there is evidence that the nucleus of the myths about the Argonauts is real. Their adventures can be located in the Black Sea area back in the thirteenth century BCE.[10] According to such evidence, the Argonauts were merchants expanding their business from today's Greece – although, back then, the ancient Greek culture had still to be born – moving north and eastwards. The hypothesis suggests why detailed lists of Argonauts have been transmitted since ancient times. These Argonauts could be seen as representatives of their cities appointed to care for their own interests and those of their communities, doing business with other people and villages in faraway territories. The lists of Argonauts would be similar to current provisions on the certification of astronauts – particularly commercial astronauts. Wikipedia, for example, contains entries on both the lists of Argonauts and humans launched into space. However, what is less obvious in the parallelism between the old and new Argonauts is that in order to do business through such sidereal distances, the Argonauts, like today's astronauts, ultimately depended on technology. It is not by chance that Argonauts were called after the name of their ship, the *Argo*, made of prodigious elements and blessed by the gods. Apollonius stressed this point in the *Argonautica* – the Greek epic poem written in the third century BCE – when the Argonauts found themselves sailing into a heavy fog. The intervention of Phoebus, or Apollo, can be compared to that of Pharos in Alexandria – namely, the lighthouse considered one of the Seven Wonders of the Ancient World. By speeding down from heaven, Apollo lights the way for Jason and his Argonauts, brilliantly solving their problems. In the introduction to the *Argonautica*, Lawrence Norfolk notes that 'if so, no poet has ever put the science of mechanics to more delightful use'.[11]

All in all, there would be no Argonaut out there without their magic ship, the *Argo*, just as no astronaut would exist without space technologies. In both cases, we should not overlook another convergence suggested by ancient myths: whether Argonauts or astronauts, our 'sailors' – in addition to their peculiar dependence on technology – deal with non-humans.

In the ancient myth, the crew of Argonauts was guided by Jason, the great-grandson of Hermes, herald of the gods. In today's crew of space missions, astronauts and new commercial astronauts, private astronauts or space tourists progressively interact with – and are guided by – sophisticated humanoid robots, AI systems and artificial agents. Such technological systems are already an essential

[9] See F Tronchetti, 'The Non-appropriation Principle as a Structural Norm of International Law: A New Way of Interpreting Article II of the Outer Space Treaty' (2008) 33(3) *Air and Space Law* 277; Z Paliouras, 'The Non-appropriation Principle: The Grundnorm of International Space Law' (2014) 27(1) *Leiden Journal of International* 37.

[10] R Graves, *The Greek Myths* (Baltimore, Penguin, 1990).

[11] Apollonius, *The Argonautica*, L Norfolk (ed) (London, Folio Society, 2014).

part of the security of all outer space missions and can contribute to human space flight safety as much as – if not better than what – commercial astronauts can do. The main assumption of this chapter is that an artificial agent can be an Argonaut. The crew of next-generation missions will either be a team of humans and smart robots, or an autonomous artificial spacecraft with intelligent systems aboard. The following section introduces the first candidates to become an artificial member of space crews.

II. The Crew

The formula 'new Argonauts' should be understood in a twofold way. On the one hand, as was stressed in the previous chapter, the new Argonauts regard the proliferation of roles and statuses of humans in outer space missions. In addition to traditional astronauts enrolled by NASA and other public agencies in their space activities, current trends in the privatisation of space have created other categories, such as spaceflight participants, commercial astronauts, private astronauts and space tourists. This trend will likely be strengthened in the following years. In March 2023, drawing on the work of the 'Low Earth Orbit Science and Technology Interagency Working Group', the US government released its National Low Earth Orbit Research and Development Strategy in which, for the first time, the aim was to create permanent human settlements in outer space and to multiply space stations for various purposes, such as manufacturing and tourism.[12] The Low Earth Orbit (LEO) strategy represents the backbone of the whole enterprise, although the document admits that further scientific research is 'necessary to achieve the goal of enabling human transportation and settlement within the solar system'.[13]

On the other hand, together with the human members, crews of today's space flights and tomorrow's deep space missions will include AI systems and robots equipped with AI. This conjecture rests on the initiatives of agencies such as ESA or NASA, in which the autonomy of smart robots and AI systems is increasingly playing a significant role in navigation functions, well-being and entertainment of the human members of the crew, repairing instructions – especially in conditions too prohibitive for humans – up to the management of (certain aspects of) the mission. CIMON is particularly instructive in this regard. A head-shaped robot equipped with AI algorithms and developed by Airbus and IBM (for example, the natural language capabilities of IBM Watson), CIMON is used in the ISS with funds from the German Aerospace Centre. The AI robot is not only an assistant

[12] US Government, *National Low Earth Orbit Research and Development Strategy*, 2023, https://www.whitehouse.gov/wp-content/uploads/2023/03/NATIONAL-LEO-RD-STRATEGY-033123.pdf.
[13] ibid 6.

but also a new artificial companion.[14] Rather than just simply a smart machine or a sample of traditional space technology, an AI system like CIMON can also (but not only) act, react and interact with the human members of the crew. The parallel with the ancient Greek myths is once again instructive to grasp the novelty of this scenario of non-human actors: Jason and his squad used to interact with their magic ship the *Argo* and the gods. Today, and for the first time ever, humans are interacting with artificial agents that are 'autonomous' and have an 'intelligence' of their own.

Years of debate on the material scope of the European regulation on AI – namely, the AI Act in EU law – show that the definition of AI and such properties as the autonomy and intelligence of AI systems can be complicated. The 'autonomy' and 'intelligence' of gods, semi-gods and mystical ships of ancient myths may well have been transformed into the 'autonomy' and 'intelligence' of artificial agents and systems, and yet it is crucial to prevent misunderstandings. The redemption of the myth through technology, so to speak, requires a terminological clarification. By admitting that some new Argonauts can meet the FAA's issue order on the eligibility criteria from July 2021,[15] we should prevent the risk of embracing another type of myth – that is, accepting that an artificial agent can have some sort of human-like properties. Some technical details of computer science and engineering will prevent misapprehensions when referring to the 'autonomy' and 'intelligence' of systems such as the humanoid robot CIMON.[16] The focus should be on how samples of second-order technology (ie, machines) have been complemented and even substituted by a new kind of agent: the crown jewel in the field of third-order technologies.

III. From Machines to Artificial Agents

In their seminal text *Artificial Intelligence: A Modern Approach*, Stuart Russell and Peter Norvig provide eight definitions of AI, which can be divided into four main categories: systems that either think humanly or rationally, or that can act humanly or rationally.[17] An alternative definition is provided by the Institute of Electrical and Electronics Engineers (IEEE), which refers to the formula of 'autonomous and intelligent systems' – ie, 'A/IS' rather than 'AI' – in some documents. For example, in the *Recommended Practice for Assessing the Impact of Autonomous*

[14] R Aylett, PA Vargas and N Sharkey, '10 Emotions: Could Robots have Feelings?' in *The Living with Robots: What Every Anxious Human Needs to Know* (Cambridge, MA, MIT Press, 2021) 161–78.

[15] Federal Aviation Administration, 'Commercial Space Astronaut Wings Program', order 8800.2, 2021, https://www.faa.gov/documentLibrary/media/Order/FAA_Order_8800.2.pdf.

[16] Q Gao, J Liu and Z Ju, 'Robust Real-Time Hand Detection and Localization for Space Human–Robot Interaction Based on Deep Learning' (2020) 390 *Neurocomputing* 198.

[17] S Russell and P Norvig, *Artificial Intelligence: A Modern Approach* (Harlow, Pearson, 2014).

and Intelligent Systems on Human Well-Being, the IEEE provides the first industry standard for the field: IEEE 7010-2020. The definition is as follows:

> An A/IS is a semi-autonomous or autonomous computer-controlled system programmed to carry out some tasks with or without limited human intervention capable of decision making by independent interference and successfully adapting to its context.[18]

The IEEE definition of A/IS can be extended to that of a robot, according to the 'sense-think-act' paradigm of AI research in robotics.[19] Based on their sensors, AI algorithms and actuators, smart robots are physical artefacts that can have the ability to 'perceive something complex and make appropriate decisions'.[20] The IEEE definition also draws attention to why such AI systems and robots are not just intelligent machines, but rather also proper artificial agents.[21] As occurs with other agents such as humans and animals, the agency of AI entails three different properties. First, agency means that both AI systems and smart robots can perceive their environment and respond to stimuli by changing the values of their own properties or inner states – in a nutshell, artificial agents are 'interactive'. Second, they are 'adaptable' since AI systems and smart robots improve the rules through which their own properties or inner states change. Finally, and more importantly, they are 'autonomous', for AI systems and smart robots can modify such inner states or properties without external stimuli, thereby exerting control over their own actions without any direct human intervention.[22]

The feature of AI that has attracted the most attention from scholars and the public at large is, by far, the 'autonomy' of such systems and robots equipped with them. As the NASA website is keen to inform us,[23] there is a long list of such autonomous systems in space technologies. These include improved ground collision avoidance systems (iGCAS), miniaturised radar for small, unmanned aircraft systems and their integration in the national airspace system (NAS), global elevation data adaptive compression systems (GEDACS), multi-level autonomous piloting systems (MAPS), peak-seeking control for trim organisation, optimal landing location in emergency situations and automated cooperative trajectories (ACT), among others. In addition to this bunch of autonomous systems, the Development Strategy of the Federal Government in the US and NASA have been

[18] IEEE Standard Association, 'IEEE Recommended Practice for Assessing the Impact of Autonomous and Intelligent Systems on Human Well-Being', IEEE 7010-2020, 2020, 16, 1–96, https://doi.org/10.1109/IEEESTD.2020.9084219, at 18.

[19] GA Bekey, *Autonomous Robots: From Biological Inspiration to Implementation and Control* (Cambridge, MA, MIT Press, 2005).

[20] The definition of Sebastian Thrun, former director of the AI Laboratory at Stanford, California, cited in P Singer, *Wired for War: The Robotics Revolution and Conflict in the 21st Century* (London, Penguin, 2009) 77.

[21] L Floridi and J Sanders, 'On the Morality of Artificial Agents' (2004) 14(3) *Minds and Machines* 349.

[22] U Pagallo, *The Laws of Robots: Crimes, Contracts, and Torts* (Dordrecht, Springer, 2013).

[23] See https://www.nasa.gov/feature/autonomous-systems.

developing highly advanced humanoid robots, such as Robonaut-2. Developed to assist astronauts, Robonaut is a dexterous humanoid robot that is able to use its hands for construction and discovery in a way that far exceeds that of a suited astronaut, going to places where risks would be too great for humans. Together with CIMON, it is probable that the likes of Robonaut are among the strongest candidates to be the new members of a space crew.

This assumption rests on work in human-robot interaction (HRI), applied ethics and social robotics, showing that the anthropomorphic features of these systems can be fruitful in outer space.[24] The design of AI applications and robots that present humanoid features – to induce humans to ascribe their own properties or characteristics to such artificial agents – does not simply rest on the inspiration of sci-fi movies, such as C-3PO in *Star Wars*, or the pulp science-fiction hero Captain Future, 'the flying man', after which the anthropomorphic features of CIMON have been modelled. The tendency has mostly to do with the benefits of the approach. For example, empirical research has drawn attention to the advantages of humanoid robots that depend on functional purposes, such as interaction with human tools and environments.[25] Such functional purposes go hand in hand with the benefits that AI robotics promises in terms of addressing the mental and emotional challenges of deep space missions. Communication and meaningful engagement are key components of HRI, particularly regarding AI systems that support human activities, such as humanoid robots and other artificial companions for healthcare and the well-being of humans. A recent survey displays an overall preference for anthropomorphic features in healthcare.[26] Although the research did not consider the scenario of HRI in outer space, the outcomes of the research suggest that communication is a key determinant of robot preference: 'The majority of research to date emphasizes a high degree of anthropomorphism with respect to robot appearance and communication to support positive perceptions of robots.'[27] In addition, as regards meaningful engagement with humanoid robots: 'Robots, because of their anthropomorphic features, are more likely to evoke empathy than tablet computers, and thus robots can be more effective in promoting pro-social behaviour.'[28]

The benefits (also but not only in outer space missions) of the AI systems and smart robots that the IEEE defines as 'autonomous' and 'intelligent' systems pose the question of how much leeway such artificial agents should have in terms of either interacting with humans or as part of a mission of their own. The problem not only concerns humanoid or anthropomorphic robots; it also relates to

[24] H Chen and C Breazeal, 'Toward Designing Social Human-Robot Interactions for Deep Space Exploration', *arXiv*, 2105.08631, 2021, https://arxiv.org/abs/2105.08631.

[25] Gao et al (n 16).

[26] K Klüber and L Onnasch, 'Appearance is Not Everything: Preferred Feature Combinations for Care Robots' (2022) 128 *Computers in Human Behavior* 107128.

[27] ibid.

[28] SY Lo et al, 'Robots and Sustainability: Robots as Persuaders to Promote Recycling' (2022) 14 *International Journal of Social Robotics* 1261.

AI systems for space data services or support of human activities. These systems vary from rovers and walkers to landers and rotorcrafts, to rappelers and deep melt probes that should provide for cargo logistics and in situ resource utilisation plants, power generation, storage and distribution systems, science and exploration activities and technology demonstration packages, among others. NASA and ESA have been developing further projects with private partners, such as the Rollin' Justin robot, to understand how astronauts in orbit could oversee such smart machines on alien planets.[29] Whether dealing with AI systems and robots for collision avoidance, for space data services or as support for human activities, all these systems raise a common concern: how much autonomy should these intelligent systems have?

IV. The Autonomy of Intelligent Systems

The next-generation Argonauts will increasingly be smart robots and AI systems that augment or replace analysis and decision making by humans, making sense of vast streams of data or defining and modifying decision-making rules autonomously. Rather than human-like properties such as consciousness and free will, moral sense or intentions, the autonomy of these artificial agents refers to the technical – ie, engineering – understanding of these terms: it means that an AI robot can modify its properties without external stimuli, thereby exerting control over its own actions without any direct intervention from humans. On this basis, the new robotic Argonauts represent a third-order technology par excellence. The autonomy of AI systems and robots should be grasped holistically – that is, considering the use of AI and smart robots as part of a more complex ecosystem. In the wording of NASA, autonomy means 'the ability of a system to achieve goals while operating independently of external control'.[30] Whilst a system is made of parts that work together to create the capability required in order to achieve a particular goal, the elements of such a system may include personnel and equipment, hardware and software, facilities, processes and procedures needed for the purpose.[31] Accordingly, an autonomous system not only refers to the components and networks of an AI application or smart robot, but may also involve a combination of astronauts and machines that are independent of an external entity, such as ground control or an orbiting crew.[32]

[29] See L Filthaut, 'Cosmic Troubleshooting: Designing Supervised Autonomy for Astronaut–Robot Coaction in Space', Doctoral dissertation, Delft University of Technology, 2023; P Schmaus et al, 'Extending the Knowledge Driven Approach for Scalable Autonomy Teleoperation of a Robotic Avatar', *2023 IEEE Aerospace Conference*, IEEE, 2023, 1–10.

[30] NASA, *Autonomous Systems Taxonomy*, NASA Technical Reports Server, Document ID 20180003082, 14 May 2018.

[31] NASA, *Systems Engineering Handbook*, US Government Printing Office, NASA/SP-2016-6105 Rev2, 2018.

[32] IA Nesnas, LM Fesq and RA Volpe, 'Autonomy for Space Robots: Past, Present, and Future' (2021) 2 *Current Robotics Reports* 251.

The autonomy and potential unpredictability of AI systems raise the problem of determining and enforcing a 'meaningful human control' (MHC) over the entire technological cycle and functioning of such autonomous systems. Since the mid-2010s, the problem has been discussed in the field of international humanitarian law (IHL) under the auspices of the Convention on Certain Conventional Weapons (CCW) and protocol groups of the UN. In this field, the challenges of autonomous technologies concern the analysis of the 'human element' in the use of lethal force, the classification of the systems under investigation, the review of potential military applications of related technologies, and their impact on the principles and rules of IHL.[33] Also, but not only in IHL, the lesson learned from this debate is that 'human control of autonomous technologies' is not an oxymoron. No such alternative exists between human control over autonomous technologies and the further development of autonomous systems that make crucial decisions by themselves. MHC is the subject of academic courses on risks and threats posed by possible losses of control of AI systems to keep them in check.[34] Rather than a zero-sum game, what is at stake is a fair balance between human control and AI autonomy. In the field of space technologies, it is evident that the autonomy of AI systems and smart robots should be strengthened for the management of complex constellations that aim to reduce the workload of ground operators, or for the guidance, navigation, and control of rovers that should remove human scheduling errors and find their way across unspecified fields, such as navigating around obstacles on the Moon or Mars.[35]

In addition to operational constraints that depend on the goals of the outer space mission, the need for autonomous artificial agents and systems hinges on the remoteness and extreme conditions of the environment. We should never forget that outer space is a faraway, unfriendly and dangerous place. Scholars have accordingly stressed the kind of unexpected changes that make using autonomous AI systems and robots necessary – that is, a requirement rather than a simple option for space missions.[36] Consider changes in the environment or the spacecraft, such as erupting plumes or gusty winds on the tiny moons of Saturn vis-a-vis possible degradations, faults or failures of the spacecraft. Since some of these changes can be unpredictable, the real-time ability of AI systems and robots to make sense of vast amounts of data in order to define decision-making rules autonomously becomes essential for collision avoidance, support of human activities or the overall success of the mission. This is particularly true when the response time to an unexpected scenario or change is shorter than the next communication cycle with

[33] M Taddeo and AA Blanchard, 'Comparative Analysis of the Definitions of Autonomous Weapons Systems' (2022) 28 *Science and Engineering Ethics* 37.

[34] U Pagallo, 'From Automation to Autonomous Systems: A Legal Phenomenology with Problems of Accountability' (2017) *International Joint Conference on Artificial Intelligence* 17.

[35] U Pagallo, E Bassi and M Durante, 'The Normative Challenges of AI in Outer Space: Law, Ethics, and the Realignment of Terrestrial Standards' (2023) 36 *Philosophy & Technology* 23.

[36] IAD Nesnas et al, 'Autonomous Exploration of Small Bodies toward Greater Autonomy for Deep Space Missions' (2021) 8 *Frontiers in Robotics and AI*, https://doi.org/10.3389/frobt.2021.650885.

ground control – that is, when the spacecraft has to react to a situation where there is no possible help from Mother Earth.

As such, the delegation of crucial cognitive tasks and decision-making processes to autonomous artificial agents and systems is at times a necessity that may entail different kinds of problems. A first issue was stressed with the increasing autonomy of AI systems in outer space missions and the MHC over their functioning. The field of autonomous vehicles (AVs) suggests two preliminary conditions that will need to be satisfied in order to achieve MHC over AI technologies: 'tracking' and 'tracing'.[37] Tracking relates to the relation between human controllers and controlled intelligent systems, namely, the degree to which a system can respond to the intentions or reasons of the designated controllers. Tracing concerns the conditions that make such control meaningful – that is, only inasmuch as humans 'are cognitively, physically and morally capable to perform their assigned tasks and fulfil their obligations'.[38] Tracking and tracing are the pillars of the regulatory model that will govern the 'enveloping effect' of third-order technology, such as AI systems displayed in outer space. Drawing on the preliminary conditions for attaining MHC over AI, we will return to the specificities of MHC in space law below in the next chapter, which deals with misuses or overuses of AI systems.

A second kind of problem with the delegation of cognitive tasks to autonomous and intelligent systems relates to matters of trust, since the more humans delegate crucial cognitive tasks and decision-making processes to smart robots and AI systems, the more they rely on the ability of such artificial agents to get things right. For a while, scholars claimed that trust would necessarily depend on shared norms and ethical values governing social – human – interaction.[39] However, it seems fair to admit that trust does not necessarily entail any identifiable direct human interaction and is feasible both in HRI and among artificial agents.[40] This viewpoint became popular when, in 2019, the European Commission's High-Level Expert Group on the ethical principles of AI published the 'Ethics Guidelines for Trustworthy AI'.[41] Trust and conditions for a trustworthy AI do not mean that the autonomy of artificial agents raises no risks; rather, trust and risk should be conceived as two sides of the same coin. Dealing with the complexity of the world, humans have to choose and select, thus exposing themselves to the contingency

[37] FS Santoni de Sio et al, 'Realising Meaningful Human Control over Automated Driving Systems: A Multidisciplinary Approach' (2022), *Minds & Machines*, https://doi.org/10.1007/s11023-022-09608-8.

[38] ibid.

[39] H Nissenbaum, 'Privacy as Contextual Integrity' (2004) 79(1) *Washington Law Review* 119.

[40] See C Castelfranchi and R Falcone, 'Principles of Trust for MAS: Cognitive Anatomy, Social Importance, and Quantification', *Third International Conference on Multi-agent Systems*, Paris, IEEE Computer Society, 1998; M Durante, 'What is the Model of Trust for Multi-agent Systems? Whether or Not e-Trust Applies to Autonomous Agents' (2010) 23(3–4) *Knowledge, Technology & Policy* 347; U Pagallo, 'Robotrust and Legal Responsibility' (2010) 23(3–4) *Knowledge, Technology and Policy* 367; and, M Taddeo, 'Modelling Trust in Artificial Agents: A First Step toward the Analysis of e-Trust' (2010) 20 *Minds & Machines* 243.

[41] A Jobin, M Ienca and E Vayena, 'The Global Landscape of AI Ethics Guidelines' (2019) 1 *Nature Machine Intelligence* 389.

of their own decisions and the corresponding risks.[42] As the German sociologist Niklas Luhmann noted:

> Trust is a solution for specific problems of risk. But trust has to be achieved within a familiar world, and changes may occur in the familiar features of the world which will have an impact on the possibility of developing trust in human relations. Hence we cannot neglect the conditions of familiarity and its limits when we set out to explore the conditions of trust.[43]

Luhmann's 'conditions of familiarity' introduce a third kind of trouble: the delegation of tasks to autonomous and intelligent systems. This problem reminds us of how trust necessarily requires time, just as positive outcomes grow so long as the act of trusting encourages more trust. Such a recursive effect still has problems of its own. The operational and environmental constraints of all space missions suggest that changes may occur and can put the very conditions of trust at risk. This is the problem that law makers aiming to regulate the use and behaviour of AI systems and smart robots are well aware of: technology is not a simple 'out of the box' machine, a sort of product in traditional consumer law regulation. On the contrary, AI robots progressively gain knowledge or skills from their interaction with living beings and other artificial agents inhabiting the surrounding environment so that, as a kind of prolonged epigenetic developmental process, more complex cognitive structures emerge in the state-transition system of the artificial agent. This scenario partially overlaps with the earlier issues of meaningful human control and 'artificial trust' in HRI, and yet the unpredictability of AI behaviour should be further understood in connection with the risks of possible misuse of the technology.

Since these new kinds of risk that hinge on the autonomy of artificial agents are particularly relevant for the following parts of the analysis, misuses and unpredictability of AI systems will be examined separately in the next section. How law makers will ultimately deal with the autonomy of AI and smart robots with potential bad uses of technology, also but not only in outer space, affects not only the *nomos* of space law, but also its *ethos*. The following section aims to explain why.

V. Ethos and Trust

Anthropomorphic robots equipped with AI will progressively play a crucial role in the evolving ethos of outer space. After all, robot Argonauts already play a significant role in entertaining and taking care of the human members of the crew, making the mission safer or more secure through their navigation

[42] N Luhmann, 'Familiarity, Confidence, Trust: Problems and Alternative' in D Gambetta (ed), *Trust: Making and Breaking Cooperative Relations*, electronic edition (Oxford, Department of Sociology, University of Oxford, 2000) 94–107.

[43] ibid.

functions, repair instructions, collision avoidance systems, or management of (certain aspects of) the mission. The interplay between astronauts and robotic Argonauts may positively affect the public attitude towards current trends in the field, such as the colonisation of space and the 'democratisation of missions' with promises of space tourism, space hotels, mass exploration, lunar settlements and the like. Still, the adaptiveness, autonomy and interactivity of such artificial agents can result in unexpected or unforeseen circumstances that may affect not only provisions and regulations of the law, but also the social acceptability of the risk inherent in the delegation of cognitive tasks or decision-making processes to AI systems.[44] Three possible drivers or causes of potential unforeseeable behaviour should be examined. These are either endogenous or exogenous (or both).

AI unpredictability is endogenous when the autonomous system's unexpected outcome, behaviour or decision has to do with the functioning of the deep neural network, large language model or unsupervised machine learning (ML) algorithms of the system. Even designers and engineers can find it difficult (or even impossible) to ascertain the reasons for a given decision, behaviour or output. Moreover, even the most powerful AI model is sensitive to small changes and perturbations, so that a tiny perturbation in the input data can dramatically impact the output and lead to completely different results. In the words of the ESA:

> AI, and in particular ML, still has some way to go before it is used extensively for space applications … the complicated models and structures necessary for ML will need to be improved before it can be extensively useful.[45]

On the other hand, the reasons for the unpredictability of AI behaviour are exogenous when the unforeseeable outcome depends on the complexity of the surrounding environment in which the AI system or smart robot has to adapt and react through its actuators. In the legal domain (as was noted in Chapter 3), the trade-off between the probability of events and potential damages is typically defined through the premium of insurance contracts – that is, the factor through which the sum to be charged for a certain amount of insurance coverage is established. The exogenous and endogenous causes of AI unpredictability have a further broader effect on society because they affect pillars of human responsibility, such as the notion of the 'reasonable person' who guards against 'foreseeable harms'. Since the pioneering research of Lawrence Solum and Curtis Karnow in the 1990s, scholars have stressed that the autonomy of AI impacts canonical notions of reasonability and foreseeability, thus redefining the content of further legal notions, such as due diligence, apportioned liability and the fault of

[44] U Pagallo and M Durante, 'The Pros and Cons of Legal Automation and its Governance' (2016) 7(2) *European Journal of Risk Regulation* 323.

[45] See VR Saxena, P Singh and A Tiwari, 'Role of Artificial Intelligence Based Applications Used for Space Technologies' (2022) 2(1) *Journal of Applied Science and Education* 1.

unreasonable persons.[46] Legal responsibility has traditionally hinged on the Aristotelian idea that we should take into account *id quod plerumque accidit* in the physical domain – that is, to focus on that which generally will be the most probable outcome of a given act, fact, event or cause. AI systems may break the chain of legal causation as well as challenge social expectations on that which is good or bad, reasonable or predictable.

The unpredictability of AI can indeed be fatal: a smart robot killing a human worker in a factory; an autonomous vehicle running over a pedestrian on a public road; drones falling down all at once in urban centres; autonomous out-of-control spacecrafts. Public expectations concerning the regulation of AI technologies arguably relate to the area of trust. In the previous section, we noted that the idea according to which humans can trust their artificial companions is well grounded, plausible or even justified.[47] However, this side of trust should not be confused with the public expectations on how the behaviour of such artificial companions must be regulated – for example, the legal standards that set the trustworthiness of such AI systems. This distinction between trust and public expectation is often overlooked by those philosophers who think that trust is a virtue, although – despite appearances[48] – it is not. Rather, trust is a property or value which, according to Luhmann teachings on human interaction, applies to AI systems; it is a solution for specific problems of risk. This means that trust can also be the glue that solidifies or strengthens a band of bandits or, according to Seneca's *Medea*, the self-confidence, arrogance, insolence, vanity and conceit of the Argonauts.

In addition to public expectations of not being involved in AI accidents, on Earth or via space-based services, attention should be paid to how misuses of technology affect trust. The recent Russian aggression to Ukraine has made this scenario apparent. On 24 February 2022, one hour before its invasion of Ukraine, Russia launched a cyberattack against Viasat to disconnect the Ukrainian government, armed forces and security services from the satellite services of the US company. The effects of the cyberattack soon affected thousands of people in France, Germany, Greece, Hungary, Italy and Poland.[49] In general terms, the panoply of AI systems for collision avoidance, AI and space data, or AI supporting human activities suggests that the only limit to the misuse of technologies in outer space activities and space-based services is the human imagination.

[46] See LB Solum, 'Legal Personhood for Artificial Intelligence' (1992) 70 *North Carolina Law Review* 1231; and CEA Karnow, 'Liability for Distributed Artificial Intelligence' (1996) 11 *Berkeley Technology Law Journal* 147.

[47] JP Sullins, 'Trust in Robots' in J Simon (ed), *The Routledge Handbook of Trust and Philosophy* (New York, Routledge, 2020).

[48] See Y Shionoya, 'Trust as a Virtue' in Y Shionoya and K Yagi (eds), *Competition, Trust, and Cooperation* (Berlin, Springer, 2001); N Potter and N Nyquist, *How Can I be Trusted? A Virtue Theory of Trustworthiness* (Lanham, MD, Rowman & Littlefield, 2002); and, L D'Olimpio, 'Trust as a Virtue in Education' (2018) 50(2) *Educational Philosophy and Theory* 193.

[49] European Space Policy Institute, 'The War in Ukraine from a Space Cybersecurity Perspective', Report 84, Vienna, 2022.

The wilful misuse of technology – and how legislators should tackle it – arguably affects the moral grounds on which current human societies increasingly delegate cognitive tasks and decisions to autonomous systems. In terms of space-related activities and missions, four major risks raised by the use of AI should be under scrutiny:

(i) devaluing human skills;
(ii) removing human responsibility;
(iii) reducing human control; and
(iv) eroding human self-determination.[50]

Some of these risks of misuse of AI were previously stressed in this chapter by highlighting the meaningful control humans should retain over the behaviour of increasingly autonomous and intelligent systems through tracking and tracing functions. In the criminal law field, further examples of AI misuse relate to old crimes that could be perpetrated through new means, such as hacking satellites through AI systems, as well as new crimes including offences against the person, as well as theft and non-corporate fraud.[51] If not properly tackled, such illegal and immoral uses of AI technologies can create general distrust and, hence, lead a society not to use such technologies to their full potential or to use them for the wrong reasons.[52] These reasons include ignorance, fear, misplaced concerns or excessive reactions, which might in turn generate the underuse of some fruitful AI robotic applications, such as the smart humanoid systems discussed in this chapter because of potential privacy concerns in mass explorers' deep space missions.[53]

By drawing attention to both the advantages and constraints of AI technologies, the aim of this section has not been to suggest that opportunities and threats of AI in outer space are a sort of double-edged weapon depending on the use that humans make of technology. Instead, such good and bad uses of AI raise a new set of legal and moral questions that must be properly regulated and wisely governed. A smart robot can either become the 'new face' of a space mission or add further problems to the troubles of space law. Although the autonomy and even unpredictability of AI systems can be a necessary feature in space activities, it is also arguable that such autonomy triggers some thorny issues that affect their own trustworthiness, namely: (i) the meaningful human control over such autonomous systems; (ii) the balance to be struck between trust and risk; and (iii) the overuses or underuses of technology. Each of these problems clearly affects the moral grounds on which all space activities lie. The final section of this chapter focuses on how legislators have intended to address the trustworthiness of AI systems.

[50] L Floridi et al, 'AI4People – An Ethical Framework for a Good AI Society: Opportunities, Risks, Principles, and Recommendations' (2018) 28(4) *Minds and Machines* 689.

[51] W Barfield and U Pagallo, *Advanced Introduction to the Law and Artificial Intelligence* (Cheltenham, Edward Elgar, 2020).

[52] Floridi et al (n 50).

[53] U Pagallo and M Durante, 'The Good, the Bad, and the Invisible with its Opportunity Costs' (2022) 5(1) *J* 139.

VI. Strict Law for New Argonauts

The analysis of this chapter has focused on some engineering features of AI systems – ie, their peculiar autonomy, adaptability and interactivity – and how the increasing delegation of cognitive tasks and decision making to such systems may raise problems of governance, trust and ethos in relation to space activities. Since the 1990s, attention has been paid to issues of liability and responsibility that can make it increasingly difficult to ascertain which human actor (if any) is responsible, accountable or liable for the behaviour and decision making of these artificial agents.[54] Over the past few years, law makers have been very active in tackling the normative challenges of AI.[55] New regulations in EU law, such as the AI Act, will likely affect not only the legal framework but also the moral grounds of Europe. In the 2019 Ethical Guidelines of the High-Level Expert Group (HLEG) set up by the European Commission to explain the ethical principles of AI, the requirements that AI must satisfy in order to be considered trustworthy included environmental robustness, the protection of societal and environmental well-being, and a 'human-centric approach' to the challenges of AI. In the words of the Expert Group:

> The common foundation that unites these rights can be understood as rooted in respect for human dignity – thereby reflecting what we describe as a 'human-centric approach' in which the human being enjoys a unique and inalienable moral status of primacy in the civil, political, economic and social fields.[56]

This approach has inspired some legislation, (such as the AI Act in EU law) as well as international institutions (for example, the Council of Europe, the Organisation for Economic Co-operation and Development (OECD) or the 2023 G7 meetings in Japan), all revolving around the 'human-centric' development and use of 'trustworthy' AI.[57] The next chapter expands on this response of national and international legislators to the normative challenges of AI, drawing on Seneca's interpretation of the Argonauts and his threefold warning. First, attention will focus on whether new laws are necessary,[58] then whether 'the sacred federations of the world will be kept intact'[59] and, finally, whether certain actions should be punished.[60] Against the traditional issues faced by public actors in international space law examined in Chapter 2 and the troubles posed by private actors in national space law discussed in Chapter 3, the focus will move on to the legal

[54] See Solum (n 46); Karnow (n 46).
[55] Floridi et al (n 50).
[56] High-Level Expert Group on Artificial Intelligence, *Ethics Guidelines for Trustworthy AI* (Brussels, European Commission, 2019), available at: https://digital-strategy.ec.europa.eu/en/library/ethics-guidelines-trustworthy-ai.
[57] H Habuka, 'Japan's Approach to AI Regulation and its Impact on the 2023 G7 Presidency' (2023) *Center for Strategic & International Studies* 14.
[58] Seneca (n 3) 351.
[59] ibid 602.
[60] ibid 611–12.

challenges generated by such actors – as artificial agents, AI systems and smart robots – that were described in this chapter. Such challenges concern other fields of legal regulation – cybersecurity and data governance, data protection and environmental law – that complement the regulations of national and international space law covered in this volume.

5

AI Meets the Law

The impact of AI systems on the law has reverberated throughout its entire fabric, including the field of space law. The autonomy of such systems and a certain degree of unpredictability and opacity surrounding their development raise thorny issues concerning the military and civilian uses of AI. On the one hand, this chapter examines current initiatives at the international level, such as the CCW under the UN auspices on how to govern the use of autonomous lethal weapons; on the other hand, the focus is drawn to tricky problems of civil law involving contractual and tortious obligations that include damages to be covered for the behaviour of AI systems. Such obligations must be complemented with further sectorial regulations in the fields of machine safety and cybersecurity, data governance and personal data protection, environmental law and the corresponding liability regimes. It is against this framework that we can appreciate the impact of AI systems and smart robots in outer space, finally making the science-fiction scenarios of a few years ago possible.

I. The Uniqueness of AI

We live 'in the age of Artificial Intelligence' – as the subtitle of this book claims – because of the unique features and properties of such technological systems. In Chapter 4, we focused on the engineering notions of autonomy, interactivity and adaptability. These properties are often summed up with the IEEE's formula 'autonomous and intelligent systems' (A/IS). In the Report of the High-Level Expert Group on liability and new technologies formation, set up by the European Commission in 2018, that which makes AI unique is summed up with a list of features, namely complexity, opacity, openness, predictability, data-drivenness and vulnerability of computers that mimic human intelligence.[1] The legal impact of AI depends not only on each of these features or properties taken singularly, but also on their cumulative effect. In the words of the Report on *Liability for Artificial*

[1] HLEG, *Liability for Artificial Intelligence and Other Emerging Technologies*, Report from the European Commission's High-Level Group of Experts on Liability and New Technologies, Brussels, 2019, https://op.europa.eu/en/publication-detail/-/publication/1c5e30be-1197-11ea-8c1f-01aa75ed71a1/language-en.

Intelligence: 'Each of these changes may be gradual in nature, but the dimension of gradual change, the range and frequency of situations affected, and the combined effect, results in disruption.'[2]

Since the mid-2010s, scholars and institutions have increasingly been focusing on the disruption of AI in space-related activities. In 2016, the ESA released two reports entitled 'Robots in Space' and 'What is Space 4.0?' to stress the benefits and also limits of AI applications. In the opinion of the ESA, after the first studies of astronomy in ancient times (Space 1.0), the Apollo missions and moon landings of the 1960s and 1970s (Space 2.0) and the ISS (Space 3.0), AI systems and smart robots have opened up the new scenarios of Space 4.0.[3] These include a myriad of AI systems, ranging from collision avoidance and space data processing to spacecraft location estimation, space weather forecasting and support of human activities that span the whole spectrum of space technologies, missions and activities.[4] There are, in fact, AI systems that can help humans find and remove space junk (such as the Clear-Space 1 programme of the ESA) or prolong satellite lifecycles through the manoeuvrability and optimisation of on-orbit services.[5] In addition, AI systems can improve maintenance procedures, orbit adjustments or the upgrading and replacing of instruments onboard.[6] Furthermore, in relation to AI systems for space-based services, technologies include the use of the Global Navigation Satellite System (GNSS) to support an increasing set of essential services, such as emergency-response services, or maritime and agriculture services.[7] Likewise, the use of satellite data by AI systems can help monitor production changes of car makers or plane traffic at airports.[8]

Some of the reasons for the success of AI systems displayed in outer space relate to the exponential increase of computing power (for example, Moore's law), the availability of big data (for example, massive datasets for machine learning techniques) and new methods to exploit this scenario (for example, adversarial networks). However, the dramatic decrease in costs, together with the increase in AI activities, should also be assessed against the risks that such autonomous

[2] ibid 32.

[3] ESA, 'What Is Space 4.0?', 2016, https://www.esa.int/About_Us/Ministerial_Council_2016/What_is_space_4.0.

[4] M Madi and O Sokolova, *Artificial Intelligence for Space: Trends, Applications, and Perspectives* (Boca Raton, FL, CRC Press, 2023).

[5] T Maury, P Loubet, SM Serrano, A Gallice and G Sonnemann, 'Application of Environmental Life Cycle Assessment (LCA) within the Space Sector: A State of the Art' (2020) 170 *Acta Astronautica* 122.

[6] 'ESA Moves Ahead with In-Orbit Servicing Missions', 2023, https://www.esa.int/Enabling_Support/Preparing_for_the_Future/Discovery_and_Preparation/ESA_moves_ahead_with_In-Orbit_Servicing_missions2.

[7] See AB Nader, A Gavrilov and W Khalaf, 'Artificial Intelligence-Based Methods for Accuracy Improvement of Integrated Navigation Systems during GNSS Signal Outages: An Analytical Overview' (2020) 11, *Gyroscopy and Navigation* 41; A Siemuri, H Kuusniemi, MS Elmusrati, P Välisuo and A Shamsuzzoha, 'Machine Learning Utilization in GNSS: Use Cases, Challenges and Future Applications', *2021 International Conference on Localization and GNSS (ICL-GNSS)*, Tampere, Finland, 2021, 1–6.

[8] U Pagallo, E Bassi, E and M Durante, 'The Normative Challenges of AI in Outer Space: Law, Ethics, and the Realignment of Terrestrial Standards' (2023) 36 *Philosophy & Technology* 23.

systems pose due to their potentially unpredictable behaviours. Traditional issues on fault and liability, due diligence and other legal standards will be revisited here together with the further set of issues posed by 'the development of space, and its companion, space law'[9] – that is, the troubles of space law with AI technologies.[10]

Attention has progressively been drawn to how the interactivity, opacity and unpredictability of autonomous 'space objects' may affect principles and rules in space law field concerning, for example, the damages to be covered, the procedures to be followed once such damages occur, or whether – and to what extent – a state is internationally liable for damages provoked by autonomous space objects (such as AI systems) that depend on the fault of private persons or companies.[11] These liability issues also relate to the use of AI systems for space-based services, such as AI systems using GNSS signals to support emergency-response services.[12] Drawing on a 30-year-old debate on the different ways in which the interactivity, autonomy and adaptability of AI robotics affect the pillars of the law,[13] the first legal tenet to focus on should be the notion of 'legal causation'.

Legal causation concerns the link between how certain events or states of affairs come about and whether – or to what extent – they are related to the actions or omissions of individuals, making them accountable, responsible or liable. A certain degree of risk and predictability in AI behaviour may seriously affect the ways in which the law has tackled matters of causality in social interaction. The failure of legal causation may concern either cases of distributed responsibility – in which unjust damages are caused by local interactions that are in themselves not illegal, but, rather, morally neutral[14] – or the whole functioning of complex digital ecosystems, including AI in outer space, where it is difficult to foresee which types of harm may supervene and who should be considered accountable in the case of unjust damages. Since his seminal work in the mid-1990s, Curtis Karnow has insisted on this point:

> No judge can isolate the 'legal' causes of injury from the pervasive electronic hum in which they operate, nor separate causes from the digital universe which gives them their mutable shape and shifting sense. The result is a snarled tangle of cause and effect as impossible to sequester as the winds of the air, or the currents of the ocean.[15]

[9] F Lyall and PB Larsen, *Space Law: A Treatise* (Abingdon, Routledge, 2018).

[10] A-S Martin and S Freeland, 'The Advent of Artificial Intelligence in Space Activities: New Legal Challenges' (2021) 55 *Space Policy* 101408.

[11] I Bratu, AR Lodder and T van der Linden, 'Autonomous Space Objects and International Space Law: Navigating the Liability Gap' (2021) 18(3) *Indonesian Journal of International Law* 423.

[12] I Bratu, 'Blaming Galileo: Liability for Damage Caused by Artificial Intelligence Operating Based on GNSS' (2021) 64(6) *Proceedings of the International Institute of Space Law*, http://dx.doi.org/10.2139/ssrn.3969363.

[13] See LB Solum, 'Legal Personhood for Artificial Intelligence' (1992) 70 *North Carolina Law Review* 1231; and CEA Karnow, 'Liability for Distributed Artificial Intelligence' (1996) 11 *Berkeley Technology Law Journal* 147.

[14] L Floridi, 'Faultless Responsibility: On the Nature and Allocation of Moral Responsibility for Distributed Moral Actions' (2016) 374 *Philosophical Transactions of the Royal Society A* 201601122.

[15] Karnow (n 13) 192.

The complexity of today's digital ecosystems can be illustrated by the intricacies of the supply chain in the design, manufacturing and use of AI systems. Consider cases of apportioned liability among the many actors of the supply chain, or the accountability horizon beyond which humans in the supply chain of AI products and services may not be able to know about data flows and interconnections that go beyond the parties with whom they directly interact and, in some instances, with whom such first-step actors further interact in turn. Humans may, in fact, have 'incomplete information although they do know who is up or downstream of them'.[16] Therefore, how to sever the chain of responsibilities between designers, manufacturers, operators, end users and third parties that interact with AI systems and smart robots can be difficult not only in everyday people's interaction but also in network management for utility networks, local interaction management in telecommunication networks, control system management in industrial plants, and simulation and training applications in defence domains. This also occurs in the field of intellectual property law, although here, dealing with the creativity of artificial agents, it can be challenging, if not impossible to identify the humans responsible or compensable for the final outcome, behaviour or decision of the artificial agent.[17] Cases of distributed responsibility and failures of legal causation illustrate the problems of the law with the traditional idea of the reasonable person who guards others against foreseeable harm. The duty of individuals to guard against such harms is increasingly challenged by the growing autonomy and intelligence of robotic behaviour, and cases where no human would be accountable for the unforeseen results or output of their decision-making processes – ie, the 'accountability gap' of AI.

The impact of AI clearly affects all branches of the law, as the disruption is both epistemic and normative. The epistemic challenges raised by the delegation of cognitive tasks and decision-making processes to AI concern inconclusive evidence leading to unjustified actions, inscrutable evidence leading to opacity and misguided evidence leading to biases.[18] The normative concerns depend on unfair outcomes that can end up either with discrimination or with transformative effects that induce challenges to human autonomy.[19] These challenges motivate a final overarching concern on traceability issues,[20] namely, the moral responsibilities and dilemmas of automation that regard the acceptability of replacing or augmenting human decision making with autonomous and intelligent systems.

[16] J Cobbe, M Veale and J Singh, 'Understanding Accountability in Algorithmic Supply Chains', *Proceedings Association for Computing Machinery*, New York, 2023.

[17] W Barfield and U Pagallo (eds), *Research Handbook on the Law of Artificial Intelligence* (Cheltenham, Edward Elgar, 2018).

[18] B Mittelstadt, P Allo, M Taddeo, S Wachter and L Floridi, 'The Ethics of Algorithms: Mapping the Debate' (2016) 22 *Big Data & Society* 1.

[19] U Pagallo, 'Algo-rhythms and the Beat of the Legal Drum' (2018) 31 *Philosophy and Technology* 507.

[20] M Durante and L Floridi, 'A Legal Principles-Based Framework for AI Liability Regulation' in J Mökander and M Ziosi (eds), *The 2021 Yearbook of the Digital Ethics Lab* (Cham, Springer, 2022).

AI may trigger various disproportionate difficulties and costs, which may be related to determining the safety of these systems, or defining either the relevant standard of care or proving its violation. However, the law may also appear inadequate or ineffective, as is the case for hacker attacks, where it can be difficult, both in outer space and on Earth, for the victim to identify a human tortfeasor.[21]

We can further appreciate how AI systems raise specific challenges in outer space by focusing on two legal fields: military and civil. The first field regards the use of lethal force through autonomous weapons systems (LAWS) displayed in outer space, while the second concerns legal issues posed by AI systems and smart robots in contracts and tort law. In both cases, the use of autonomous and intelligent systems adds a further layer of intricacy to the complexity of today's space law: in the first case – the militarisation of space – AI and smart robots update traditional debates on the interplay between provisions and principles of space law and IHL; in the second case, the level of risk and predictability of autonomous systems may require departing from established tortious liability doctrines. The following sections of this chapter investigate each of these problems separately.

II. AI Meets the Laws of War

It is a well-established opinion that principles and provisions of IHL – which essentially refer to the four Geneva Conventions of 1949 and the two additional Protocols of 1977 – apply to space activities. The opinion rests on: (i) the specific wording of treaties of space law, for example, Article IV of the 1967 Outer Space Treaty; (ii) case law of the International Court of Justice, also but not only as regards IHL – for example, the 'customary nature' of some principles and provisions of IHL; and (iii) the overall architecture of the international legal system.

Regarding the wording of outer space treaties and conventions, Article IV of the 1967 Outer Space Treaty prohibits the placement in orbit around the Earth of any object carrying nuclear weapons or any other kind of weapons of mass destruction. The placement of such weapons on celestial bodies or the stationing of such weapons in outer space is also prohibited. Yet, the Treaty does not prohibit further space weapons systems, such as anti-satellite weapons, or the partial orbit of a weapon of mass destruction. Although Article IV determines that the Moon and other celestial bodies shall be used exclusively for peaceful purposes, several military activities are considered acceptable under the terms of the Treaty.[22] However, limits to military and warfare activities of states in outer space not only hinge on a strict interpretation of international space law, but international law principles and norms, such as principles and provisions of IHL, also define the limits of military activities in outer space. In fact, Article III of the Outer Space Treaty establishes

[21] HLEG (n 1).
[22] C Christol, *The Modern International Law of Outer Space* (New York, Pergamon Press, 1982).

that all activities in outer space shall be conducted 'in accordance with international law', of which IHL is part.

One way in which norms and principles of IHL may apply to space law can be illustrated by some provisions of IHL, such as Articles 35(3) and 55 of Additional Protocol I. These norms establish obligations on states for general environmental reasons and concern risks relating to 'the health or survival of the population'. Arguably, space, as much as land, sea or air, should be considered part of the natural environment of our species, crucial to preserving both the health and survival of the entire world population. Filling the gaps in outer space treaties and conventions, the IHL provisions – namely, Articles 35(3) and 55 – reasonably apply to military activities in outer space to limit possible uses of weapons systems. The assumption rests on the case law of the International Court of Justice and its interpretation of the IHL framework, according to which IHL 'applies to all forms of warfare and to all kinds of weapons, those of the past, those of the present and those of the future'.[23] Moreover, many principles and provisions of IHL should be deemed customary law. Customs bind all activities of states on land, sea, air or space, regardless of whether states are signatories of international agreements or conventions. Examples of this hierarchy of legal sources are both the principle of distinction between civilians and combatants, and between civilian and military objectives enshrined in Article 48 of Additional Protocol I. To some, the principle according to which attacks shall be limited strictly to military objectives, enshrined in Article 52(2) of Additional Protocol I, is also a valid example.[24]

The applicability of IHL to outer space activities does not mean, of course, that all problems are solved. Indeed, scholars have discussed the open issues that the applicability of such principles, such as the principle of distinction or proportionality, raises in terms of the use of lethal force.[25] These issues could arise in relation to astronauts involved in a star wars scenario – that is, military astronauts. The legal regime for the activities of such military astronauts has been a topic of debate. On the one hand, they would fall under the provisions and principles of IHL for all combatants. On the other hand, in accordance with Article V of the 1967 Treaty, they would be considered 'envoys of mankind' – that is, astronauts – and, therefore guaranteed protection, aid and assistance at all times under the 1968 Rescue Agreement. Although in this case, IHL – or the customary norms and principles of international law that are enshrined in IHL – should be considered *lex specialis*, it must be conceded that 'the special protection afforded to astronauts under the

[23] International Court of Justice, *Legality of the Threat or Use of Nuclear Weapons*, Advisory Opinion, ICJ Rep 226 [*Nuclear Weapons*], 2016.

[24] See Y Sandoz, C Swinarki and B Zimmerman (eds), *Commentary on the Additional Protocols of 8 June 1977 to the Geneva Conventions of 12 August 1949* (Geneva, Martinus Nijholf Publications, 1987) 598; Permanent Court of Arbitration, Eritrea-Ethiopia Claims Commission, Partial Award, *Western Front, Aerial Bombardment and Related Claims*, 2005, https://legal.un.org/riaa/cases/vol_XXVI/291-349.pdf.

[25] C Steer and D Stephens, 'International Humanitarian Law and Its Application in Outer Space' in C Steer and M Hersch (eds), *War and Peace in Outer Space* (Oxford, Oxford University Press, 2021).

Outer Space Treaty and the Rescue and Return Agreement must be given particular attention where military personnel, who are astronauts during a time of armed conflict, are *not* engaged in belligerent actions, for instance, if they are engaged in scientific or other truly neutral activities'.[26]

The applicability of IHL provisions and principles to space weapon systems should be further understood in connection with how IHL applies to AI systems and smart robots in outer space – that is, in the jargon of IHL, LAWS. Since the early 2000s, scholars have dissected the manifold ways in which the use of LAWS can affect pillars of the laws of war, such as: (i) the just reasons to resort to the use of force (*ius ad bellum*); (ii) that which can justly be done in war (*ius in bello*); and (iii) the fundamental right to life.[27] In retrospect, it is not hard to understand why AI systems and smart robots can disrupt the pillars of the laws of war and IHL. Indeed, the increasing autonomous and intelligent behaviour of such AI systems poses two formidable problems. The first relates to the technical difficulties of designing artificial agents and systems that abide by the law – namely, embedding a complex set of legal rules into a piece of software so that it can distinguish combatants from civilians and military targets from civilian ones.[28] Then, once this first difficulty is overcome – and this is a big 'if' – the further problem raised by the use of AI systems and smart robots is whether actions that are permitted to humans only in strictly special circumstances (for example, the use of lethal force) should ever be permitted to any AI system, robot or autonomous spacecraft.

As stated by Philip Alston, Special Rapporteur on extrajudicial, summary or arbitrary execution, in his 2010 Report to the UN Assembly, the question of the lawful use of LAWS still concerned whether a certain agent, either human or artificial, would abide by the rules of *ius ad bellum*, *ius in bello* and IHL.[29] However, the problem is not simply technical – that is, robot soldiers that 'can perform more ethically than human soldiers are capable of'.[30] The question of whether the use of lethal force could ever be up to the autonomous decisions of AI systems involves a 'matter of principle'.[31] In a 2019 tweet from the UN Secretary-General António Guterres, emphasis was placed on 'autonomous machines with the power and discretion to select targets and take lives without human involvement'.[32] Guterres claimed that such design solutions would be 'politically unacceptable, morally repugnant and should be prohibited by international law'. AI military systems and robot soldiers should not decide whether they may take human life on land, sea, air or space; any opposing view would be either paradoxical or contradictory. In the words of a US Navy-sponsored piece of research on *Autonomous Military*

[26] ibid 37.
[27] U Pagallo, 'Robots of Just War: A Legal Perspective' (2011) 24 *Philosophy and Technology* 307.
[28] RC Arkin, *Governing Lethal Behaviour: Embedding Ethics in a Hybrid Deliberative/Hybrid Robot Architecture*, Report GIT-GVU-07-11, Georgia Institute of Technology's GVU Center, Atlanta, 2007.
[29] U Pagallo, *The Laws of Robots: Crimes, Contracts, and Torts* (Dordrecht, Springer, 2013) 59.
[30] Arkin (n 28).
[31] R Dworkin, *A Matter of Principle* (Oxford, Oxford University Press, 1985).
[32] See https://twitter.com/antonioguterres/status/1110232038081204224?lang=en.

Robotics: 'It is morally unjustifiable to deploy military robots before we have any idea of their risk to non-combatants … we may paradoxically need to use the first deaths to determine the level of risk.'[33]

However, bans on LAWS also trigger some problems of their own. It is not easy to flesh out the different degrees of autonomy and automation that can make legal regulations effective. For example, in the field of Unmanned Aircraft Systems (UAS) operations, the focus has been on the many autonomous functions relating to the purposes of the aircraft: taking off, flying to the target area, identifying targets, arming weapons for launch etc. As a 2014 United Nations Institute for Disarmament Research (UNIDIR) study on the automation of weapons technology stressed, in the future, it may be challenging to identify a particular 'bright line' between an unmanned aircraft – or spacecraft – with many autonomous functions, and aircraft and spacecrafts that are fully autonomous.[34] An additional issue concerns the dual use of autonomous technologies that are equally employable for intelligence, surveillance and reconnaissance (ISR) missions, as well as the lethal use of force. The Russian aggression to Ukraine in 2022 and the subsequent Ukrainian resistance and counteroffensive show the difference between small drones that are increasingly capable of carrying lethal payloads at long ranges and beyond visual line of sight (VLOS), and drones that are primarily used for ISR missions, such as the US RQ-4 Global Hawk or Hermes 900. How a ban on LAWS should address such dual uses of technologies remains an open problem, as does the dual uses of satellites in current space law.[35]

In any event, strict human responsibility for using AI must be strengthened with mechanisms for improving the transparency, oversight and accountability of military uses of AI.[36] These efforts must address the challenges that the autonomous functions of any weapon system pose: whether the autonomy of the system should be considered an attribute of a weapon system as a whole or attached to different tasks of weapons systems; or whether the environment of deployment, specific constraints on time of operation, or scope of movement over an area are relevant from the stance of international law regulations, among others. After a decade of scholarly discussions and pressure on the UN institutions, the international community finally addressed these issues in the mid-2010s. The forum of choice turned out to be the CCW, since the Convention deals with weapons that may be deemed excessively injurious or having indiscriminate effects. The Convention hinges on fundamental IHL principles, such as proportionality and distinction between civilians and combatants. In accordance with most international law agreements and conventions discussed in this volume (for example,

[33] P Lin, G Bekey and K Abney, *Autonomous Military Robotics: Risk, Ethics, and Design*, Report for US Department of Navy, Office of Naval Research Ethics + Emerging Sciences Group at California Polytechnic State University, San Luis Obispo, CA, 2008.

[34] UN Institute for Disarmament Research, *The Weaponization of Increasingly Autonomous Technologies: Considering How Meaningful Human Control Might Move the Discussion Forward* (Geneva, UN, 2014).

[35] Steer and Stephens (n 25).

[36] Pagallo (n 29).

the ICAO and IHL), CCW also has its protocols. So far, there are five: Protocol I on Non-detectable Fragments; Protocol II on Prohibitions or Restrictions on the Use of Mines, Booby-Traps and Other Devices (as amended on 3 May 1996); Protocol III on Prohibitions or Restrictions on the Use of Incendiary Weapons; Protocol IV on Blinding Laser Weapons; and Protocol V on Explosive Remnants of War. The modular design of the CCW has thus suggested to the international community that it is the proper forum to host discussions about the impact of autonomous technologies in the field of LAWS.

III. The LAWS of the CCW and the GGE

After a series of informal discussions held between 2014 and 2016 at the CCW in Geneva, the Fifth Review Conference of the High Contracting Parties to the CCW established, with a formal mandate, a Group of Governmental Experts (GGE) in December 2016. The topic of the first formal meeting of the GGE, held in November 2017, was the emerging technologies in the area of lethal autonomous weapons systems in the context of the objectives and purposes of the CCW. So far, the GGE has delivered annual reports, with the exception of 2020 due to the COVID-19 pandemic. Such documents include a list of guiding principles that, concerning the autonomy of intelligent systems, can be adequately expanded to the military challenges of AI systems and robots in space. Certain specimens of autonomous technologies, for example, should certainly be prohibited. This is the case for every 'weapons system … of a nature to cause superfluous injury or unnecessary suffering, or if it is inherently indiscriminate, or is otherwise incapable of being used in accordance with the requirements and principles of IHL', as proposed by the GGE.[37]

However, between possible bans of technology and fair military uses of AI in space – for example, ISR missions – lie the grey areas of the law. GGE declarations recommend restricting the focus of the analysis to three types of observables: (i) the characterisation of the AI systems to be regulated; (ii) the review of their potential military applications; and (iii) how they are related to the human element in the use of lethal force. A guideline for this work in progress on the regulation of LAWS in the context of CCW efforts is provided by the GGE with a list of principles that will govern this crucial domain of technological innovation. The guiding principles concern:

> The applicability of IHL to LAWS; non-delegation of human responsibility; accountability for use of force in accordance with international law; weapons reviews before deployment; incorporation of physical, non-proliferation and cyber security safeguards;

[37] The CCW reports are available at: https://meetings.unoda.org/meeting/67246/documents. The Report of the 2019 session of the Group of Governmental Experts on Emerging Technologies in the Area of Lethal Autonomous Weapons Systems at https://documents.unoda.org/wp-content/uploads/2020/09/CCW_GGE.1_2019_3_E.pdf. See Point 17 (h) of the Report CCW/GGE.1/2019/3, at 4.

> risk assessment and mitigation during technology development; consideration of the use of emerging technologies in the area of LAWS in compliance with IHL; non-harm to civilian research and development and use; the need to adopt a non-anthropomorphic perspective on AI; and the appropriateness of CCW as a framework for dealing with this whole set of issues.[38]

This list can be conveniently exported to the regulation of military uses of AI in space, starting with the principle that humans shall always remain strictly responsible for the behaviour of their autonomous systems, regardless of the degree of control over those very systems. As a further UN unit, the Advisory Board on Disarmament Matters, affirms in a 2014 report, this strict human responsibility for the use of technology must be strengthened with mechanisms for improving the transparency, oversight and accountability of military uses of AI.[39] One of the lessons learned from current international initiatives on the regulation of LAWS is, in fact, that regulations are most effective when they focus on how a specific model or technological application is used rather than on what the autonomous system should be. Attention must correspondingly be drawn to the levels of predictability and reliability deemed appropriate in the autonomous functions of robotic or AI operations, according to the constraints on time of operation, deployment and scope of movement over an area. At the time of writing, the GGE meetings at the CCW in Geneva have continued on an annual basis. In the conclusions of the May 2023 Report – drawing on the decision of the High Contracting Parties of the Convention held in November 2022 – the GGE stressed that 'the work of the open-ended Group of Governmental Experts related to emerging technologies in the area of lethal autonomous weapons systems … is to continue, to strengthen the Convention'.[40]

Admittedly, most work on the military disruption of AI technologies and their regulation is still to be done. In October 2023, the First Committee of the UN General Assembly approved a new draft resolution on LAWS in which – 'underlining the significant progress' made by the GGE on LAWS – the Secretary-General is requested to 'seek the views of Member States and observer States on lethal autonomous weapons systems, inter alia, on ways to address the related challenges and concerns they raise from humanitarian, legal, security, technological and ethical perspectives and on the role of humans in the use of force'.[41] While the Speaker of the First Committee, following the 2019 tweet of the UN Secretary-General, warns that 'an algorithm must not be in full control of decisions involving killing',

[38] ibid.

[39] U Pagallo, 'The Governance of AI and its Legal Context-Dependency' in J Cowls and J Morley (eds), *The 2020 Yearbook of the Digital Ethics Lab* (Cham, Springer, 2021).

[40] See the Report at https://docs-library.unoda.org/Convention_on_Certain_Conventional_Weapons_-Group_of_Governmental_Experts_on_Lethal_Autonomous_Weapons_Systems_(2023)/CCW_GGE1_2023_2_Advance_version.pdf.

[41] UN General Assembly, First Committee, *General and Complete Disarmament*, Doc A/C.1/78/L.56, October 2023, https://documents-dds-ny.un.org/doc/UNDOC/LTD/N23/302/66/PDF/N2330266.pdf?OpenElement.

the devil is once again in the legal detail. The regulation and governance of what makes AI unique on the battlefield – also but not only in outer space – requires all sources and means of the law, such as (i) a political declaration of the UN on, for example, the principle of non-delegation of human responsibility; (ii) a new legally binding instrument for autonomous systems on, for example, dual uses of AI technologies; (iii) guidelines and codes of conduct, the military outer space counterpart of the ICAO's manuals in civil aviation law; and (iv) improvements in the implementation of existing legal requirements, which comprises strict reviews of weapons.

In the following chapter, we will return to this military side of the analysis of the new laws of outer space. For now, we must complement the scrutiny of LAWS and further military uses of autonomous and intelligent systems with the investigation of the civil – as opposed to the military – side of the law. The focus should be on non-contractual claims and contractual obligations relating to the use of AI systems. The aim is to cast light on a further set of normative challenges unique to AI – namely, issues of civil liability that depend on multiple regulatory fields involved in the use of AI systems in space activities.

IV. AI Meets Civil Liability

The civilian impact of AI on the law can be appreciated through the voluntary agreements between parties to a contract and the obligations between private persons imposed by the government to compensate for damages caused by wrongdoing. In Chapter 3, we noted that contractual clauses and terms of services by private companies have, in a certain sense, shaped the rules of space law. Conversely, in the field of tort law, several provisions can be extended to complement dispute settlement among private companies and potential third parties – for example, through the strict liability rules for ground damages enshrined in the US Restatement (Second) of Torts or the strict liability regime enshrined in the new 2024 Product Liability Directive of EU law. As a method of accident control, strict liability policies can help strengthen the level of legal protection by shielding consumers and individuals who 'can do little, at reasonable costs' to prevent rare AI failures.[42] Strict liability rules may properly tackle complex cases of distributed responsibility or failures of legal causation in dealing with autonomous and intelligent systems. This is because individuals often find it difficult to demonstrate the existence of a defect in an AI service or product: legal protection against damages provoked by AI systems should not be weaker than that implemented when damages are caused by other technological artefacts or humans.[43]

[42] R Posner, 'The Jurisprudence of Skepticism' (1988) 86(5) *Michigan Law Review* 827.
[43] HLEG (n 1).

However, no-fault liability policies are not the magic bullet. At times, they are simply not effective,[44] may require over-frequent revision to cope with technological progress[45] or even hinder sound technological innovation.[46] Strict liability policies are always complemented by fault-based doctrines on how to tackle risks and unpredictability of AI behaviour, such as ML algorithms. Tort law doctrines include duties of care, theories of agency and procedural standards on burdens of proof and presumptions. Experts have proposed the extension of tortious liability doctrines, such as the burden of proving defect, to tackle the 'accountability gaps' of AI.[47] Such a burden should be reversed under several circumstances, such as: (i) disproportionate difficulties or costs relating to determining the safety of the AI system or that a certain level of safety has not been met; (ii) cases in which the victim has no reasonable access to the information, or when the information has not been logged, thereby 'triggering the presumption that the condition of liability to be proven by the missing information is fulfilled';[48] (iii) disproportionate difficulties and costs that exist for determining either the relevant standard of care or to prove its violation. Some of these recommendations have been endorsed by the European Commission in its 2021 proposal for a new 'AI Liability Act'.[49]

These recommendations could be fruitfully extended to tackle some liability issues of space law that shape current privatisation trends. Since most experts predict that liability issues of space law will increasingly relate to private parties, it is likely that a new generation of tortious claims and contractual issues will concern the ways in which private companies may guarantee the rights of their customers, but also the protection of basic rights of space tourists, space explorers or space settlers.[50] On 2 May 2022, CNN announced that the first space hotel orbiting the Moon was scheduled to open in 2025.[51] Cases of distributed responsibility or inextricable legal causation will be expected, for example, concerning hacking issues. These cases are increasing in outer space,[52] showing that the current

[44] A Bertolini and F Episcopo, 'The Expert Group's Report on Liability for Artificial Intelligence and Other Emerging Digital Technologies: A Critical Assessment' (2021) 12(3) *European Journal of Risk Regulation* 644.

[45] E Bassi, 'From Here to 2023: Civil Drones Operations and the Setting of New Legal Rules for the European Single Sky' (2020) 100 *Journal of Intelligent Robotic Systems* 493.

[46] U Pagallo, 'LegalAIze: Tackling the Normative Challenges of Artificial Intelligence and Robotics through the Secondary Rules of Law' in M Corrales, M Fenwick and N Forgó (eds), *New Technology, Big Data and the Law: Perspectives in Law, Business and Innovation* (Singapore, Springer, 2017).

[47] HLEG (n 1).

[48] ibid no 15.

[49] U Pagallo, 'The Politics of Data in EU Law: Will it Succeed?' (2022) 1 *Digital Society* 20.

[50] See S Freeland and R Jakhu, 'What's Human Rights Got to Do with Outer Space? Everything!' in R Moro-Aguilar, PJ Blount and T Masson-Zwaan (eds), *Proceedings of the International Institute of Space Law*, 2014; J Lim, 'Charting a Human Rights Framework for Outer Space Settlements', *71st International Astronautical Congress (IAC) – The CyberSpace Edition*, 2020, https://www.jusadastra.org/assets/files/IAC-20,E7,2,11,x60311(1).pdf.

[51] See https://edition.cnn.com/travel/article/space-hotel-orbital-assembly-scn/index.html.

[52] D Hechler (ed), 'Cybersecurity in Outer Space Unprepared?' (2023) 9(3) *Tag CYBER Security Annual*.

rules of tort law may prove insufficient to defend victims of cyberattacks: it can be impossible for the individual victim of a cyberattack to identify a tortfeasor. Accordingly, in their recommendations to the European Commission, the HLEG's report suggested the insertion of compensation schemes: 'compensation funds may be used to protect tort victims who are entitled to compensation according to the applicable liability rules, but whose claims cannot be satisfied'.[53] Therefore, in addition to the extension of current doctrines of tort law to some new scenarios of space law, liability issues of AI systems may recommend stepping away from traditional approaches in the field and endorsing new kinds of responsibility and liability for space law, such as the compensation mechanisms for victims of hacking mentioned above.

The legal protection of humans dealing with increasingly autonomous and intelligent systems in space-related activities – through the means of strict liability rules, fault-based liability norms or new compensation schemes – should be complemented with further sets of rules that, in the jargon of EU lawyers, are either 'horizontal' or 'vertical'. Horizontal regulations apply to AI systems in all sectors, such as data protection in EU law; on the contrary, vertical regulations are sectorial, such as machinery safety in health law. Arguably, such provisions and principles are potentially relevant for all space-related activities and their liability issues. At an international level, in 2019, the UN Committee on the Peaceful Uses of Outer Space (COPUOS) started focusing on the use of AI in space, in particular regarding the 'convergence of space-derived data and information with neural network-based artificial intelligence and blockchain for sustainable development'.[54] However, no particular outcomes should be expected on this front any time soon. In the wording of the Report of the international forum on 'Access to Space4All':

> Participants expressed the view that solutions offered through new technology developments, such as artificial intelligence, blockchain or cloud computing, could provide very useful tools to tackle a variety of issues currently on the agenda of the Committee, and consequently proposed that the Committee could consider including exchanges on these developments in the future.[55]

For the moment, all crucial regulations of AI activities in outer space, or related to space services that entail civil liability problems, are up to national or regional legislators. The following section introduces national and regional regulation fields that complement traditional principles of international law on space-related activities.

[53] HLEG (n 1) nos 18 and 34.

[54] T Blagojevich, 'A Brave New World: In-Space AI and Space-Related AI and its Soon-to-Be Fitting Legal Robe' (2023) *Observatorio Jurídico Aeroespacial* 11.

[55] Committee on the Peaceful Uses of Outer Space, *Report on the United Nations/Austria World Space Forum 'Access to Space4All'*, Scientific and Technical Subcommittee Fifty-Seventh Session, Vienna, February 2020, https://www.unoosa.org/res/oosadoc/data/documents/2020/aac_105c_12020crp/aac_105c_12020crp_11_0_html/AC105_C1_2020_CRP11E.pdf, at no 34.

V. National and Regional Regulations of AI in Outer Space

Against the general framework of the laws of contracts and tortious liability under scrutiny in the previous section, attention should be paid to general and sectorial provisions of legislators aiming to govern the opportunities and challenges of AI. As noted earlier, some of these regulations are general or, in the jargon of EU lawyers, 'horizontal'. Consider the Artificial Intelligence Act (AIA), the first all-encompassing legal regulation of AI systems in the world. One of the most relevant political decisions enshrined in this piece of EU legislation is that certain uses of AI systems shall be prohibited. According to Article 5 of the AIA, the ban includes: (i) the deployment of 'subliminal techniques beyond a person's consciousness' (Article 5.1(a)); (ii) the abuse of people's 'vulnerabilities' due to their age, physical or mental disability (Article 5.1(b)); or (iii) real-time biometric identification systems that, however, admit certain exceptions in the ability of robots – either to scan an individual's face for facial recognition[56] or to detect the emotions of individuals.[57] These provisions represent a general condition for every legitimate use of such systems in space. In addition, the EU legislation establishes a further set of duties and obligations for designers, providers and end users of AI systems considered to be 'high-risk' systems. Provisions on, for example, AI systems for biometric identification and categorisation of natural persons, management and operation of critical infrastructures, education and vocational training, employment or management of workers are most likely to affect many uses of AI systems and smart robots in space activities and missions.[58]

Another instance of 'horizontal regulation' concerns personal data protection law, for example, the General Data Protection Regulation (GDPR) in EU law, which applies to the regulation and governance of data-driven technologies, such as AI and robots. Privacy concerns in space law have traditionally been associated with technologies, such as remote sensing, that gather Earth data from outer space. Google Earth services, for example, made this technology popular in the early 2000s. Today's privacy concerns not only refer to the collection and use of satellite data, but also the way in which such data may be exploited by a machine learning algorithm. In 2022, in the 59th session of the Scientific and Technical Sub-Committee of UNCOPUOS, a side-event was devoted to 'Data Protection and AI'.[59] Although no possible legislative outcome of such events and international

[56] M Smith and S Miller, 'The Ethical Application of Biometric Facial Recognition Technology' (2022) 37 *AI & Society* 167.

[57] S Pal, S Mukhopadhyay and N Suryadeyara, 'Development and Progress in Sensors and Technologies for Human Emotion Recognition' (2021) 21(16) *Sensors* 5554.

[58] Pagallo et al (n 8).

[59] See the 59th session of the Scientific and Technical Sub-Committee of the United Nations Committee on the Peaceful Uses of Outer Space (UNCOPUOS), *CEST Data Protection and AI*, Vienna, February 2022, 14–15, https://www.unoosa.org/documents/pdf/copuos/stsc/2022/CANEUS_Side_Events_Feb_15_1.pdf.

activities should be expected in the short to medium term, national regulators have been very active.[60] In some jurisdictions, such as EU law, provisions on data protection are undoubtedly relevant for all space-related activities in the civilian sector. Although exceptions for the collection and use of personal data for public and national purposes exist, as a general rule, personal data processing of space-related activities arguably falls under the provisions of the GDPR, regardless of whether the data subjects are space tourists, users of satellite services or scientists in the Columbus Laboratory of the ISS.

Regarding 'vertical regulations' that may affect the use of AI systems and robots in space activities, the focus should be on rules of machinery products, cybersecurity and environmental law. In EU law, most of the legal fields of technological regulation which affect the use of AI systems and smart robots are under current revision or in progress. The proposal of a new regulation on machinery products of April 2021, for example, aimed to 'cover new risks stemming from emerging technologies (in particular robots using artificial intelligence technologies)'.[61] The provisions entered into force in July 2023 as Regulation (EU) 2023/1230 and apply to the design of smart robots in the safety and security of the machinery in the HRI field.

Such design should also consider provisions of connectivity and cybersecurity. EU Regulation 2019/881, which established the new European Union Agency for Cybersecurity (ENISA) (as amended with further provisions – for example, NIS2 Directive 2022/2555, or Regulation (EU) 2023/588), is intended to safeguard the functioning of robots and AI systems that may be related to space activities. The aim is to strengthen the resilience of the connectivity networks on which such autonomous intelligent systems act, react and interact. Supplementing the first 2016 NIS Directive on cybersecurity, NIS2 Directive 2022/2555 adds cybersecurity of space activities to the list of sectors – such as health and water, energy and transport, banking and financial markets, or digital infrastructures – considered 'of high criticality'. All duties and obligations set up with NIS2 shall apply to 'operators of ground-based infrastructure, owned, managed and operated by Member States or by private parties, that support the provision of space-based services'. Likewise, in the field of satellite law, Regulation (EU) 2023/588 aims to strengthen secure access to some of such services. In the wording of Article 3(1)a of the Regulation:

> The general objectives shall be … uninterrupted access to secure, autonomous, high-quality, reliable and cost-effective satellite governmental communication services to government-authorised users, by establishing a multi-orbital, secure connectivity system.

[60] FG von der Dunk, 'Outer Space Law Principles and Privacy' in D Leung and R Purdy (eds), *Evidence from Earth Observation Satellites: Emerging Legal Issues* (Leiden, Brill, 2013) 243–58.

[61] See COM (2021) 202, https://www.europarl.europa.eu/thinktank/en/document/EPRS_BRI(2021)694206.

The provisions of EU law thus set up a new set of duties and obligations for private providers of some critical space-based services. Leaving aside the merits of these EU cybersecurity policies that include space activities in a complex integrated network (for more on this, see Chapter 8), it seems fair to admit that cybersecurity is by far one of the most vibrant sectors in the field of space law.

Another critical sector concerns environmental law. We noted that provisions such as Articles 35(3) and 55 of the Additional Protocol I of IHL provide some basic principles of international space law. However, despite being under the auspices of the 17 Sustainable Development Goals of the UN 2030 Agenda, most of the work is once again up to national or regional legislators.[62] It is well known that AI systems may affect the environment. This is the result of: (i) high energy requirements and the carbon footprint of AI;[63] (ii) increasing volume of e-waste and pressure on rare-earth elements generated by the computing industry;[64] (iii) risks of dependency from private actors who own and operate AI models and infrastructures;[65] and (iv) environmental harm via hacking, because AI systems for monitoring environment mostly rely on data collection by sensors and transmission through communication networks.[66] In addition to these environmental concerns, we should be attentive to the use of kerosene and liquid oxygen used to power today's space rockets, which inject black carbon into the upper atmosphere, creating problems of re-entry – for example, aluminium coming back into the atmosphere.[67] In some jurisdictions, such as EU law, 'promoting sustainable development' and acting 'in accordance with the principle of sustainable development' are basic principles of the legal system enshrined in Article 11 of the Treaty on the Functioning of the European Union (TFEU) and Article 37 of the Charter of Fundamental Rights (CFR) respectively. Correspondingly, space law regulations of EU law – for example, Regulation (EU) 2023/588 on the Union Secure Connectivity Programme 2023–2027 – must abide by Regulation (EU) 2021/1119 on 'climate neutrality', ie, the so-called European Climate Law. The aim should be to attain the overall sustainability of space-related activities. We will return to this aspect of space law in Chapter 8.

[62] D Gugunskiy and N. Emelianova, 'Space Activities and Sustainable Development Goals' in EG Popkova and BS Sergi (eds), *Modern Global Economic System: Evolutional Development vs. Revolutionary Leap* (Cham, Springer, 2021).

[63] N Jones, 'How to Stop Data Centres from Gobbling up the World's Electricity' (2018) 561 *Nature* 163.

[64] E Alonso et al, 'Evaluating Rare-Earth Element Availability: A Case with Revolutionary Demand from Clean Technologies' (2012) 46(6) *Environmental Science and Technology* 3406.

[65] See M Bolton, R Raven and M Mintrom, 'Can AI Transform Public Decision-Making for Sustainable Development? An Exploration of Critical Earth System Governance Questions' (2021) 9 *Earth System Governance* 100116; and A Zuiderwijk, Y-C Chen and F Salem, 'Implications of the Use of Artificial Intelligence in Public Governance: A Systematic Literature Review and a Research Agenda' (2021) 38 *Government Information Quarterly* 101577.

[66] World Economic Forum, *Harnessing Artificial Intelligence for the Earth*, 2018, https://www.pwc.com/gx/en/services/sustainability/publications/ai-for-the-earth.html.

[67] D Werner, 'Aerospace Corp Raises Questions about Pollutants Produced during Satellite and Rocket Reentry', *SpaceNews*, 11 December 2020, https://spacenews.com/aerospace-agu-reentry-pollution.

Drawing on this bunch of vertical and horizontal regulations relating to the civil – as opposed to the criminal or military – side of the law, the result is that traditional civil liability issues of space law will be complemented with the further set of regulations that relate to both axes of national or regional legislation. These provisions may relate to either strict liability policies, fault-based regulations or a mix of hard and soft law. As was noted earlier, such provisions include: (i) general top-down rules of legislators, such as the AIA or the GDPR in EU law; (ii) machinery regulations that establish standards of security and safety for HRI; (iii) rules and norms of personal data protection and data governance, for example, both the Data Act and the Data Governance Act in EU law;[68] (iv) integration with the cybersecurity provisions of the legal system; and (v) integration with the environmental regulations on the sustainability of space activities and missions. It is within this framework that we can appreciate the specificities of each national space law regulation and their connectivity programs, for example, Regulation (EU) 2023/588.

Therefore, a piece of space legislation like the EU Secure Connectivity Programme 2023–2027 cannot be grasped alone, but rather in accordance with a coherent interpretation of several regulations that traditionally fall outside the radar of experts in space law, such as regimes of product liability. The legal challenges of AI are inextricably connected to problems of data governance, cybersecurity and environmental protection that technological advancements raise both in space and on Earth. Such new fields of space law add a further layer of complexity to traditional discussions on the national, regional and international dimensions of the field.

VI. The Mid-2020s Boom

The chapter has discussed the many problems raised by the increasing use of AI systems and smart robots in space activities. Although in many cases, it is AI which makes these activities possible or that changes and improves what other third-order technologies do, we should be attentive to the set of unique moral and legal challenges in the military and civilian sectors. On the one hand, the chapter has focused on the current works of the CCW in regulating LAWS at the international level. On the other hand, attention has been drawn to liability issues that may recommend stepping away from traditional approaches of the field, such as compensation mechanisms. Constraints and affordances of AI systems are inextricably connected to the further regulation of data governance issues, cybersecurity concerns or sustainability problems examined in the previous sections of this chapter. The boom of space activities in the mid-2020s emphasises this inextricable

[68] Pagallo (n 49).

connection of technological innovation and normative constraints. In the words of the US National Academies of Science, Engineering, and Medicine:

> The past decade experienced a very large expansion in new routes to space and new uses for space exploration, with concomitant increased capacities and utilization of space science platforms. One example of the results of this expansion is the science output from the ISS, driven by international academia, government researchers, and the commercial sector … The world is entering a new era fueled by humanity's connection to space and marked by greater opportunities, interest, resources, and innovation than ever before, rivaling and indeed exceeding the magnitude and relevance of the Apollo era. At the same time, there are many significant challenges in Earth-based societies, such as impact of population growth and climate change on the environment and civil organization.[69]

The flourishing of space activities and their normative challenges include: (i) new space stations for scientific research or mass tourism; (ii) thousands of satellites recorded in the Master International Frequency Register (MIFR) on an annual basis; (iii) asteroid mining; (iv) further improvement in the search for the physical and biological principles that guide the long-term and safe habitation of space; and (v) further improvement for the physiological adaptation of terrestrial organisms to space, which goes hand in hand with a dozen lunar programmes in the making, such as NASA's Artemis programme and China's Lunar Exploration Program (also known as the Chang'e Project). Such space activities and projects critically depend on technological advancements and how law makers intend to govern them. The challenges revolve around the balance to be struck between the pros and cons of AI systems with their unique properties and features, as well as the interdependence of AI solutions with the functioning of a single complex digital ecosystem. The new frontiers of cybersecurity space law and the impact of technological innovation on traditional issues of space law tackled in the previous chapters of this book can be further illustrated by the thorny issue on the appropriability of space resources. Asteroid mining techniques make this appropriability real at decreasing costs.

Against these trends, the next chapter focuses on arguably the most fascinating project in the mid-2020s boom of space activities and missions – the colonisation of the Moon and, generally speaking, the establishment of permanent human colonies on celestial bodies. Projects of several national governments and space agencies shed light on this legal novelty – that is, how provisions and principles of national and international space law are related to the regulation of those which were dubbed the new fields of space law (cybersecurity space law, machinery safety for HRI, AI data governance and data protection, and environmental space law). Dramatic technological advances have made it necessary to deal with these normative challenges urgently. In the next chapter, attention will be drawn to how this interplay works out on the Moon.

[69] National Academies of Sciences, Engineering, and Medicine, *Thriving in Space: Ensuring the Future of Biological and Physical Sciences Research: A Decadal Survey for 2023–2032* (Washington DC: National Academies Press, 2023).

6

Colonies

We can reasonably expect to see hundreds of colonies in outer space over the following decades. Self-assembling 3D bio-printers that exploit lunar resources to build artificial colonies on the Moon are all but futuristic. However, what laws should be applied to this context is – and will increasingly be – controversial. The current drawbacks of international space law, trends on the privatisation of space activities, and technology disruption – and not only for military purposes – suggest several cautionary tales. Rather than the idyllic sort of a new Greek colony with its space Argonauts, such cautionary tales concern the risk of a new form of sidereal colonialism. This would entail the unilateral exploitation of natural resources with growing space debris and overpopulated orbits, which may go hand in hand with a lack of agreement and goodwill among sovereign states on how to amend the old space law treaties from the 1960s and 1970s. The problem not only relates to the enforcement of principles and rules of this legal framework, but also to how this legal framework falls progressively short in terms of coping with the new challenges of outer space activities.

I. A Warning from the Ancient World

Historical research on Greek colonies has shown how everything started with a community of migrants who founded villages in the wilderness with no neighbours in sight.[1] Although the account of Greek colonisation spanned centuries and was particularly complex and context-dependent, we can hold on to what, centuries later, Aristotle wrote in the *Politics* about those pristine communities: 'the village according to the most natural account seems to be a colony from a household'.[2] Lest we start imagining extra-terrestrial beings and AI super-intelligences, this is what we should expect with the first human colonies on the Moon or Mars: harsh environments with no (intelligent) life around.

However, what laws should be applied to this context is – and will increasingly be – quite controversial, just as the issues of law and the constitution were in ancient times. Aristotle suggests that Greeks initially settled their colonies based

[1] GR Tsetskhladze (ed), *Greek Colonisation* (Leiden, Brill, 2018).
[2] Aristotle, *Politics*, J Barnes (ed and trans) (Princeton, Princeton University Press, 2017) 1252 B.

on the values, norms and ethos of their own villages, and only later opened up to multiple political orders over the centuries. This evolution example is critical, as it draws attention to the role that a growing population may play in the exploration of new territories – scale matters. Aristotle was well aware of the critical differences between the first Greek colonies in unpopulated areas around 1000 BCE and his own portrayal of the laws and constitutions of such colonies. It was none other than Aristotle's master Plato who clarified this social change in the *Republic*. States develop from 'primitive communities' to societies that progressively flourish and thrive as a result of multiplying commercial activities, sophisticated mores and social expectations. And then, in the words of Plato:

> (Socrates): The country, too, which was large enough to support the original inhabitants, will now be too small. If we are to have enough pasture and plough land, we shall have to cut off a slice of our neighbours' territory; and if they too are not content with necessaries, but give themselves up to getting unlimited wealth, they will want a slice of ours.
>
> (Glaucon): That is inevitable, Socrates.
>
> (Socrates): So the next thing will be, Glaucon, that we shall be at war.[3]

Plato's link between colonies and wars reminds us of why, since the Middle Ages, the Crusades and the conquest of the Americas in modern times, 'colonisation' may entail a practice of domination, such as the subjugation of one population by another. Today, it is arguable that any colonisation process on Earth should be considered pejorative.[4] However, in the field of space law, scholars still refer to current projects to establish the first human long-term settlements on the Moon as colonisation efforts.[5] The formula refers to the technological advancements supporting such efforts as 3D bio-printing,[6] and their legal grounds, which relate to principles and provisions of international space law such as 'freedom of scientific investigation' under Article I of the Outer Space Treaty, prohibition of 'national appropriation' in Article II, 'international responsibility' for national activities in Article VI, and more.

Projects of long-term and even permanent human colonies on the Moon are not science fiction. Today, there are more than a dozen programmes relating to lunar activities, such as: (i) the HAKUTO-R Missions under the direction of the Japanese Aerospace Exploration Agency (JAXA); (ii) the Chandrayaan-3 programme of the Indian Space Research Organization (ISRO); (iii) Russia's Luna-Glob and China's Chang 6; (iv) the US Peregrine Missions and the Intuitive

[3] Plato, *The Republic*, F MacDonald Cornford (ed) (London, Oxford University Press, 1945) 373 D.

[4] R Young, *Postcolonialism: An Historical Introduction* (Oxford, Blackwell, 2001).

[5] See R Zubrin, *Entering Space* (New York, Jeremy P Tarcher/Putnam, 1999); O Dunnett, The Spaces of Outer Space, in *The Routledge Handbook of Social Studies of Outer Space* (Abingdon, Routledge, 2023); M Balistreri and S Umbrello, 'Modifying the Environment or Human Nature? What is the Right Choice for Space Travel and Mars Colonisation?' (2023) 17(1) *NanoEthics* 5.

[6] T Ghidini, 'Regenerative Medicine and 3D Bioprinting for Human Space Exploration and Planet Colonisation' (2018) 10 *Journal of Thoracic Disease* S2363.

Machines missions with the Nova-C Landers; (v) the ESA's Argonaut Project (see Chapter 4); and (vi) the US-led Artemis programme under the coordination of NASA. In addition, the International Lunar Research Station project (ILRS) was launched by China's National Space Administration in collaboration with Russia's Roscosmos in 2021.

After Eugene Cernan's moonwalk with the Apollo 17 mission in 1972, the next return of astronauts to the Moon is scheduled for the end of 2025. A new space race is expected, raising questions as to what legal principles and norms should govern places such as the human colonies on the Moon or Mars. The principles of international space law only provide partial answers and, furthermore, projects of human establishments on celestial bodies rest on highly controversial grounds. Chapter 2 stressed that some national legislation – that of US and Luxembourg – has sparked controversy among experts with its provisions on the appropriability of space resources.

This controversy shall be properly understood in terms of 'good' or 'bad' colonisation. In the *Republic* – finalising his story on the establishment of the ideal community, with its expansion through colonies and the risks of resorting to war – Socrates draws attention to 'what kind of natures are suited for the guardianship of a state'.[7] Governance issues that follow the public and private 'greatest disasters' of the war not only concern who should guard against the guardians, but also how to assess and govern social practices. Experts of space law do not necessarily have to buy into Socrates's arguments on the 'philosopher king'; however, they still share the Greek philosopher's problem of distinguishing what is just or unjust and – in particular, vis-a-vis multiple lunar activities and programmes involving long-term settlements on the celestial body – the different kinds of colonisation.

The dilemma between good and bad colonisation is not a theoretical exercise. The following section illustrates this moral problem through the most important space colonisation programme today, namely, the Artemis Programme, under the leadership of the US government and its space agency NASA. After Greek and European colonies – initially in the Americas, then around the world – the classic question of which regulations and principles of the law will be established in new territories now concerns the Moon (and its environment).

II. The Artemis Accords

The Artemis Programme is a US-led project, formally established in 2017, which aims to return astronauts to the Moon by 2025. The overall aim is to create a sustainable presence on the Earth's satellite, paving the way for next-generation missions to Mars. After a first uncrewed Moon-orbiting mission – Artemis-1,

[7] Plato (n 3) 374 E.

which was launched in November 2022 – the members of the first crewed mission were presented on 4 April 2023. The 'faces' of Artemis-2 are those of commander Reid Wiseman, pilot Victor J. Glover and mission specialists Jeremy Hansen and Christina Koch. We 'met' Christina Koch in Chapter 3 when dealing with the physical and mental challenges of long space missions. From a legal viewpoint, these plans of 'scientific discovery, economic benefits, and inspiration for a new generation of explorers: the Artemis Generation'[8] hinge on Title IV of the US 2015 Commercial Space Launch Competitiveness Act, namely, the 'Space Resource Exploration and Utilization'.

The 2015 US Act set up three key provisions. The first was illustrated in Chapter 2: the rights of US citizens 'engaged in commercial recovery of an asteroid resource or a space resource' to the resource thus obtained. The second concerns a mandate to create a US regime for the authorisation and supervision of such commercial activities in accordance with US obligations under international law. The third requires the US President to 'promote and facilitate through appropriate federal agencies, commercial space resources exploration and extraction and to promote the rights of US citizens to engage in such activities in accordance with international obligations'.[9]

Drawing on these legal bases, in April 2020, President Trump signed an Executive Order on 'Encouraging International Support for the Recovery and Use of Space Resources'. Though some scholars claim that such an order points towards the right direction,[10] it is not hard to understand why the Executive Order appears controversial, as it states the following:

> Americans should have the right to engage in commercial exploration, recovery, and use of resources in outer space, consistent with applicable law. Outer space is a legally and physically unique domain of human activity, and the United States does not view it as a global commons. Accordingly, it shall be the policy of the United States to encourage international support for the public and private recovery and use of resources in outer space, consistent with applicable law.[11]

Moreover:

> [The] US does not consider the Moon Agreement to be an effective or necessary instrument to guide nation states regarding the promotion of commercial participation in the long-term exploration, scientific discovery, and use of the Moon, Mars, or other celestial bodies.[12]

[8] NASA, 'Why We Are Going to the Moon', 2023, https://www.nasa.gov/specials/artemis/#why.

[9] M de Zwart, 'To the Moon and beyond: The Artemis Accords and the Evolution of Space Law' in M de Zwart and S Henderson (eds), *Commercial and Military Uses of Outer Space* (Singapore, Springer, 2021).

[10] P Stimers, 'The President's Space Resources Executive Order: A Step in the Right Direction', *Space Review*, 2020, https://www.thespacereview.com/article/3925/1.

[11] White House, Executive Order 13914, 2020, https://trumpwhitehouse.archives.gov/wp-content/uploads/2020/04/Fact-Sheet-on-EO-Encouraging-International-Support-for-the-Recovery-and-Use-of-Space-Resources.pdf.

[12] ibid.

Drawing on this Executive Order, the US government prepared the blueprint for a series of bilateral agreements on how to promote the commercial exploration and exploitation of space resources. Similarly minded nations and their space agencies were involved in this ambitious plan of space colonisation through long-term human settlements on the Moon. On 13 October 2020, eight states –Australia, Canada, Italy, Japan, Luxembourg, the United Arab Emirates, the UK and the US – signed the Accords. Ukraine joined a month later. Although not legally binding, the Accords have highly relevant political meaning since the explicit goal is to influence and develop space law through adherence and practice to the terms of the agreements. At the time of writing, there are 34 Artemis partners. India joined in June 2023, Germany in September, the Netherlands and Bulgaria in November, and Angola in December. The Accords remain open for signature indefinitely.

The Artemis Accords comprise 13 sections.[13] Section 1 defines the purpose and scope of the Accords, while section 2 is devoted to their implementation. Rather than consensus and international cooperation under the auspices of the UN, the Accords suggest more flexible forms of legal governance. In the words of section 2:

> Cooperative activities regarding the exploration and use of outer space may be implemented through appropriate instruments, such as Memoranda of Understanding, Implementing Arrangements under existing Government-to-Government Agreements, Agency-to-Agency arrangements, or other instruments. These instruments should reference these Accords and include appropriate provisions for implementing the principles contained in these Accords.

The implementation phase of the Accords regards principles such as its 'peaceful purposes' (section 3); 'transparency' (section 4); 'interoperability' (section 5); 'emergency assistance' (section 6); 'registration of space objects' (section 7); 'release of scientific data' (section 8); and mitigation of 'orbital debris' (section 12). Arguably, most of these principles are not controversial; they are either a copy and paste of the current tenets of international space law – such as paragraph 2 of Article IV of the Outer Space Treaty on 'peaceful purposes' – or they complement such principles with further provisions, as the ISS IGA did over 20 years ago. It seems fair to concede that such provisions on, say, transparency, release of data or emergency assistance specify duties and obligations of current international space law. In some cases, such as the principle of interoperability with the development of new standards, the Accords aim to fill an obvious and increasingly relevant gap in today's legal framework regarding advancements in technology. Under section 5 of the Accords:

> The Signatories recognize that the development of interoperable and common exploration infrastructure and standards, including but not limited to fuel storage and delivery systems, landing structures, communications systems, and power systems, will enhance space-based exploration, scientific discovery, and commercial utilization. The

[13] See https://www.nasa.gov/wp-content/uploads/2022/11/Artemis-Accords-signed-13Oct2020.pdf.

> Signatories commit to use reasonable efforts to utilize current interoperability standards for space-based infrastructure, to establish such standards when current standards do not exist or are inadequate, and to follow such standards.

Two provisions of the Artemis Accords are particularly critical. On the one hand, section 10 on the utilisation of space resources is devoted to the issue of utilising 'space resources', such as ice and water-bearing minerals from the lunar South Pole or water and minerals from asteroids, which could provide support for safe and sustainable operations. Although section 10 refers to the binding norm of Article II of the Outer Space Treaty – according to which outer space 'is not subject to national appropriation, by claim of sovereignty, by means of use or occupation, or by any other means' – it remains an open question as to whether the extraction of space resources under section 10 entails no national appropriation. In 2020, Jim Bridenstine, the NASA administrator under the Trump presidency, proposed viewing the issue through the analogy of fishing on the high seas, 'where a fish cannot be owned while in the ocean but can be owned as soon as it is caught'.[14] As noted earlier, US law has established the rights of US citizens over resources obtained in their commercial activities and, still, the analogy to fishing begs the question of how to distinguish between private and national appropriation. In the wording of the second paragraph of section 10:

> The Signatories affirm that the extraction of space resources does not inherently constitute national appropriation under Article II of the Outer Space Treaty, and that contracts and other legal instruments relating to space resources should be consistent with that Treaty.

On the other hand, section 11 concerns 'deconfliction of space activities' through provisions relating to due regard and harmful interference. In the wording of paragraph 7 of this section:

> In order to implement their obligations under the Outer Space Treaty, the Signatories intend to provide notification of their activities and commit to coordinating with any relevant actor to avoid harmful interference. The area wherein this notification and coordination will be implemented to avoid harmful interference is referred to as a 'safety zone'. A safety zone should be the area in which nominal operations of a relevant activity or an anomalous event could reasonably cause harmful interference.

Several scholars have welcomed the Accords. Some claim that they provide for sound international Moon cooperation through interoperability, registration, transparency and data-sharing clauses,[15] while others think that 'this bold pursuit of uncharted territories is to be applauded'.[16] After all, the Artemis Accords did not come out of the

[14] Bridenstine's analogy is given in A Boley and M Byers, 'US Policy Puts the Safe Development of Space at Risk' (2020) 370(6513) *Science* 174–75.

[15] C Johnson, 'SpaceWatchGL Feature: The Space Law Context of the Artemis Accords: Part II', *Space Watch Global*, 2020, https://spacewatch.global/2020/05/spacewatchgl-feature-the-spacelaw-context-of-the-artemis-accords-part-2/.

[16] JK Schingler, 'Imagining Safety Zones: Implications and Open Questions', *Space Review*, 2020, https://www.thespacereview.com/article/3962/1.

blue; in fact, they align with many recommendations of the international community, such as the guidelines of the Hague Working Group – a consortium of academic institutions open to the engagement of all stakeholders, such as government representatives, civil society groups, NGOs and space industries.[17] The overall argument in support of the series of bilateral agreements is that after decades of international deadlock, following the stalemate of the Moon Agreement, the Artemis Accords offer a proper framework for next-generation exploration and exploitation of celestial bodies and resources that rely on more agile forms of legal governance, such as those set up in section 2 of the Accords.

However, the very idea of the appropriation of space resources with the establishment of long-term settlements and the corresponding safety zones has sparked criticism. Unsurprisingly, Russia has called the Artemis Accords a form of 'space colonialism' and is not expected to sign them anytime soon.[18] What is even more interesting is that this criticism is not only popular in some parts of the world where such reactions are to be expected, such as Russia or China; many Western scholars have also strongly criticised the Accords.

The following section aims to deepen the analysis of these claims on space colonialism and how the law should tackle them. It is not only a matter of geopolitical confrontation between Russia, China and the US and its like-minded allies: the new human settlements on the Moon entail a discussion on legal and moral principles that will distinguish between 'good' and 'bad' colonisation.

III. The Threat of Sidereal Colonialism

According to many scholars, the original sin of the Artemis Accords should be traced back to Trump's 2020 Executive Order and the very idea that outer space is not – or at least no longer – a 'commons'.[19] This means that most critical regulations of space law are devolved to national regulations, in particular US law. And since the US is by far the leading licensing nation for most of the world's space companies, this leadership would make the US – and its powerful private companies – the de facto gatekeeper of celestial bodies. The Artemis negotiations in the international arena, guided by a more powerful actor, such as the US, would represent a sort of prisoner's dilemma. In this scenario, negotiations with the US would either deny all Artemis partners the opportunity to communicate with each other or, at the very least, create a system where the bilateral nature

[17] R Deplano, 'The Artemis Accords: Evolution or Revolution in International Space Law?' (2021) 70(3) *International & Comparative Law Quarterly* 799.

[18] P Stimers and A Jammes, 'The Artemis Accords after One Year of International Progress', *Space Review*, 2021, https://www.thespacereview.com/article/4267/1.

[19] O Neto, 'Outer Space as a Global Commons and the Role of Space Law' in K-U Schrogl, C Giannopapa and N Antoni (eds), *A Research Agenda for Space Policy* (Cheltenham, Edward Elgar, 2021).

of such negotiations would make the coordination strategies of the Artemis partners more difficult.[20] After all, one of the lessons learned from centuries of colonisation on Earth is the central role played by private companies in controlling target territories, often by establishing colonies and possibly settling them.[21] The US-led colonisation of space in the mid-2020s would fortify the trends of space privatisation examined in Chapter 3 of this book.

Critics of the Artemis Accords claim that the US-led colonisation of space, with its heavyweight contractors, raises four critical issues. First, leaving regulations to national governments can entail a 'race to the bottom' and even the emergence of 'flags of convenience'.[22] Such trends were not created by the Artemis Accords, but this legal framework might exacerbate the negative externalities of these trends. The exploration and exploitation of celestial bodies and space resources can turn into sources of depletion and destruction. Earlier we mentioned Jim Bridenstine's parallelism between outer space activities, such as extraction of celestial resources and fishing. The opinion of NASA's leader under the Trump 2016–20 administration follows a long-standing opinion of legal experts on the separable nature of mines, the surface of the land or the capture of fish on the high seas.[23] However, according to Bridenstine, the appropriability of fish on the high seas as soon as they are caught reminds us of how fishing without science-based regulation may lead to over-exploitation and destruction of stocks. Nonetheless, the Artemis Accords are silent on the duties and responsibilities of private actors as regards the negative externalities of their outer space activities. What standards and practices the project partners will adopt remains to be seen.

The second concern is that 'space mining, especially if conducted by loosely regulated private companies, could hinder science. Inconsistent practices in resource extraction, a likely result of purely national regulations, would only exacerbate the losses in scientific opportunities'.[24] An example of how space mining can generate operational concerns relates to lunar dust. According to this argument, without the cooperation of all actors, not only could the limited number of useful lunar orbits quickly become filled with space debris, but meteoroid debris streams could also threaten lunar operations or satellites' motion in Earth's orbit.[25] The Artemis Accords are silent on the duties and obligations of private companies for their space mining activities, devolving such definitions of duties and obligations to the governance mechanisms of section 2 of the Artemis Accords. However, this mechanism can once again trigger a 'race to the bottom' effect, either as a

[20] Boley and Byers (n 14).

[21] F Cooper, *Colonialism in Question: Theory, Knowledge, History* (Berkeley, University of California Press, 2005).

[22] Boley and Byers (n 14).

[23] J Su, 'Legality of Unilateral Exploitation of Space Resources under International Law' (2017) 66(4) *International & Comparative Law Quarterly* 991.

[24] Boley and Byers (n 14).

[25] N Boone, and R Bettinger, 'Simulation of Debris Events in Selected Low Lunar Orbits' (2023) 70(3) *Journal of the Astronautical Sciences* 16.

consequence of unilateral regulations at the national level or as a result of the prisoner's dilemma set up by the Artemis Accords.[26]

The third concern is that the 'safety zones' envisioned in section 11 of the Accords may provoke another tragedy of the commons. Surely, such safety zones do not necessarily raise threats of colonisation. In the opinion of the Hague Space Resources Working Group, international law 'should permit States and international organizations responsible for space resource activities to establish a safety zone, or other area-based safety measure, around an area identified for a space resource activity as necessary to assure safety and to avoid any harmful interference' with that activity.[27] The ISS is protected by a 200 metre radius 'keep out' zone and no state has questioned the legitimacy of such a measure. Yet, the safety zones of section 11 could 'provide a space actor with many of the benefits of territory while relieving it of long-term obligations of stewardship'.[28] The risk is evident when considering the 'orphan' oil wells and abandoned mine tailings on Earth. Rule making and oversight of the Accords relate to areas beyond national jurisdiction, and yet they are left to individual nations rather than agreements of international law.

Finally, the fourth fear concerns the challenging geopolitical problems that the 'safety zones' of the Artemis Accords raise. 'Safety zones' could become critical if the lunar surface is divided, therefore breaching the fundamental principle of non-appropriation of celestial bodies under Article II of the Outer Space Treaty.[29] A divided lunar surface could prevent states from exercising their rights to exploration, use and free access in accordance with Article I, paragraph 2 of the 1967 Treaty. Furthermore, setting up 'safety zones' entails tricky issues of enforcement, for example, whether the use of military force should be deemed legitimate to protect zones such as the 'safety zones' of the Artemis partners in the light of similar projects undertaken by China and its allies.[30] The 'ultimate result could be a "fracturing" of the Moon along legal lines, with different states operating under different rules. This would adversely impact the safety of space operations'.[31]

The legal problems of the Artemis Accords add to – and sometimes are even a result of – inconsistencies and vagueness of the international legal framework.[32] Many critics of the Accords concede that applicable provisions of international law are often too vague or general, allowing states to understand them differently or develop national rules that differ from those of other states, and enforcing

[26] Boley and Byers (n 14).
[27] Deplano (n 17).
[28] Boley and Byers (n 14).
[29] JW Nelson, 'The Artemis Accords and the Future of International Space Law' (2020) 24(31) *American Society of International Law*, available at https://www.asil.org/insights/volume/24/issue/31/artemis-accords-and-future-international-space-law.
[30] D O'Brien, 'The Artemis Accords: Repeating the Mistakes of the Age of Exploration', *Space Review*, 2020, https://www.thespacereview.com/article/3975/1.
[31] Nelson (n 29).
[32] WA Smith, 'Using the Artemis Accords to Build Customary International Law: A Vision for a US-Centric Good Governance Regime in Outer Space' (2021) 86 *Journal of Air Law & Commerce* 661.

them with differing levels of consistency.[33] Critics of the Accords stress that such fragmentation of the law – which follows the shortcomings of the international legal framework – would nonetheless end up with a 'bad' US-led colonisation. Some scholars assert that the US is indeed going full speed ahead with a 'dominance model' of space development.[34] Others claim that the 'Artemis Accords are an attempt by the Americans to walk softly to legitimise their deviation from the Outer Space Treaty',[35] and yet others reckon that the Artemis Accords are a part of the US government's aim to gather consensus around its interpretation of the Outer Space Treaty regarding the exploitation of the Moon's resources.[36] At best, the Accords entail 'the risk of diverging from 53 years of international law';[37] at worst, new forms of space governance through bilateral agreements would end up with a new form of domination. In the wording of the US Vice-President Mike Pence back in 2018: 'Space is a warfighting domain … It is not enough to have an American presence in space; we must have American dominance in space.'[38]

Against this backdrop – which reminds us of Plato's warnings on wars and colonies in the *Politics* – we should not jump to conclusions. A 'race to the bottom' colonisation of the Moon that hinders scientific research and paves the way towards the militarisation of space does not necessarily follow the Accords. Considering the shortcomings of international law, it is indispensable to determine whether the Accords will trigger a 'good' or 'bad' colonisation, so that supporters and opponents of the bilateral agreements shall adopt more nuanced interpretations. Some stress that 'a global approach may eventually emerge, but it is better to begin by stimulating the market and implementing imperfect regulation than to wait'.[39] Others note that 'the Artemis Accords may not end up being the final word on what commercial missions to the Moon will look like, but they reflect a reasoned and sensible attempt to move the dialogue on these issues along'.[40] After all, a critical part of the Accords rests on manifold forms of cooperation, not only among the partners of the programme but also between them and the international community.

The following section draws attention to these forms of collaboration and how they may tackle the unique class of legal issues posed by the Accords. They include the governance – under section 2 of the Accords – of the first human colonies on the Moon with the development of standards for communications systems and

[33] Boley and Byers (n 14).

[34] O'Brien (n 30).

[35] The opinion of Stephan Hobe, Director of the Institute of Air Law, Space Law and Cyber Law at the University of Cologne in Germany, cited in A Stirn, 'Do NASA's Lunar Exploration Rules Violate Space Law?', *Scientific American*, 2020, https://www.scientificamerican.com/article/do-nasas-lunar-exploration-rules-violate-space-law.

[36] The opinion of Frans von der Dunk, a professor of space law at the University of Nebraska–Lincoln, cited in Stirn (n 35).

[37] Schingler (n 16).

[38] Cited in O'Brien (n 30).

[39] J Sills, A Gilbert, M Bazilian and G Sowers, 'US Space Policy: Multilateral Mining' (2020) 370(6520) *Science* 1045.

[40] De Zwart (n 9).

landing structures, power systems or fuel storage. The cooperative efforts concern not only the enforcement of principles and rules of international space law, but also how the latter has fallen progressively short in terms of coping with the new challenges of outer space and its ethos.

IV. Pragmatism and Cooperation

The polarisation of today's debate on the Artemis Accords recommends pragmatism: the focus should not only be on real-world problems, but also on solution-oriented discussions.[41] The extraordinary economic investments necessary to create a self-sustaining lunar base, such as the 'Moon Base Camp' of the Artemis Project with its corresponding orbital station – the 'lunar Gateway' – rest on manifold forms of cooperation. The assumption can be illustrated by the wording of the Accords. Drawing on the former cooperation and ethos of the ISS activities over the past few decades, the Artemis Accords provide some principles of cooperation, 'underscoring the continuing importance of existing bilateral space cooperation agreements', 'considering the necessity of greater coordination and cooperation between and among established and emerging actors in space' and regulating the cooperative activities that relate to the exploration and use of outer space that 'may be implemented through appropriate instruments' (such as those in section 2 of the Accords).

Provisions on notification and coordination between partner nations can help to clarify these forms of cooperation. The aim is to respect the safety zones of section 11 to prevent harmful interference, in accordance with Article IX of the Outer Space Treaty and the principle of due regard. Conversely, the provisions on the extraction and utilisation of space resources shall be conducted under the norms of the Outer Space Treaty, particularly those in Articles II, VI and XI. In the wording of section 11.2 of the Artemis Accords:

> The Signatories affirm that the exploration and use of outer space should be conducted with due consideration to the United Nations Guidelines for the Long-term Sustainability of Outer Space Activities adopted by the COPUOS in 2019, with appropriate changes to reflect the nature of operations beyond low-Earth orbit.

Moreover, according to section 10.4 of the Accords:

> The Signatories intend to use their experience under the Accords to contribute to multilateral efforts to further develop international practices and rules applicable to the extraction and utilisation of space resources, including through ongoing efforts at the COPUOS.

After the 2019 Guidelines for the long-term sustainability of outer space activities, it is worth noting that the UN Committee on the Peaceful Uses of Outer Space

[41] NJ Salkind, *Encyclopedia of Research Design* (London, SAGE Publications, 2010).

created a Working Group on Space Resources within its Legal Subcommittee in 2021 – that is, the year after the Artemis Accords. Such international discussions on 'space sustainability' are complemented by further proposals, such as the recommendations of the Hague Working Group mentioned in the previous section; the Moon Village Principles; the Model Implementation Agreement drafted by the Space Treaty Project; or the *Lunar Policy Handbook* of the Open Lunar Foundation.[42] The engagement between the international community and the multiple stakeholders is crucial for considering the manifold critical facets of every colonisation. Forms of cooperation concern: (i) the prevention or mitigation of potential harmful interferences among lunar resources activities; (ii) interoperability and standards development to cut the costs of manufacturing, use and replacement of space objects and spacecrafts; (iii) new standards of information sharing on the nature, location, conduct and results of space resource activities, including forms of active orbital data sharing; and (iv) the development of standards for network communications, such as NASA's LunaNet project and the ESA's Moonlight initiative, which include traffic relay and message formats on which AI systems, robots and lunar services rely – for example, positioning, navigating and timing of activities on or around the Moon.

Of course, forms of cooperation to develop new standards of interoperability and information sharing do not mean that all problems are solved. The development of standards does not occur overnight. Moreover, what should be standardised remains uncertain – for example, whether 'harmful interference' of the safety zones of section 11 includes economic harm and not just safety, or whether private actors will be required to follow the same rules as states.[43] In addition, the extraction and utilisation of space resources may well be admissible, since extracting ice and water-bearing minerals from the lunar South Pole will likely be indispensable to support safe and sustainable missions and operations on the Moon, or from a colony on the Moon to Mars. However, many national approaches – for example, the US repudiation of the controversial 1979 Moon Agreement – show the incongruencies of some jurisdictions in terms of operationalising their normative commitments to international law. Remarkably, in 2020, the US space agency administrator Jim Bridenstine announced that, once extracted, NASA would purchase small amounts of lunar regolith from private companies,[44] even going so far as to sign contracts for future purchases with four of such companies.[45] The role of the US space agency in the attempt to shape the 'subsequent practice' of international law does not necessarily mean that NASA

[42] H Khera and H Vertadier (eds), *Lunar Policy Handbook* (Moon Dialogs, 2023).

[43] O'Brien (n 30).

[44] J Foust, 'NASA Offers to Buy Lunar Samples to Set Space Resources Precedent', *SpaceNews*, 2020, spacenews.com/nasa-offers-to-buy-lunar-samples-to-setspace-resources-precedent.

[45] 'NASA Selects Companies to Collect Lunar Resources for Artemis Demonstrations', NASA press release 20-118, December 2020, www.nasa.gov/press-release/nasaselects-companies-to-collect-lunar-resources-for-artemis-demonstrations.

is behaving badly. Yet, the very distinction between national appropriation and private appropriation of celestial resources may mean that scientific sampling of data – for example, section 8 of the Artemis Accords on the release of scientific data – could blend with the commercial uses of celestial resources.

A pragmatic approach to the challenges of space law does not suggest that 'anything goes'. Indeed, NASA's purchases of lunar regolith may be an incentive for private partners, despite remaining legally problematic or even redundant. Some scholars oppose any appropriation of celestial resources without international consensus; others think that national space agencies may interpret the extraction and utilisation of space resources – since they are indispensable to support safe and sustainable missions and operations – not to mean any 'appropriation', but rather 'freedom to use' outer space resources for peaceful purposes.[46] What current discussions on Artemis and further projects of space colonisation make clear is that problems of legitimacy revolve more around a new ethos of outer space and the 'subsequent practices' of states (and private companies) in international space law[47] than around formal interpretations of the agreements from the 1960s and 1970s. Attempts to influence and develop the new laws of outer space do not occur in a moral or legal vacuum; such attempts occur alongside attempts at cooperation that, at times, do not simply hinge on the goodwill of sovereign states.

The conjecture rests, pragmatically, on the normative constraints of the law of physics, such as the cislunar space environment with predominantly unstable orbits that pose unique challenges to situational awareness regarding the detection, tracking and characterisation of space objects.[48] By considering the multiple legal and political issues raised by the Artemis Accords, we should not overlook the uniqueness of the new territory with its physical constraints. As occurred with the first regulations of satellites in the 1960s, such physical constraints recommend further efforts of cooperation.

V. So Far, So Close, So Crowded

Many legal troubles with the colonisation of space will materialise only in the mid- to long term. In addition to the appropriability of space resources and occupation of lunar places – which will be further examined in the following chapters – problems of growing amounts of lunar debris and the staggering number of satellites orbiting the Earth may appear futuristic, but they are not. The chapter began with a warning: Plato's *Politics* reminds us of the necessary distinction between good and bad colonies, whereas all processes of colonialisation bring with them

[46] D Zannoni, 'The Dilemma between the Freedom to Use and the Proscription against Appropriating Outer Space and Celestial Bodies' (2020) 19(2) *Chinese Journal of International Law* 329.

[47] P de Man, 'State Practice, Domestic Legislation and the Interpretation of Fundamental Principles of International Space Law' (2017) 42 *Space Policy* 92.

[48] TG Roberts, 'Cislunar Space Situational Awareness' in Khera and Vertadier (n 42) 21–22.

the risk of wars. China's International Lunar Research Station, in collaboration with Russia, suggests an incumbent competition for lunar orbits and even lunar places.[49] The stakes are clear:

> Since Artemis and ILRS target the same area and timeframe, the establishment of such infrastructure could either become a point of contention, a prompt for coordination or an opportunity for cooperation.[50]

The alternative casts light on the drawbacks of international space law and the efforts of spacefaring states to fill the gaps in this legal framework. Though unilateralism and contention arguably make every space colonisation look bad, it remains an open issue whether cooperation efforts will prevail over unilateralism and contention. What is at stake is the crucial challenges of this chapter, such as: (i) the proper utilisation of space resources; (ii) the deconfliction of space activities; (iii) the development of new standards on interoperability, transparency, data sharing and registration; (iv) the further development of standards for the use of autonomous and intelligent systems; (v) the duties and obligations of private companies, with the attendant risks of 'flags of convenience' and a 'race to the bottom' effect; and (vi) a new ethos of outer space.

Drawing on the clauses of the Artemis Accords, this chapter has stressed manifold forms of cooperation that should prevent another tragedy of the commons on the Moon. Such forms include memoranda of understandings and implementing arrangements under bilateral agreements as well as cooperation between the Artemis partners and the whole international community, such as COPUOS. However, it has been noted that international treaties, agreements or resolutions are extremely difficult to attain and, in the best-case scenario, need time. Consensus among increasingly space-capable and space-interested states is problematic, for commercial space activities and space-related services are rapidly expanding, and COPUOS membership since 1975 has more than doubled (as of today, it includes 102 members). The fact that dozens of national governments are becoming signatories of the Artemis Accords can hardly be underestimated and yet this should not prevent further cooperation efforts. This need not only concerns the development of new standards or preventing old risks of unilateralism and contention, disagreement and militarisation; the subsequent colonisation of the Moon should also consider collaboration efforts in accordance with a broader – and common – legal framework. This framework relates to the oldest of human space activities: the functioning of artificial satellites flying around the Earth.

Overpopulated orbits, radio-frequency interferences or collision risks – which increase with the proliferation of space objects and activities – are not only the problem of responsible law makers and scholars dealing with next-generation projects of celestial colonisation. These scenarios are also the bread and butter of

[49] JV Berge and L Odgaard, 'NATO in the Global Commons: Defending Outer Space against Threats from China' (2023) 78(4) *International Journal*, DOI:10.1177/00207020231217119.

[50] A Salmeri, 'Infrastructure Activities' in Khera and Vertadier (n 42).

two generations of experts dealing with the decreasing costs of manufacturing, and the use and replacement of satellites proliferating into Earth's orbit. Satellite law with its success stories, but also multiple drawbacks, casts further light on today's debate on good or bad space colonisation. A holistic approach is necessary, given that space missions aiming towards colonies on the Moon must already go through more than 16,403 satellites around the Earth.[51] In the best-case scenario of a good colonisation, an efficient space traffic management system should govern the exponential increase of space activities and lunar missions; in the worst-case scenario, we will not be able to leave Mother Earth to reach such celestial colonies due to an ungovernable proliferation of space debris.

[51] UNOOSA, 'Online Index of Objects Launched into Outer Space', 2023, https://www.unoosa.org/oosa/osoindex/search-ng.jspx?lf_id=.

7

Satellites

Satellites are strictly regulated at the international law level. However, the present landscape presents overpopulated orbits, radio-frequency interferences and unresolved issues on how to allocate spectra and provide services, often under the agenda of well-known multi-billionaires, such as the role of Elon Musk's satellites in Ukraine's resistance to the aggression of Russia. On the one hand, advancements in technology, from the miniaturisation of satellites to their teamwork through swarms or constellations, have burdened traditional regulations and governance of space communications law. On the other hand, both the use of satellites and the states' development of anti-satellite weapons raise thorny issues for international law. From the 1985 US Air Force test to China's 2007 anti-satellite experiment, to India's 2019 ground-based missile interceptor and Russia's 2021 destruction of Kosmos 1408, the results have been catastrophic. Such cases draw attention to the environmental impact of the entire satellite ecosystem and how peaceful uses of technology should entail a fair organisation, assignment and coordination of satellite activities.

I. Thinking Big

Satellite law is a branch of international law that concerns regulations and governance of artificial space objects orbiting celestial bodies. Since the first satellite launch into low elliptical Earth orbit in October 1957 – ie, the first Soviet Union Sputnik – governments and law makers have been attentive to how to govern this scenario. The challenge not only concerns military uses of technology but also its commercialisation, in particular, the promise of a revolution in broadcasting and communications. This is why, at the very beginning of its history, the 'law of satellites' was governed by provisions of space telecommunications law under the regulatory powers of the International Telecommunications Union (ITU), as was illustrated in Chapter 2. The commercialisation of space telecommunications services, like broadcasting, required legal incentives to develop a commercial and international satellite communications system. In 1962, the US Congress passed the Communications Satellite Law, in which a publicly traded company – the Communications Satellite Corporation (COMSAT) – was established.

A year later, in 1963, the UN General Assembly approved Declaration 1962 (XVIII), a list of eight legal principles for all state activities in outer space. It was in this spirit that in 1964, COMSAT created the International Telecommunication Satellite Organization (INTELSAT), with the help of Western Europe, Japan, Canada and Australia. The definitive arrangements of INTELSAT were agreed upon in 1971, although the joint venture only became fully operational in February 1973. These were the golden years: the early 1970s, when people started watching 'live and via satellite' TV. The wording of the INTELSAT agreement also reflects the ethos of that era:

> Desiring to continue the development of this telecommunications satellite system with the aim of achieving a single global commercial telecommunications satellite system as part of an improved global telecommunications network which will provide expanded telecommunications services to all areas of the world and which will contribute to world peace and understanding,
>
> Determined, to this end, to provide, for the benefit of all mankind, through the most advanced technology available, the most efficient and economic facilities possible consistent with the best and most equitable use of the radio frequency spectrum and of orbital space,
>
> Believing that satellite telecommunications should be organized in such a way as to permit all peoples to have access to the global satellite system and those States members of the International Telecommunication Union so wishing to invest in the system with consequent participation in the design, development, construction, including the provision of equipment, establishment, operation, maintenance and ownership of the system.[1]

Further commercial and international satellite communications systems directed at public services were set up a few years later. The European Telecommunications Satellite Organization (EUTELSAT) was created in 1977 as a network of 16 joint ventures. The International Maritime Satellite Organization (INMARSAT) was established in 1979 at the behest of the International Maritime Organization and pursuant to the International Mobile Satellite Organization (IMSO), which was signed by 28 countries in 1976. In addition, in 1979, Canada, France, the US and the Soviet Union started a satellite-aided search and rescue initiative called the International Cospas-Sarsat Programme. Both the ground stations on Earth and the satellites in the network providing global positioning signals were owned and operated by the partners of the Programme, along with India, the European Community and the European Organisation for the Exploitation of Meteorological Satellites (EUMETSAT). In 2016, IMSO had 102 members, while at the time of writing, the Programme includes 45 'participant states'.

By the end of the 1990s, this scenario of cooperation and governmental activism had changed dramatically. We mentioned in Chapter 2 and again in Chapter 6

[1] The text of the agreement is available at https://treaties.un.org/doc/Publication/UNTS/Volume%201220/volume-1220-I-19677-English.pdf.

that the failure of the Moon Agreement reverberated throughout the 1980s and the early 1990s. Technological advances in the satellite industry also affected the field. While in the beginning, satellites used to be big and launched individually, today technology has provided for their miniaturisation. The first small satellite, CubeSat, was launched in 1993. Rather than a 'micro' or 'pico-satellite', CubeSat is a nano-satellite with a mass of 1.33 kg and a form factor of 10 cm cubed.[2] The miniaturisation of satellites provided not only new opportunities for exploiting low Earth orbits at dramatically decreasing costs but also new business models. The traditional world of space telecommunications and international broadcasting through big satellites was progressively complemented – and, after all, mostly overcome – by smart satellite services set up by private companies.

This shift, also dubbed the privatisation of outer space, can be traced back to the mid- and late 1990s, under the US administration of President Bill Clinton. Between 1998 and 2000, COMSAT merged with Lockheed Martin in a US$2.7 billion merger, becoming a part of the subsidiary Lockheed Martin Global Telecommunications (LMGT). Likewise, in 1999, EUTELSTAT was privatised; the European Commission oversaw the whole privatisation process with its 48 former members. In 2000, the US Congress passed the ORBIT Act. According to section 625 of the Act, the aim was for the business sector to call for the privatisation of outer space. As a result, in 2001, INTELSAT was privatised; parties to the intergovernmental agreement became the first shareholders. By this time, some 35 countries depended on the services of INTELSAT for their national and international communications. The same happened to INMARSAT plc: in the early 2000s, the private company and its subsidiaries started providing telecommunication services at commercial rates through a dozen satellites. By the end of the 2010s, another private company, EUTELSAT SA, was thriving thanks to its 40 satellites.

Issues of jurisdiction and valid law relating to the privatisation of satellite organisations and companies are often the crux of experts. Chapter 3 stressed the absence of internationally consistent rules capable of establishing a corporation's nationality in any given case. The privatisation of INTELSAT is a good example of how valid law and jurisdiction issues affect the international community. Although most of its company facilities are incorporated in Luxembourg, the Federal Communications Commission (FCC) considers INTELSAT to be a US enterprise. This classification implies that INTELSAT is subject to compliance with US law and, furthermore, that the privatisation of the satellite companies and the commercialisation of their services, coupled with the corresponding competition among national and commercial service providers, still has to replace the 1970s ethos, aligning instead with the pursuit of global public interests.[3]

[2] International Telecommunication Union Radiocommunication Sector Report, *Characteristic, Definition and Spectrum Requirement of Nanosatellites and Picosatellites, as well as Systems Composed of Such Satellites*, 2014, ITU-R SA.2312-0.

[3] See B Warf, 'Geopolitics of the Satellite Industry' (2007) 98(3) *Tijdschrift voor economische en sociale geografie* 385–97; RJ Zelnio, 'Whose Jurisdiction over the US Commercial Satellite Industry?

In addition to the power of private actors in the field – today, Space X's Starlink controls a large amount of the Earth's most desirable orbits – attention should be paid to the intricacy of legal regulations. Most governments and institutions have developed their own satellite programmes and alliances to safeguard autonomy and sovereignty in the field of satellite communications. It is no coincidence that Russia, China and India have all developed their system of governance and regulation of satellite communications networks.[4] The same is true of like-minded allies of the US: the EU Member States have pursued their space strategy and have advanced some sovereignty claims over the past few years, such as the creation or consolidation of strong national aerospace companies (for example, EUTELSAT, Hispasat and SES). However, under the regulatory powers of the ITU and the treaties and conventions of the 1960s and 1970s, trends in satellite law and most of today's programmes and services must be grasped at the national or regional level. Complementing efforts of cooperation illustrated in the previous chapters of this book with the Artemis Accords or the ISS, the focus should be on the specificities of regional initiatives and programmes, such as those of the EU in satellite law. The following section aims to clarify some reasons for the competition between the US and the EU.

II. A New Brussels Effect?

The Treaty on the Functioning of the European Union (TFEU) states that the EU shall draw up a European space policy. This power is set up in Article 189 of the Treaty, which also allows for a space programme to promote scientific and technical advancements, and to coordinate the exploration and exploitation of space. Regardless, Article 189(2) of the TFEU excludes 'any harmonisation of the laws and regulations' of the Member States, at least in relation to space law. Such a political compromise meant that all previous space regulations of Member States were safeguarded. Still, the European Commission had considerable leeway in terms of addressing the new legal challenges of outer space. In June 2018, the Commission proposed a first Regulation 'establishing the space programme' and creating an ad hoc European Union Agency for the Space Programme (EUSPA). By increasing the space budget to foster competitiveness and innovation in the EU, the aim

Factors Affecting International Security and Competition' (2007) 23(4) *Space Policy* 221–33; and, more recently, J Guyot, R Akhil and S Rouillon, 'Oligopoly Competition between Satellite Constellations Will Reduce Economic Welfare from Orbit Use' (2023) 120(43) *Proceedings of the National Academy of Sciences* e2221343120.

[4] See D Kong, 'Shaping a Legal Framework for China's BeiDou Navigation Satellite System' (2017) 42 *Space Policy* 26; J Sanyal and K Hashwani, 'Changing Landscape of Satellite Communication Laws in India', International Bar Association, 2022, https://www.ibanet.org/changing-landscape-of-satellite-communication-laws#:~:text=%5B1%5D%20The%20Satcom%20Policy%20was,operating%20an%20Indian%20satellite%20system.

was to bring all the main EU-led space programmes under the control of a single body, thus replacing the old European Global Navigation Satellite System Agency with the EUSPA. Regulation (EU) 2021/696 of the European Parliament and of the Council, which established the Union Space Programme and EUSPA, entered into force in May 2021, with retroactive effect from 1 January 2021.

The regulatory powers of EUSPA have affected the powers of the ESA, which had been essential to many EU space activities in the ISS. The ESA, an independent and intergovernmental organisation, was created in 1975 as a result of the merger of the European Launcher Development Organisation and the European Space Research Organisation. These organisations were established in 1962 to develop, respectively, launch systems and spacecrafts. In 2004, the ESA and the EU entered into a framework agreement, the aim of which was to: (i) provide operational arrangements based on the principles of efficiency and mutual benefit; (ii) prevent unnecessary duplications of efforts; and, (iii) attain a sound advancement of the whole European space policy. Therefore, as a result of the new EU Regulation 2021/696, the ESA and the Commission had to enter into a new financial framework and partnership agreement. The deal was signed in June 2021, updating the roles and responsibilities of the Commission, the ESA and EUSPA. In March 2022, EUSPA signed a memorandum of understanding with the UN Office for Outer Space Affairs (UNOOSA).

The EU space programmes include the European Geostationary Navigation Overlay Service (EGNOS), Galileo, Copernicus, the Space Situational Awareness (SSA) programme, the EU Space Surveillance and Tracking (EU SST) programme and GOVSATCOM. In particular, EGNOS, the European regional satellite-based augmentation system that strengthens the performance of global navigation satellite systems (GNSS) – such as the US GPS initially and Galileo later on – started operations in July 2005.

Galileo, Europe's own GNSS, became operative in December 2016. Currently, the system consists of 28 satellites offering positioning, navigation and timing information for services and users under civilian control in the EU. Moreover, Galileo is interoperable with the US and Russian standards: GPS and Glonass.

In 2021, it was time for Copernicus, previously known as the Global Monitoring for Environment and Security Programme, to support the new EU Earth observation initiative. Its aim is to 'improve the management of the environment, understand and mitigate the effects of climate change and ensure civil security'. Remarkably, the programme endorses a free and open data policy regarding its own services. These include six categories: atmosphere, climate change, emergency, land, marine, and security.[5]

[5] See SC Alvarado, 'The Regulation of the "Open Data" Policy and its Elements: The Legal Perspective of the EU Copernicus Programme' in *Space Law in a Networked World* (Leiden, Brill Nijhoff, 2023); L Paseri, S Varrette and P Bouvry, 'Protection of Personal Data in High Performance Computing Platform for Scientific Research Purposes' in N Gruschka, LFC Antunes, K Rannenberg and P Drogkaris (eds), *Privacy Technologies and Policy* (Cham, Springer, 2021).

Further EU programmes include the EU Space Surveillance and Tracking (EU SST) programme, which is part of the SSA Programme, and the GOVSATCOM programme. The SSA programme deals with space surveillance and tracking of artificial objects, space weather monitoring and forecast, and near-Earth objects monitoring. The GOVSATCOM programme is a part of the Global Strategy for the EU's Foreign and Security Policy adopted in June 2016. Its aim is to guarantee reliable, secure and cost-effective communications capabilities to EU agencies, institutions and Member States for critical missions and operations. GOVSATCOM became a part of the 2021–27 EU Space Programme under the EU Space Regulation.

In February 2022, the Commission adopted two new initiatives to boost satellite-based secure connectivity and Space Traffic Management (STM). On the one hand, the aim was to create an EU space-based secure connectivity system. In the words of the European institution:

> The EU space-based secure connectivity system will ensure worldwide access to secure and cost-effective satellite communications services, for governmental communications and commercial use. It aims to protect critical infrastructures, support surveillance and crisis management, as well as enable high-speed broadband everywhere in Europe to best anticipate future challenges of our economy.[6]

On the other hand, the proposed regulation aims to address the new legal challenges of STM. The miniaturisation and proliferation of satellites have created an urgency to the problems of traffic, viability and debris. In the words of the 2022 proposal on the establishment of an EU secure space-based connectivity system:

> The exponential applications of space services involve more and more satellites, thus more traffic in space. As the congestion of satellites and debris threaten the viability of space infrastructure, the European Commission and the High Representative of the Union for Foreign Affairs and Security Policy have presented an EU approach on Space Traffic Management (STM). This would further strengthen the Union's space surveillance and tracking capabilities (already providing collision avoidance services to more than 260 European spacecraft), and set clear standards and regulation for a safe, sustainable and secure use of space.[7]

In March 2023, the European Parliament and the Council passed Regulation (EU) 2023/588 on 'establishing the Union Secure Connectivity Programme for the period 2023–2027' in record time. This regulation goes hand in hand with the Commission's proposal for the launch of an EU swarm of multi-orbit satellites, namely, 170 satellites that should guarantee robust and secure space-based connectivity in Europe, as much as cloud-based services in the private sector. The project is named the Infrastructure for Resilience Interconnectivity Security by

[6] European Commission, 'EU Space Programme', Defense Industry and Space, Brussels, 2023, https://defence-industry-space.ec.europa.eu/eu-space-policy/eu-space-programme_en.

[7] European Commission, 'Joint Communication to the European Parliament and the Council An EU Approach for Space Traffic Management', (2022) 4.

Satellite (IRIS). The 'infrastructure' comprises three layers: governmental; shared; and self-standing commercial. The plan is that IRIS will be implemented one step at a time, starting its services by 2024 or 2025, and then increasingly reaching full speed by 2027. The manifold uses include people struggling with poor terrestrial internet speed who could see their problem solved thanks to satellite technology.

Another use of the European space-based connectivity system relates to civil aviation, in particular, supporting the next-generation air traffic management system in accordance with the Single European Sky Air Traffic Management Research (SESAR) programme and under the leadership of the European Commission. The first trial flights started in 2018. The IRIS datalink service will soon become operational on commercial flights across Europe. The overt aim is to expand its use in other global regions, such as Asia and the Americas. IRIS Global – the next step of the system – should further integrate the management of civil aviation operations and satellite internet services between the European Aviation Security Agency (EASA) and the new STM to safely coordinate, for example, the flight of drones and other autonomous aircraft that deliver aid to remote communities or medical supplies between hospitals.[8] By the end of this decade, the hope is that, on the one hand, IRIS will optimise flights across the globe, either with or without humans aboard. On the other hand, the goal concerns the datalink: in the words of the Commission, it should become 'the primary means of communications between pilots and air traffic controllers, making flights greener and more efficient'.[9]

The European space industry has welcomed the Commission's 'secure connectivity satellite constellation' initiatives. In a 2021 joint position paper, SES, Eutelsat and Hispasat affirmed that they were ready to take part in the EU-wide approach to the use of satellites, particularly in relation to the use of low Earth orbit (LEO): 'Eutelsat, Hispasat and SES strongly believe a European satellite infrastructure would strengthen the strategic autonomy of the EU by providing it with the ability to compete.'[10] As noted earlier, a year later, in February 2022, the EU proposed the regulation on the 'secure connectivity satellite constellation', which was finally adopted in Regulation (EU) 2023/588. In 12 months, much was the work carried on: (i) the announcement of the launch of the new EU large satellite constellations; (ii) the publication of the Space Strategy for Security and Defense adopted by the European Commission; (iii) the Draft Opinion of the Council on 'Fair and Sustainable Use of Space';[11] and (iv) the publication of the

[8] E Bassi, 'From Here to 2023: Civil Drones Operations and the Setting of New Legal Rules for the European Single Sky' (2020) 100 *Journal of Intelligent Robot Systems* 493.

[9] European Commission (n 6).

[10] G Tricco, 'The Upcoming of Iris2: Bridging the Digital Divide and Strengthening the Role of the EU in International Space Law' (2023) 2(2) *Journal of Law, Market & Innovation* 17.

[11] Council of the European Union, *Draft Council Conclusions on 'Fair and Sustainable Use of Space'*, 8962/23, 2023, https://data.consilium.europa.eu/doc/document/ST-8962-2023-INIT/en/pdf#:~:text=The%20conclusions%20recall%20that%20space,and%20sustainable%20use%20of%20space.

EU approach to STM.[12] These legal steps and accomplishments clearly show the relevance of space and satellites in the politics of the EU. The overall aim of the strategy is not only to 'strengthen the strategic autonomy of the EU' in certain aspects and technologies of outer space activities and satellite data services, but also to present the EU as a model for the rest of the world.[13]

The idea that EU law can be adopted and applied in other jurisdictions – thus exerting power beyond its own boundaries in fields like data protection, environmental law or antitrust law – became popular more than 10 years ago with Anu Bradford's formula of 'the Brussels effect'.[14] The non-divisibility of data and compliance costs of multinational corporations that deal with multiple regulatory regimes may prompt most technological manufacturers and service providers to adopt and adapt themselves to the strictest international standards across the board – that is, in many cases, just EU law.[15] EU law has arguably embraced some of the strictest standards for outer space missions, presenting itself as the champion of responsible behaviour in outer space – in particular, by proposing a proper space traffic management framework, a serious space debris removal mitigation plan, a transparent licensing and registration of space objects under the international responsibility of the EU, and attempts to tackle overpopulated orbits and frequency attributions.

The governance model of the EU Space Programme revolves around the close cooperation of EU Member States, EUSPA, the ESA, EUMETSAT and other stakeholders. The EU-led programmes on satellite constellations embrace the soft law of international commitments and guidelines, such as the 2019 COPUOS Guidelines on the long-term sustainability of space activities. We noted this strength of soft law in Chapter 6 when discussing similar provisions of the Artemis Accords.[16] However, whether and to what extent the EU space strategy will be successful does not only depend on the overall coherence or fragmentation of EU policies; although this is a 'big if', attention should also be paid to: (i) the formidable competition of the US government with its private companies, such as SpaceX; (ii) further competition with Japan, Australia, Canada or the UK; and (iii) the problems currently facing law in terms of the regulation and governance of satellite services at the international level.

From Chapter 2 onwards, we have noted the legal powers of the ITU regarding the frequency assignment notices submitted by the launching states and their administrations, as well as the procedures for space-related assignment

[12] European Commission (n 6).

[13] G Pavesi and J Wouters, 'The Final Frontier? The European Union and the Governance of Outer Space' (2023) 45(8) *Journal of European Integration* 1199.

[14] See A Bradford, 'The Brussels Effect' (2012) 107(1) *Northwestern University Law Review* 1; and, more recently, A Bradford, *The Brussels Effect: How the European Union Rules the World* (Oxford, Oxford University Press, 2020).

[15] U Pagallo, 'Online Security and the Protection of Civil Rights: A Legal Overview' (2013) 26 *Philosophy and Technology* 381.

[16] P Martinez, 'UN COPUOS Guidelines for the Long-Term Sustainability of Outer Space Activities' (2021) 8(1) *Journal of Space Safety Engineering* 98.

or allotment plans of satellites – whether big satellites in geosynchronous orbit (GEO) or swarms of satellites in LEO. Such a proliferation of satellites multiplies – and, in many cases, makes it difficult to properly address – governance problems on the demand of licences, duties of registration, or distribution of frequencies and orbits. Many of these problems fall outside the powers of single regions or countries. Therefore, EU efforts on, say, respect for the long-term sustainability of space activities can only be addressed at the international level. The transformation of satellite law from the early years of space telecommunications law to the current troubles with satellite internet services can be illustrated by Rwanda's filings for 327,320 satellites on behalf of Marvel Space Communications in 2021 – that is, more than 50 times the number of all the satellites currently in operation.[17]

It has been estimated that between 1 January 2021 and 31 January 2022, 'over 1.5 million satellite slots were filed in the ITU's "as-received" database, only about 0.4 per cent of the proposed satellite slots (for this one year alone) would need to be used to exceed the current number of active satellites'.[18] Finding reasonable solutions for these striking problems is in the interests of all parties. Indeed, it is vital to address legal certainty and efficiency issues that far exceed the regulatory efforts of states and organisations like the EU with their satellite programmes and space strategies to shape the new laws of outer space – for example, new standards of STM. Although such national and regional efforts can be commendable and can reinforce the ethos of the field, they have clear limits as regards the governance of the whole sector.

In the previous section, such limits were traced back to the trends in the mid-1990s of privatisation and technological innovation; here the focus is on the state of the art 30 years later. National and regional policies and regulations must still be complemented with the enforceability of old space law provisions, and yet the regulatory powers of the ITU have increasingly been tested in the new world of space-based internet services. No good news or any possible Brussels effect is likely to be expected. The following section illustrates the complex governance of a new legal world brought about by technological innovation with the regulation of satellite mega-constellations.

III. The Problems with Satellite Services

The problems of international law with the regulation and governance of satellite internet services and operations will be divided into two groups regarding: (a) their commercial and civilian use – mostly provided by private companies; and b) their military use, which includes the dual uses of technology. This

[17] S Millwood, *The Urgent Need for Regulation of Satellite Mega-constellations in Outer Space* (Cham, Springer, 2023).

[18] M Byers and A Boley, *Who Owns Outer Space? International Law, Astrophysics, and the Sustainable Development of Space* (Cambridge, Cambridge University Press, 2023) 75.

section focuses on the non-military uses of satellites. Such focus draws attention to how the provisions of space law fall increasingly short in terms of coping with the proliferation of swarms and mega-constellations of satellites. The first kind of problem raised by this scenario is quantitative. At the time of writing, the US heavyweight SpaceX's Starlink had around 2,700 satellites in LEO, with the aim of ending up with a whole constellation of 42,000 satellites. Blue Origin aims to create its own constellation with the Kuiper project: so far, the Federal Communications Commission (FCC) has approved the launch of 3,236 satellites. Kuiper's commercial services will start once 578 satellites of the float are in orbit. It is worth bearing in mind that the previous section stressed that over a million and a half satellite slots were filed in the ITU 'as-received' database from January 2021 to January 2022.

Traditionally, in the old world of big satellites, the ITU adopted a 'first come, first served' approach.[19] This meant that once a launching state submitted the frequency assignment notice in accordance with its duties of coordination with other systems and against possible harmful interference, the assignment was entered on – and protected by – the Master International Frequency Register (MIFR). Scholars have insisted on the limits of this mechanism, in particular, dealing with swarms of satellites in LEO.[20] As shown by Rwanda's filings for 327,320 satellites in 2021, 'an ITU state member may seek to derive income by in effect acting as an agent for commercial interests'.[21] Moreover, the proliferation of satellites, filings and assignments raises questions about the satellite orbits and frequencies to be used, as well as new risks of 'paper satellites' or 'flag of convenience'.[22] In 2019, the ITU adopted a 'milestone-based regulatory approach', according to which the listing of a 'non-geosynchronous (non-GSO) satellite system' in the MIFR hinges on percentages of use, namely, 10 per cent of the non-GSO satellites should be deployed within two years 'of the end of the current regulatory period for bringing into use' and 50 per cent within five years.[23] On this basis, the ITU aims to disincentivise the rush of private companies and governments to require as much spectrum and orbital space as possible in the shortest time.

Yet, the proliferation of satellites and satellite networks as 'systems of systems' also affects another pillar of space law: the registration of space objects.[24] According

[19] F Lyall and PB Larsen, *Space Law: A Treatise* (Abingdon, Routledge, 2018) 216.

[20] S Freeland, 'Legal Issues Related to the Future Advent of Small Satellite Constellations' in *Handbook of Small Satellites: Technology, Design, Manufacture, Applications, Economics and Regulation* (Cham, Springer, 2020).

[21] Lyall and Larsen (n 19) 217.

[22] H Wong, 'The "Paper Satellite" Chase: The ITU Prepares for its Final Exam in Resolution' (1998) 18 *Journal of Air Law & Commerce* 849.

[23] International Telecommunication Union, 'ITU World Radiocommunication Conference Adopts New Regulatory Procedures for Non-geostationary Satellites', November 2019, www.itu.int/en/mediacentre/Pages/2019-PR23.aspx.

[24] HR Hertzfeld, 'Unsolved Issues of Compliance with the Registration Convention' (2021) 8(3) *Journal of Space Safety Engineering* 238.

to a NASA report,[25] there are over 20,000 human-created space objects larger than 10 cm, but only 7,949 space objects are present in the UN registry. The drawbacks of international law are further illustrated by agreements such as that between a Chinese space company – Hong Kong Aerospace Technology Group – and the government of Djibouti in January 2023. The aim of this agreement is to build a rocket launch facility in Obock. However, Djibouti has not signed the main treaties governing outer space activities – from the Outer Space Treaty to the Registration Convention – and, arguably, lacks experience with any form of space law. Against this background, it is far from clear which rules of international space law should govern Chinese commercial operators overseas.[26] Hopes for any effective oversight of Chinese satellite activities originating from Djibouti are not high.

However, the overpopulation of LEO with low-cost, mass-produced satellites is here to stay and does not simply depend on the intentions of the government of Djibouti. As stressed in Chapter 3, many flag states sell citizenship by investment;[27] however, this is only part of the problem. The decentralisation of the system with the regulatory powers of national or regional authorities helps lower the standards of due effective oversight. In order to stimulate business, for example, some jurisdictions require small insurance premiums or, for some space objects like nano-satellites from 1 to 10 kg, no insurance at all.[28] The international community is aware of these problems. A proper space traffic management framework and a strict space debris removal mitigation plan are at the top of the agenda of the international community. This is the hope and goal of the European Council on 'Fair and Sustainable Use of Space'[29] and of the EU approach to STM,[30] in addition to the Guidelines for the long-term sustainability of space activities that COPUOS approved in 2019. However, even in the best-case scenario of law-abiding uses of satellite technologies, the staggering numbers – according to some, '100,000 satellites in LEO by 2030'[31] – suggest a further critical problem: environmental protection issues.

The environmental concerns and overall sustainability of outer space activities depend on the commercialisation of satellite services as well as military uses of satellite and anti-satellite weapons (ASAT). So far, the worst catastrophes in outer space have been triggered by sovereign states: the US, China, India and

[25] AL Allison, 'Requirements for Obtaining Spectrum and of Orbital Approvals for Small Satellite Constellations' in *Handbook of Small Satellites: Technology, Design, Manufacture, Applications, Economics and Regulation* (Cham, Springer, 2020).

[26] B Silverstein, 'China's Space Dream is a Legal Nightmare', *Foreign Policy*, April 2023, https://foreignpolicy.com/2023/04/21/china-space-law-treaty-djibouti-obock-launch-facility-ost.

[27] A Taghdiri, 'Flags of Convenience and the Commercial Space Flight Industry: The Inadequacy of Current International Law to Address the Opportune Registration of Space Vehicles in Flag States' (2014) 19 *Boston University Journal of Science & Technology Law* 405.

[28] Tricco (n 10).

[29] Council of the European Union (n 11).

[30] European Commission (n 6).

[31] Byers and Boley (n 18) 76.

Russia. To put the environmental challenges of outer space activities into context, the following section explores the consequences of: (i) the US Air Force's 1985 test; (ii) China's 2007 use of ASAT; (iii) India's 2019 ground-based missile defence interceptor; and (iv) Russia's 2021 ground-based missile attack on Kosmos 1408. These cases clarify what 'sustainable activities' and 'environmental protection' should mean in outer space, in addition to the kerosene and liquid oxygen of SpaceX's rockets, or the amount of aluminium re-entering the atmosphere with the satellites of the mega-constellation Starlink. All these space-related activities will be understood in accordance with a more complex ecosystem, in which the laws of legislators will take into account the constraints of the laws of physics. The focus is now on what happens when an anti-satellite weapon strikes a satellite in outer space, both from a physical and a normative standpoint.

IV. The Kessler Syndrome

There are four sorcerer's apprentices in this section – namely, in the spirit of J.W. Goethe's poem, those who were unable to control a situation they created. The first is the US. In 1985, the US Air Force, despite the opposition of NASA scientists, tested an air-launched missile against a satellite. The result was the scattering of 285 pieces of trackable debris and many thousands of smaller pieces. Luckily, further tests were soon cancelled, and within a year, the US Department of Defense released its first debris mitigation guidelines. The George HW Bush administration promoted space debris mitigation with other states and international organisations, including the creation of a new US-Soviet Orbital Debris Working Group. In 1993, the Clinton administration fostered the creation of the Inter-Agency Space Debris Coordination Committee (IADC). Whilst the Russian Space Agency (today's Roscosmos) joined from the start, the China National Space Administration (CNSA) joined two years later.

The second sorcerer's apprentice of this section is China. In 2007, China tested a ground-based missile against a defunct satellite. The result was appalling. The US military's satellite catalogue (USSPACECOM) listed 3,527 pieces of debris and inferred 150,000 pieces larger than 1 cm as a result of the strike. China calculated the explosion at an altitude of 850 km. More than 700 satellites and the ISS were at risk of collision, whereas some were actually struck: years later, in 2013, a Russian satellite was disabled by a collision with the 'Chinese debris'. Scholars discussed whether the Chinese Ministry of Foreign Affairs was aware of the 2007 ASAT test in advance.[32] In fact, China's test represents the worst space debris-generating event so far. The destruction created fragments travelling in

[32] PC Saunders and CD Lutes, 'China's ASAT Test: Motivations and Implications' (2007) 46 *Joint Force Quarterly* 3, available at apps.dtic.mil/sti/pdfs/ADA517485.pdf.

orbit from 3,000 to 7,600 metres per second – that is, around 27,000 km per hour. Some of this debris will be in orbit for centuries.

The third sorcerer's apprentice is India. In 2019, a ground-based missile defence interceptor was tested. A satellite, Microsat-R, was launched and then, on 27 March, India conducted an ASAT test against it. The explosion occurred at an altitude of 283 km. Although India tried to minimise the impact of the test, the USSPACECOM catalogue identified out about 130 pieces of debris. This means that such objects were so far in orbit that they were tracked and classified with a number.

The last sorcerer's apprentice is Russia. In 2021, the target was a defunct Soviet-era satellite weighing 1,750 kg, orbiting at an altitude of 480 km. Russia's military used a ground-based missile to strike Kosmos 1408. 'Due to the high impact energies involved in such a strike, debris ended up on highly eccentric orbits that cross the orbital altitudes of thousands of other satellites twice per revolution.'[33] In the wording of Bill Nelson, the then NASA Administrator: 'I'm outraged by this irresponsible and destabilizing action.'[34]

Scholars have dissected the manifold ways in which the use of ASAT can affect provisions and principles of IHL, such as the principle of proportionality or the distinction between combatants and non-combatants, or between military and civilians. Attention has been drawn, for example, to the collateral damages expected in targeting a dual-use object such as a satellite. The challenge is to strike a balance between the 'definitive military advantage' gained through such collateral damages, the effects on civilians and the 'reverberating collateral effects' that may catastrophically follow.[35] A controversial Nuclear Weapons Advisory Opinion of the International Court of Justice from 1977 states that 'an extreme circumstance of self-defence, in which the very survival of a State would be at stake' makes a nuclear attack 'proportionate'.[36] However, scientific evidence suggests that most uses of ASAT would have dire consequences, often summed up as the 'Kessler syndrome'.[37] Knowing some astrophysical properties of outer space helps to refine traditional legal notions of foreseeability, proportionality and liability.

In particular, the 'Kessler syndrome' draws attention to the main potential factor changing orbital environments – namely, collisions. Some scenarios can easily end up with a collisional chain reaction and the corresponding runaway proliferation of space debris. This is the lesson learned from the US Air Force's 1985 test, China's 2007 use of ASAT, India's 2019 defence interceptor and Russia's 2021 ground-based missile strike on Kosmos 1408. However, space debris and

[33] Byers and Boley (n 18) 270.

[34] ibid 326.

[35] C Steer and D Stephens, 'International Humanitarian Law and its Application in Outer Space' in C Steer and M Hersch (eds), *War and Peace in Outer Space* (Oxford, Oxford University Press, 2021).

[36] U Pagallo, *The Laws of Robots: Crimes, Contracts, and Torts* (Dordrecht, Springer, 2013) 63.

[37] DJ Kessler and BG Cour-Palais, 'Collision Frequency of Artificial Satellites: The Creation of a Debris Belt' (1978) 83(A6) *Journal of Geophysical Research: Space Physics* 2637.

collisional chain reactions can also depend on a lack of communication. In December 2021 – so claims China – its Space Station had to avoid potential collisions with some Starlink satellites. SpaceX and the Chinese National Space Agency (CNSA) lacked effective communication channels in a situation in which coordination would be essential. All in all, the more orbits are overpopulated, the greater the risk of collisions and runaway debris, which must be balanced against current state-of-the-art technology – for example, AI systems for avoiding satellite collision and space traffic management networks.[38] A collisional chain reaction may render orbits unsafe for centuries, either due to irresponsible ASAT tests by sovereign states or as a consequence of a lack of coordination and communication – for example, the lack of a proper STM framework between SpaceX and CNSA.

Leaving aside cases of negligence and fault-based liability, the intentional triggering of collisional chain reactions should be deemed unacceptable under international law. There is no legitimate gain in triggering the runaway proliferation of space debris. This military decision would clearly infringe the crucial principles of IHL and the very ethos of international space law. On the one hand, according to Article I of the 1967 Outer Space Treaty, 'outer space, including the Moon and other celestial bodies, shall be free for exploration and use by all States … and there shall be free access to all areas of celestial bodies'. On the other hand, Articles 35(3) and 55 of Additional Protocol I of IHL establish obligations on states for general environmental reasons. Indeed, space, as much as land, sea or air, is a part of the natural environment of our species and can be critical to preserving the health and survival of the global population.

The embarrassment of the Chinese government after the 2007 ASAT test, as well as the reaction of the international community to India's 2019 test and Russia's 2021 test, suggest that there is a consensus on this view: the intentional creation of dangerous debris in outer space is intolerable. The fact that Russia claimed that its 2021 weapon test created no risks for space stations and active satellites confirms this assumption. The denial was scientifically implausible, yet it acknowledged the basic principles of international law.

V. A Third-Order Formicary

The multiplication of satellites with swarms and mega-constellations of 'systems of systems' can be visualised as a thin ant nest, or formicary, incessantly moving and enveloping our world. So far this volume has examined the challenges of this enveloping effect, paying attention to how third-order technologies need no humans on the loop, but rather set the environment in which further technologies and humans interact. Today's satellites are the clearest illustration of

[38] U Pagallo, E Bassi and M Durante, 'The Normative Challenges of AI in Outer Space: Law, Ethics, and the Realignment of Terrestrial Standards' (2023) 36 *Philosophy & Technology* 23.

this enveloping effect. Satellites reshape the form of the Earth through a robotic envelopment. The proliferation of satellites in different orbits of our planet goes hand in hand with new business models, such as SpaceX's and Amazon's vertically integrated processes 'where the connectivity solution is part of a vertically integrated market, such as autonomous driving or e-commerce'.[39] Chapter 3 stressed that, by the early 2020s, the satellite industry will have generated around $270 billion in revenue worldwide. However, this chapter has illustrated the problems that this business creates, such as: (i) a transparent licensing system and registration of space objects that fall under the international responsibility of states and institutions; (ii) a more rational assignment of orbits and frequencies; (iii) a robust space debris removal mitigation strategy; and (iv) a proper system of STM. The troubles with exploiting space resources like orbits for purely for-profit purposes were complemented by the arsenal of military uses of satellites, such as ASAT and dual uses of technology that may pose vital questions of IHL.

The challenges created by technology in satellite law should not overlook its benefits. We must not throw the baby out with the bathwater. Scholars and institutions increasingly address the normative challenges of next-generation satellite swarms or mega-constellations, which promise to revolutionise how humans communicate, tackle the climate crisis or make the transport system more efficient. Next-generation satellites, increasingly supported by AI systems,[40] not only help private companies' revenues; they also tackle problems of internet connectivity in rural zones, optimising the management of civil aviation services such as drones, identifying and removing space junk,[41] or strengthening scientific research and public awareness through open data policies.[42] Furthermore, satellite data and AI systems can be beneficial in terms of improving the management of the environment, ensuring civil security for emergencies, land and marine security, or more effective ways to tackle climate change.[43]

By stressing the pros and cons of technology, the intention here is not to dwell on its neutrality, but instead to draw attention to the sustainability of the whole satellite ecosystem with incrementally overpopulated orbits. Visualising myriads of satellites in LEO as a formicary can be more disturbing once the focus is on the impact of such digital ecosystems on Earth. Reports such as those of the International Astronomical Union (IAU) in collaboration with UNOOSA on

[39] European Space Policy Institute, *Rising Opportunities in the Satellite Connectivity Market: Eutalsat and One Web Combination*, ESPI Brief No°60, 2022.

[40] E Camporeale, 'Artificial Intelligence for Space Weather Forecasting' in M Madi and O Sokolova (eds), *Artificial Intelligence for Space: Trends, Applications, and Perspectives* (Boca Raton, FL, CRC Press, 2023).

[41] T Petersen, 'Deep Learning Algorithms Helping to Clear Space Junk from Our Skies', *EPFL*, October 2020, https://actu.epfl.ch/news/deep-learning-algorithms-helping-to-clear-space-ju/.

[42] G Lapenta, F Califano, R Dupuis, ME Innocenti and G Pedrazzi, 'Using Unsupervised ML to Make New Discoveries in Space Data' in Madi and Sokolova (n 40).

[43] U Pagallo, J Ciani Sciolla and M Durante, 'The Environmental Challenges of AI in EU Law: Lessons Learned from the Artificial Intelligence Act (AIA) with its Drawbacks' (2022) 16(3) *Transforming Government: People, Process and Policy* 359.

'dark and quiet skies for science and society' show that the satellite formicary can be suffocating.[44] These growing concerns on the environmental impact of space-related activities also relate to the anthropogenic and natural injection of matter into the Earth's atmosphere,[45] and the impact of launches of suborbital rockets that could create a 'persistent layer of black carbon particles in the northern stratosphere'.[46]

Outer space is a unique environment with its own laws, both astrophysical and prudential, such as the 'Kessler syndrome' relating to the Earth's environment as a single interconnected ecosystem. For better or worse, the enveloping effect of today's satellite formicary shows that advancements in technology are a part of the problem, but also that they often offer the key to clever solutions. AI systems can indeed address overpopulated orbits and growing space debris to help achieve the sustainable development of space activities as a condition for the thriving of human societies on Earth. From a legal perspective, the environmental impact of space activities – also but not only through the use of satellites – tests the commitment of international agreements to protect the environment of the Moon and of other celestial bodies, but also several legal systems like EU law that protect the environment as a fundamental right of their citizens. The growing interdependence of Earth and space environments makes this legal commitment critical because gone are the days when ordinary people wondered what space travels and activities were for. From the first satellite TV broadcasts in the 1970s, we moved on to ultra-fast internet connections for social networks in the space of just 50 years.

The increasing impact of space-related activities on people's lives and the Earth environment makes it necessary to go 'back to Earth'. After the moral dilemmas and legal issues inspected in the previous parts of this volume with a new generation of Argonauts (Chapter 4), AI systems (Chapter 5), lunar colonies (Chapter 6) and satellites (this chapter), we must now pay attention to how such activities and space-based services affect the environment of Mother Earth, and how law makers and institutions tackle this impact. It is not only a matter of threats and catastrophes, but also of opportunity costs – namely, the price human societies pay for not using technology properly.

[44] See IAU and UNOOSA, *Dark and Quiet Skies for Science and Society – Report and Recommendations*, International Astronomical Union and UNOOSA, 2021, www.iau.org/static/publications/dqskies-book-29-12-20.pdf; IAU and UNOOSA, *Dark and Quiet Skies II for Science and Society – Working Group Reports*, 2022, doi.org/10.5281/zenodo.5874725.

[45] L Schulz and KH Glassmeier, 'On the Anthropogenic and Natural Injection of Matter into Earth's Atmosphere' (2021) 67(3) *Advances in Space Research* 1002.

[46] JA Dallas, S Raval, JA Gaitan, S Saydam and AG Dempster, 'The Environmental Impact of Emissions from Space Launches: A Comprehensive Review' (2020) 255 *Journal of Cleaner Production* 120209.

8

Back to Earth

The environmental impact of space activities not only relates to the contamination of the Earth from outer space, space debris mitigation policies or the use of nuclear power sources by spacecrafts; it also affects the impact that space-related activities with emissions from space launches have on Earth or pollutants produced during satellite and rocket re-entry. The 2030 Agenda for Sustainable Development under the auspices of the UN includes environmental and space sustainability. AI, smart robots and other emerging technologies can help human societies attain the Sustainable Development Goals (SDGs) of the 2030 Agenda, in particular, SDG 13 on climate action. However, the use of AI and robotics has its price because environmental concerns relating to space activities also depend on the digital vulnerability of space technologies and the cybersecurity of satellites. What is at stake with the environmental sustainability of space activities thus concerns a twin challenge – that is, the green and digital transformation of human societies.

I. Environmental Concerns

Environmental concerns of space law should be traced back to its own foundation. A specific provision of the 1967 Outer Space Treaty – Article IX – is devoted to contamination with 'the corresponding interest of other states'. Complementing Article VI on the responsibility of states in outer space activities, the provision states as follows:

> States Parties to the Treaty shall pursue studies of outer space, including the Moon and other celestial bodies, and conduct exploration of them so as to avoid their harmful contamination and also adverse changes in the environment of the Earth resulting from the introduction of extraterrestrial matter and, where necessary, shall adopt appropriate measures for this purpose.

Subsequent international agreements have tackled additional environmental concerns related to outer space activities. In Chapter 7, we examined initiatives and agreements on space debris and mitigation policies. In addition to the work of the IADC, attention should be paid to the Debris Mitigation Guidelines of COPUOS in 2014, which was soon followed by a code of conduct for space traffic operations between the EU, the US and other states. In 2015, the European

Cooperation for Space Standardization and the ESA, with its 22 Member States, adopted the 'Space Debris Mitigation Requirements' of the International Standardization Organization (ISO). The new Space Debris Mitigation Requirements updated such requirements and standards in October 2023. In the US, NASA released its Orbital Debris Mitigation Standard Practices (ODMSP) in 2019. Several jurisdictions – from the 2018 Australia's Space (Launches and Returns) Act to the 2023 EU law on secure connectivity – require, on a similar basis, a robust space debris mitigation plan for every launch.

Another critical environmental concern regards the use of nuclear power sources in outer space. Although Article IV of the Outer Space Treaty bans 'any objects carrying nuclear weapons or any other kinds of weapons of mass destruction', it is clear that many uses of nuclear power sources are not only legitimate but necessary. The compactness, long life and other attributes of nuclear power sources are essential for generating electric power 'on board space objects for non-propulsive purposes'.[1] In 1976, the US, the Soviet Union, China and others signed the Convention on the Prohibition of Military or Any Other Hostile Use of Environmental Modification Techniques (hereinafter 'the ENMOD Convention'). This international disarmament law agreement was specifically intended to protect the environment in the event of armed conflict. At the time of writing, ENMOD has 78 parties. In 1992, the UN General Assembly further defined the legitimate uses of nuclear power sources with a Resolution on 'Principles Relevant to the Use of Nuclear Power Sources in Outer Space'.[2] In 2009, COPUOS released the 'Safety Framework for Nuclear Power Source Application in Outer Space'.

In addition to space debris or uses of nuclear power sources, the environmental impact of space activities includes the assessment of emissions from space launches on the atmosphere and pollutants produced during satellite and rocket re-entry. The increase in these launches raises unique challenges of environmental protection that would have been simple science fiction a generation ago. The first flight of SpaceShipTwo, an air-launched suborbital spaceplane for space tourism manufactured by Spaceship under the control of Virgin Galactic, prompted public protests in 2010. However, it also generated a prediction: 'emissions from a fleet of 1,000 launches per year of suborbital rockets would create a persistent layer of black carbon particles in the northern stratosphere that could cause potentially significant changes in the global atmospheric circulation and distributions of ozone and temperature'.[3] Similar concerns relate to the use of kerosene and liquid oxygen to power the rockets of SpaceX's Falcon 9, injecting black carbon into the upper atmosphere.

[1] UN General Assembly, *Principles Relevant to the Use of Nuclear Power Sources in Outer Space*, Resolution 47/68 of the UN General Assembly, 1992, https://digitallibrary.un.org/record/159141?ln=en.

[2] ibid.

[3] JA Dallas, S Raval, JP Alvarez Gaitan, S Saydam and AG Dempster, 'The Environmental Impact of Emissions from Space Launches: A Comprehensive Review' (2020) 255 *Journal of Cleaner Production* 120209.

Environmental worries about rocket launches also entail problems of re-entry. The entire float of Starlink, which comprises around 42,000 satellites, implies a robust amount of aluminium re-entering into the atmosphere every day.[4] For some, 'the deposition of large amounts of aluminium into the upper atmosphere from re-entering mega-constellation satellites will affect the upper atmosphere, even if we do not yet know the scale of those impacts or understand all the complex interactions involved'.[5] The dramatic increase of launches for setting up and renewing growing numbers of mega-constellations makes this environmental problem of satellite re-entries more urgent and complex.[6] This is what this chapter refers to as 'the new challenges of environmental space law'.

Traditionally, environmental space law has been considered a sub-field of international environmental law, although with its own specific principles and provisions. In the wording of Article III of the Outer Space Treaty: 'State Parties to the Treaty shall carry on activities … in accordance with international law.' International environmental law is thus relevant in this context – in particular, considering the 2030 Agenda for Sustainable Development, adopted by all UN Member States in 2015. The Agenda draws on previous work of the international community under the auspices of the UN: (i) Agenda 21 of the Earth Summit in 1992; (ii) the Johannesburg Declaration on Sustainable Development and the Plan of Implementation in 2002; (iii) the Rio+20 Declaration in 2012; and (iv) the Paris Agreement on Climate Change in 2015.

Among other issues, the 2030 Agenda deals with how space activities can support many of its sustainable development goals, such as SDG 13 on climate action. The UN Department of Economic and Social Affairs (UNDESA), through its Division for Sustainable Development Goals (DSDG), will provide support and capacity building for attaining the goals of the 2030 Agenda. It is up to the DSDG to assess the overall implementation of the project and help engage all stakeholders through partnerships and collaborations. Still, most of the UN-sponsored agreements and agendas on environmental issues, including outer space, rest on the goodwill of the sovereign states – ie, their 'nationally declared contributions'. Some environmental and space law principles should be deemed customary law and thus be binding. However, most powers rest at the national level, including the quasi-federal powers of the EU.

Consider the regulatory powers of the US Federal Communications Commission (FCC), which approved the launch of Blue Origin's Kuiper project with its 3,236 satellites in 2022. In that very year, the FCC also issued a licence for about 12,000 satellites for SpaceX's Starlink. Viasat, the heavyweight provider

[4] D Werner, 'Aerospace Corp Raises Questions about Pollutants Produced during Satellite and Rocket Re-entry', *Space News*, 11 December 2020, https://spacenews.com/aerospace-agu-reentry-pollution.

[5] M Byers and A Boley, *Who Owns Outer Space? International Law, Astrophysics, and the Sustainable Development of Space* (Cambridge, Cambridge University Press, 2023) 67.

[6] EJL Larson, RW Portmann, FH Rosenlof, DW Fahey, JS Daniel and MN Ross, 'Global Atmospheric Response to Emissions from a Proposed Reusable Space Launch System' (2017) 5(1) *Earth's Future* 37.

of communications for Western militaries and internet services for commercial aircraft activities, claimed that the FCC failed to comply with the US National Environmental Policy Act, since the FCC did not conduct any environmental impact assessment for Starlink before issuing the licence.[7] Whatever the outcome of the potential lawsuits under the US jurisdiction, the case is interesting because it reminds us of the crucial role that national jurisdictions have in deciding issues that affect the Earth globally, such as emissions from space launches or re-entry of space objects. However, as past trends have shown, some jurisdictions may not adhere to the agreements of the international community in environmental law: the US withdrew from the Paris Agreement under the Trump administration in 2017, while other states have pledged their commitment to climate action, but only a few have followed such international environmental agreements to the letter.

Among the most relevant jurisdictions across the board, the EU formally endorsed the goals of the Paris Agreement on climate change in November 2016. In 2019, the European Council illustrated the aim to attain a climate-neutral EU by 2050 under the objectives of the Paris Agreement: 'all relevant EU legislation and policies need to be consistent with, and contribute to, the fulfilment of the climate-neutrality objective while respecting a level playing field'.[8] Two years later, in April 2021, the European Parliament and the European Council agreed on a new regulation for net emissions of greenhouse gases. In the wording of today's Article 1 of the European Climate Law, the EU's 2050 climate-neutrality mission represents the 'binding objective' of all measures that will be taken at both the EU level and the national level. Such a mission arguably comprises the emissions from space launches and the re-entry of space objects. This aim, as much as the 17 SDGs of the UN 2030 Agenda, crucially hinge on technological advancements. In the words of the European Commission, 'data, combined with digital infrastructure (e.g., supercomputers, cloud, ultra-fast networks) and artificial intelligence solutions, can facilitate evidence-based decisions and expand the capacity to understand and tackle environmental challenges'.[9]

The following section explores what a legal system looks like when endorsing the objectives of the Paris Agreement as well as the 17 SDGs of the UN Agenda – that is, EU law. The reason for this is twofold and depends on the relevance of the EU endorsement of the Paris Agreement for the space industry and how this endorsement could make a precedent in international space law. The key word here is 'sustainability'. Space technologies and AI solutions for monitoring climate change, forecasting weather or managing disasters through, for example, GNSS,

[7] Byers and Boley (n 5) 111.

[8] European Council, *Conclusions of 12 December 2019*, Brussels, EUCO 10/11, available at: https://data.consilium.europa.eu/doc/document/ST-10-2011-INIT/en/pdf.

[9] European Commission, 'Communication from the Commission to the European Parliament, the European Council, the Council, the European economic and social committee and the Committee of the regions, The European Green Deal, Brussels 2019' COM (2019) 640 final.

can be game changers. Next, the focus will be on how sustainability is regulated under EU law and how this principle of environmental law has been extended to outer space.

II. Sustainability

The basis of EU environmental law was set up in the 1986 Single European Act (SEA). For the first time, Article 130(r), (s) and (t) conferred competence upon the EU institutions to act for the protection of the environment. In particular, the European Commission was required to adopt a procedure for addressing the environmental implications of each piece of EU legislation proposal in accordance with the principle of 'environmental integration'. Eleven years later, in 1997, the Treaty of Amsterdam 'exported' the integration principle from the environmental field as a 'general principle' applicable to the entire European Community (EC) Treaty. Later, in 2007, Article 11 of the TFEU followed suit, mirroring Article 6 of the revised EC Treaty: 'Environmental protection requirements must be integrated into the definition and implementation of the Union's policies and activities, in particular with a view to promoting sustainable development.' A slightly different articulation of the integration principle is given in Article 37 of the CFR, according to which 'a high level of environmental protection and the improvement of the quality of the environment must be integrated into the policies of the Union and ensured in accordance with the principle of sustainable development'.

In addition to the constitutional basis of EU law, the right to 'a high level of environmental protection and the improvement of the quality of the environment' relates to the secondary legislation of the EU institutions (for example, the European Climate Law) and the case law of the Court of Justice of the European Union (CJEU). In a controversial decision, the Court claimed that each EU institution has 'a wide discretion regarding the measures it chooses to adopt in order to implement the environmental policy'.[10] When examining regulations such as the so-called Ozone Regulation 3093/94, the Court's opinion was that it should limit itself to questioning 'whether the Council, by adopting the Regulation, committed a manifest error of appraisal regarding the conditions for the application of Article 130r of the Treaty'.[11] This discretion of Member States is strengthened by how the principle of environmental integration should be understood either as a way 'to promote sustainable development' under Article 11 of the TFEU or 'in accordance with the principle of sustainable development' under Article 37 of the CFR.

[10] Case C-341/95, *Bettati v Safety Hi-Tech Srl* (European Court of Justice), https://eur-lex.europa.eu/legal-content/EN/TXT/?uri=CELEX%3A61995CJ0341.

[11] ibid.

The subordination of environmental safeguards to that which is socially, economically and financially sustainable may entail a lower level of environmental protection.[12] The potential incompatibility of the integration principle and the further principle of sustainability seems to be confirmed by the proliferation of integration principles under Articles 7–10 and 12–13 of the Lisbon Treaty.[13] A wide range of policy objectives, in addition to those relating to the environment, must be considered when defining and implementing each EU policy. Since the early 2010s, scholars have stressed that such an increase in the range and number of interests to be accommodated in the policy-making process may have made the implementation of the integration principle difficult and even decreased the relevance that the green initiatives have in the EU. In the words of JH Jans, 'like the mixture of ingredients in minestrone, decision-making on the basis of multiple integration principles could result in measures where the component elements are still visible, but not as sharply and clearly as before'.[14]

Fifteen years later, the scenario has changed radically. We noted that the EU institutions have relaunched their environmental commitment. This was done primarily through two legal instruments: Regulation (EU) 2021/1119 on 'climate neutrality', also known as the European Climate Law; and the Green Deal, the growth strategy aiming to transform the EU by 2050 into a fair and prosperous society in which no net emissions of greenhouse gases exist. Such policy commitments have been complemented with relevant case law and doctrine of courts. For example, the Hague District Court in the Netherlands handed down a watershed judgment in May 2021. The claimants were various environmental groups asserting that the aggregate greenhouse gas emissions generated by Shell via its business operations and products amounted to a breach of the standard of care and the duty of corporations to protect human rights, in particular, the right to life.[15] On the basis of the duty of care enshrined in the Dutch Civil Code and the obligation of companies to limit, or to properly address, the human rights impact of their own activities, the Court ruled that Shell should align its corporate policies with the Paris Agreement. In the words of the Court, 'Shell is ordered to reduce the CO2 emissions of the Shell Group by a net 45% in 2030, compared to 2019 levels, through the Shell Group's corporate policy'.[16]

[12] See JH Jans, 'Stop the Integration Principle?' (2010) 33 *Fordham International Law Journal* 1533; O McIntyre, 'The Principles of Integration and Interrelationships in International Law Related to Sustainable Development: Sobering Lessons from EU Law' in L Westra, P Taylor and A Michelot (eds), *Confronting Ecological and Economic Collapse: Ecological Integrity for Law* (Abingdon, Routledge, 2013).

[13] S Kingston, *Greening EU Competition Law and Policy* (Cambridge, Cambridge University Press, 2012).

[14] Jans (n 12).

[15] U Pagallo, J Ciani Sciolla and M Durante, 'The Environmental Challenges of AI in EU law: Lessons Learned from the Artificial Intelligence Act (AIA) with its Drawbacks' (2022) 16(3) *Transforming Government: People, Process and Policy* 359.

[16] Hague Court, *Shell Case*, C/09/571932/HA ZA 19–379, 2021.

The environmental commitment of EU law includes its space programmes. The wording of Recital 25 of Regulation 2023/588 on the Union Secure Connectivity Programme 2023–27 makes this point clear. Although recitals are not legally binding in EU law, their role can hardly be overestimated in regard to soft law. Recital 24 affirms:

> In line with the objectives set out in the Commission Communication of 11 December 2019 entitled 'The European Green Deal', the Programme should minimize, to the extent possible, its environmental impact. While the space assets do not themselves emit greenhouse gases while in use, their manufacturing and associated ground facilities do have an environmental impact.

Article 8 of the 2023 Regulation is devoted to environmental and space sustainability. All contracts and procedures covered in Article 19 should: (i) minimise greenhouse gas emissions generated by the infrastructure; (ii) establish a scheme to offset the remaining greenhouse gas emissions; (iii) take appropriate measures to reduce radiation pollution created by spacecrafts; (iv) use appropriate collision-avoidance technologies; and (v) implement a mitigation plan for space debris before the 'deployment phase, including orbital positioning data, in order to ensure the avoidance of space debris by the satellites of the constellation'. The contracts and procedures of Article 19 'shall include an obligation to provide data, in particular ephemeris data and planned manoeuvres, to the entities in charge of producing SST information' and 'the Commission shall ensure that a comprehensive database of the Programme's space assets, containing, in particular, data relating to environmental and space sustainability aspects, is maintained' (Article 8(2) and (3)). The Commission should take care of both the space assets owned by the EU and contractors of the Programme under Articles 5(2), 8(5) and 19(10) of the Regulation.

Environmental constraints for space activities will be complemented with policies for the beneficial use of both space technologies and AI systems to tackle the challenges of the European Green Deal and the UN 17 SDGs. The previous chapter illustrated some EU initiatives, such as Copernicus, Galileo and EGNOS, that aim to provide high-quality, updated and secure space-related data services. By enhancing the EU security and autonomy of space-related activities whilst enjoying the socio-economic benefits from the use of space data and space-based services, the overall goal is to make the EU a leading actor in the field. The further challenge is to explore how the use of AI systems may help attain sustainability and how to measure the sustainability of human behaviour through AI models.

Space data are essential for climate observation, research, science and policy. AI can help make smart use of resources, such as water and electricity,[17] strengthening the circular economy through monitoring and predictive management

[17] N Jones, 'How to Stop Data Centres from Gobbling up the World's Electricity' (2018) 561 *Nature* 163.

of the waste cycle[18] or preventing natural disasters.[19] The convergence of space technologies and AI systems can thus be a game changer in terms of tackling the climate crisis and current environmental concerns. In the words of the European Commission, the EU is taking 'measures to ensure that digital technologies such as artificial intelligence … can accelerate and maximise the impact of policies to deal with climate change and protect the environment'.[20]

However, there is another side to the coin. In Chapter 5, we mentioned that AI systems may affect the environment – just like space technologies with emissions – through high energy requirements and the carbon footprint of AI,[21] the increasing volume of e-waste and the pressure on rare-earth elements generated by the computing industry,[22] the risks of dependency on private actors who own and operate AI models and infrastructures,[23] and the risk of environmental harm via hacking, since AI systems for monitoring the environment mostly rely on data collection by sensors and transmission through communication networks.[24] It is well known that because ecosystems change rapidly as a result of climate and ecological shifts, AI models are also exposed to a form of concept drift.[25] Unsurprisingly, many scholars have recently coined the formula of 'sustainable AI'[26] to suggest a development of AI throughout its entire lifecycle – that is, from idea generation to training, retuning, implementation and governance of AI systems – that should be compatible with ecological integrity and able to support environmental resources for current and future generations.[27] In other words, the aim is to develop not only AI systems that attain sustainability, but also AI systems that are themselves sustainable.[28]

[18] M Abbasi and A El Hanandeh, 'Forecasting Municipal Solid Waste Generation Using Artificial Intelligence Modelling Approaches' (2016) 56 *Waste Management* 13.

[19] R Lamsal and TVV Kumar, 'Artificial Intelligence and Early Warning Systems' in TVV Kumar and K Sud (eds), *AI and Robotics in Disaster Studies: Disaster Research and Management Series on the Global South* (Singapore, Palgrave Macmillan, 2020).

[20] European Commission (n 9).

[21] Jones (n 17).

[22] E Alonso et al, 'Evaluating Rare-Earth Element Availability: A Case with Revolutionary Demand from Clean Technologies' (2012) 46(6) *Environmental Science and Technology* 3406.

[23] See M Bolton, R Raven and M Mintrom, 'Can AI Transform Public Decision-Making for Sustainable Development? An Exploration of Critical Earth System Governance Questions' (2021) 9 *Earth System Governance* 100116; A Zuiderwijk, Y-C Chen and F Salem, 'Implications of the Use of Artificial Intelligence in Public Governance: A Systematic Literature Review and a Research Agenda' (2021) 38 *Government Information Quarterly* 101577.

[24] World Economic Forum, 'Harnessing Artificial Intelligence for the Earth', 2018, https://www.pwc.com/gx/en/services/sustainability/publications/ai-for-the-earth.html.

[25] A Hastings and DB Wysham, 'Regime Shifts in Ecological Systems Can Occur with No Warning' (2010) 13(4) *Ecology Letters* 464.

[26] See A van Wynsberghe, 'Sustainable AI: AI for Sustainability and the Sustainability of AI' (2021) 1 *AI and Ethics* 213;F Rohde, M Gossen, J Wagner and T Santarius, 'Sustainability Challenges of Artificial Intelligence and Policy Implications' (2021) 36 *Ökologisches Wirtschaften – Fachzeitschrift* 36.

[27] C Wilson and M van der Velden, 'Sustainable AI: An Integrated Model to Guide Public Sector Decision-Making' (2022) 68 *Technology in Society* 101926.

[28] S Larsson, M Anneroth, A Felländer, F Heintz and RC Ångström, *Sustainable AI: An Inventory of the State of Knowledge of Ethical, Social, and Legal Challenges Related to Artificial Intelligence* (Stockholm, AI Sustainability Center, 2019).

In the first draft of the Commission's proposal of the AIA – so far the world's most ambitious 'horizontal regulation' of AI technologies – the environmental impact of AI, also but not only in outer space, was simply overlooked. In Article 6 of the April 2021 draft, the Commission suggested specific rules for all AI systems with 'a risk of harm to the health and safety, or a risk of adverse impact on fundamental rights'. The AIA Explanatory Memorandum included, among such rights, the right to a high level of environmental protection and the improvement of the quality of the environment, pursuant to Article 37 of the CFR. However, such mandatory requirements for high-risk AI systems did not include any commitment against adverse environmental impact, lest such AI systems pose a direct threat to 'the health and safety, or a risk of adverse impact on fundamental rights'.[29] The Report of the European Parliament's Special Committee on Artificial Intelligence in a Digital Age (AIDA) criticised such an approach for omitting 'any hazards related to the environment'.[30] Most proposals on the 'environmental sustainability' of technology, including AI, were left to voluntary initiatives put in place by providers of non-high-risk AI systems in relation to, for instance, the formation of codes of conduct.

However, further provisions of EU law mitigate the troubles of the AIA with environmental protection. Such regulations are vertical or sectorial rather than horizontal. In addition to Regulation 2023/588 on environmental and space sustainability, a critical pillar of the whole digital ecosystem, such as the connectivity on which all data-driven technologies hinge with the corresponding risk of cyberattacks, is at stake. Critical sectors of human societies, such as transport, water and healthcare, can be disrupted. Further legal provisions come into play to determine the overall sustainability of the field. The focus now moves on to cybersecurity issues and regulations on connectivity for data-driven technologies that represent the other side of the coin regarding the environmental sustainability of AI.

III. Connectivity

The environmental sustainability of space activities relates to that which the Commission sums up in the AIA Explanatory Memorandum as a twin challenge: the green and digital transformation of human societies,[31] All space activities should be as environmentally friendly as possible and uses of AI, robotics and other emerging technologies should be 'for good' – for example, implementing

[29] U Pagallo and M Durante, 'The Good, the Bad, and the Invisible with its Opportunity Costs' (2022) 5(1) *J* 139.

[30] P Gailhofer et al, *The Role of Artificial Intelligence in the European Green Deal*, Study for the Special Committee on Artificial Intelligence in a Digital Age (AIDA), Policy Department for Economic, Scientific and Quality of Life Policies, European Parliament, Luxembourg, 2021.

[31] Pagallo et al (n 15).

the UN SDGs through AI systems.[32] However, the use of such technologies does not come without risk. Key challenges concern the availability and quality of data (poor data may result in incorrect management recommendations), transfer context bias (deriving from the incorrect transfer of an AI model to a different context), lack of transparency and trust (because of the black box-natured AI models) and global inequality (considering the capabilities and resources needed for AI that may not be accessible for low-income countries).[33] Therefore, in addition to risks of dependency on private actors who own and operate AI models and infrastructures,[34] the focus should be on the misuse of AI for environmental harm via hacking. Machine learning models can, in fact, be duped by malicious inputs, triggering perverse outputs.[35] Since AI for the purposes of monitoring the environment relies on data collection by sensors and transmission through communication networks in real time, each phase can be disrupted with detrimental ecological impacts. AI models are also exposed to a type of concept drift caused by the fact that ecosystems change rapidly as a result of climate and ecological shifts.[36]

The EU space law aims to tackle some of these challenges through provisions on connectivity and cybersecurity. There would be no room for the use of AI systems and robots – as illustrated in Chapters 4 and 5 – without specific conditions of internet connectivity and cyberprotection in outer space. Regulation (EU) 2023/588 on the Union Secure Connectivity Programme aims to 'ensure the provision and long-term availability within the Union's territory and worldwide uninterrupted access to secure, autonomous, high-quality, reliable and cost-effective satellite governmental communication services to government-authorised users, by establishing a multi-orbital, secure connectivity system' (Article 3(1)(a) of the Regulation). The satellite communication services that support AI systems and robots as much as space data research, rescue agreements or drones also relate to business and commercial services. In the wording of Article 3(1)(b) of the Regulation, the goal is:

> [T]o enable the provision of commercial services, or services offered to government-authorised users based on commercial infrastructure at market conditions, by the private sector in accordance with the Union's applicable competition law, in order to facilitate, inter alia, the further development of worldwide high-speed broadband and seamless connectivity as well as removing communication dead zones and increasing cohesion across Member States' territories.

The EU connective plan aims to further develop and gradually integrate the European Quantum Communication Infrastructure (EuroQCI) into the security

[32] R Vinuesa et al, 'The Role of Artificial Intelligence in Achieving the Sustainable Development Goals' (2020) 11(233) *Nature Communications* 1.

[33] J Blumenstock, 'Don't Forget People in the Use of Big Data for Development' (2018) 561(7722) *Nature* 170.

[34] See Bolton et al (n 23); and Zuiderwijk et al (n 23).

[35] World Economic Forum (n 24).

[36] Hastings and Wysham (n 25).

connective system of the programme (Article 3(2)(c) of the Regulation). In June 2019, the EU Member States passed the EuroQCI Declaration to develop a quantum communication infrastructure with the Commission and the ESA. EuroQCI aims to deploy a certified secure end-to-end quantum communication infrastructure through the terrestrial facilities owned by the Member States. In the wording of Recital 15:

> One of the main functions of the EuroQCI will be to allow for quantum distribution of cryptographic keys (QKD). To date, QKD technology and products are not sufficiently mature to be used for the protection of EU classified information (EUCI). The main issues concerning QKD security, such as standardisation of QKD protocols, side channel analysis and evaluation methodology, still need to be solved. The Programme should therefore support the EuroQCI and allow for the inclusion of approved cryptographic products in the infrastructure when available.

The standardisation of QKD protocols and corresponding ground and terrestrial infrastructure should be developed in two main phases: 'a preliminary validation phase', in which the development and validation of several different technologies and communication protocols will be under scrutiny; and a 'full-deployment phase' for inter-satellite connectivity and data relay between satellites, ground and terrestrial infrastructures (Recital 14 of the Regulation). On this basis, the aim is to complement and integrate the current functions of GOVSATCOM, mentioned in the previous chapter, into the secure connectivity system of the EU Programme. According to Article 11(4), each programme participant shall designate one competent, secure connectivity authority to ensure that: (i) the use of governmental services abides by the general security requirements of the regulation; (ii) the access rights to the governmental services are properly managed; (iii) the general security requirements are met through proper equipment in the use of the services and associated electronic communication connections; and (iv) a central point of contact is created to 'assist as necessary in the reporting of security risks and threats, in particular the detection of potentially harmful electromagnetic interference affecting the services under the Programme' (Article 11(4)(d)).

Notably, the EU intends to develop standards such as QKD protocols, adopting open standard licences and open-source technologies.[37] In the wording of Article 7(2)(d) of the Regulation, the aim is to promote 'the use and development of open standards, open source technologies and interoperability in the architecture of the secure connectivity system, in order to allow synergies, optimise costs, improve reliability, foster innovation and reap the benefits of wide competition'. The secure connectivity system will define, design, develop, build and operate a multi-orbital connectivity infrastructure 'adjusted to the evolution of governmental demand for satellite communications and offering low latency' (Article 5(1)).

[37] J N Pelton and S Madry, 'Space Systems, Quantum Computers, Big Data and Sustainability' in M Madi and O Sokolova (eds), *Artificial Intelligence for Space: Trends, Applications, and Perspectives* (Boca Raton, FL, CRC Press, 2023).

A critical role is played by the cybersecurity features of the Programme against threats to satellites. Among the general security requirements of the connectivity framework, 'response to and recovery from such cyberattacks should therefore be duly taken into account' (Recital 60 of the Regulation). Among its specific objectives, Article 2(e) establishes the development of 'redundancy, passive, proactive and reactive cyber protection and operational cybersecurity and protective measures against cyber threats and other measures against electromagnetic threats'.

In previous chapters, we dealt with cybersecurity issues: Chapter 1 mentioned the Budapest Convention from 2001 on cybercrime; Chapter 5 referred to the liability claims of victims of cyberattacks with possible compensation schemes; and Chapter 7 examined the challenges of cyberattacks in the laws of war. Current developments in space law are also defining a new field: cybersecurity space law. One of the leading indicators taken into account by the EU 2023 Regulation was the 'annual number and severity of impact of cybersecurity incidents and number of electromagnetic disturbances related to the secure connectivity system' (indicator 7.2 of the Regulation, which still remains classified). Understandably, since the 2022 Russian aggression in Ukraine, cybersecurity space law and related cases of satellite hacking have been among the main topics of today's space agenda. As noted, satellites should be conceived of as 'things on the internet of things' as well as autonomous spacecrafts, smart robots or AI systems related to outer space activities.[38] Although this issue has become increasingly popular over the past years,[39] the Russian aggression showed Earth's dependence on space connectivity and related space-based services.

The multiplication of mega-constellations of satellites incessantly moving and literally enveloping the Earth was presented as a form of third-order formicary in the final section of Chapter 7. In that context, the formicary referred to the physical effects of satellite proliferation with the staggering numbers of rocket launches, satellites placed into Earth's orbit, and the mass of space objects in Earth's orbit (more than 11,500 tonnes). In the next section, attention will be paid to the digital counterpart of this trend – namely, the risk that cyberattacks disrupt the connectivity of space services and activities. We may well imagine the urgency of a human space tourist with fever and nausea, diffuse abdominal rigidity and sinus tachycardia diagnosed and cured by a humanoid AI doctor and its robotic arms. Such technological marvels depend on the connectivity of the digital ecosystem and parameters such as latency, reliability, autonomy and worldwide access to the network. The European Commission aims to assess the implementation of its connectivity programme by June 2026 in relation to the parameters of latency, reliability, autonomy and universal access (Article 42(3) of the 2023 Regulation).

[38] PJ Blount, 'Satellites are Just Things on the Internet of Things' (2017) 3 *Air and Space Law* 273.

[39] S Lohani and R Joshi, 'Satellite Network Security', *2020 International Conference on Emerging Trends in Communication, Control and Computing (ICONC3)*, Lakshmangarh, India, 2020, 1–5.

IV. Cybersecurity for the Global Village

In 1962, the great Canadian philosopher Marshall McLuhan coined the term 'Global Village' to sum up the pervasive effects of information and communication technologies (ICTs). ICTs would shrink the physical boundaries of states and territories by connecting people worldwide and would allow for the sharing of information and culture through 'continuous and instantaneous electronic media'.[40] This vision materialised decades later with the digital transformation of human activities and their data-driven dependency – from the emergence of the internet in the early 1980s to the World Wide Web in the early 1990s. The new scenario meant that, conversely, sharing data and information in the Global Village would raise common connectivity and security problems in cyberspace. Integrating outer space activities with protecting critical digital infrastructures on Earth illustrates how the Global Village has progressively expanded to encompass spacecrafts, satellites and lunar colonies – that is, the enveloping effect of third-order technology.[41]

Some scholars stress commonalities between cyberspace and outer space: they are both open, limitless, transborder, shared, and somewhat intangible and unregulated domains of military, civil or commercial operations.[42] Others insist on the vulnerabilities of the digital world that expose satellites and other space objects to cyberattacks. For example, according to the UN Institute for Disarmament Research (UNIDIR), the complexity of the supply chain, its transnational dimension and overall digital management make satellites highly vulnerable to cyber-risks, either considering the software supply chain or the hardware supply chain, such as backdoors.[43] In addition, the increasing use of cheaper components – the so-called Commercial off the Shelf (COTS) – as well as the use of standardised hardware and software solutions can make cyber-risks even more likely since once a COTS component becomes vulnerable, all satellites using such a component become vulnerable as well.[44]

Chapter 5 examined cases of apportioned liability among the many actors of the supply chain, together with the accountability horizon beyond which humans may not know about interconnections going beyond the parties with whom they interact or with whom such actors further interact in turn.[45] How to sever the chain of responsibilities of designers, manufacturers, operators, end

[40] M McLuhan, *Understanding Media: The Extensions of Man* (Cambridge, MA, MIT Press, 1994).

[41] L Floridi et al, 'AI4People – An Ethical Framework for a Good AI Society: Opportunities, Risks, Principles, and Recommendations' (2018) 28(4) *Minds and Machines* 689.

[42] A Froehlich (ed), *Outer Space and Cyberspace* (Dordrecht, Springer, 2020).

[43] O Demidov and G Persi Paoli, *Supply Chain Security in the Cyber Age: Sector Trends, Current Threats and Multi-stakeholder Responses* (UNIDIR, United Nations, 2020).

[44] European Space Policy Institute, *The War in Ukraine from a Space Cybersecurity Perspective*, Report 84, Vienna, 2022.

[45] J Cobbe, M Veale and J Singh, 'Understanding Accountability in Algorithmic Supply Chains', *Proceedings Association for Computing Machinery*, New York, 2023.

users and third parties that interact with digital space infrastructures and services (for example, digital satellite services) can be difficult, and this difficulty increases in the event of a cyberattack. It may be impossible for individual victims of cyberattacks to identify a tortfeasor; furthermore, satellite operators do not always know whether an interference is caused by natural space weather conditions or a cyberattack. Moreover, some cyberattacks are perpetrated or organised by states. These cases illustrate the limits of current regulations regarding both the cybersecurity obligations of private companies and the international responsibility of sovereign states. Unfortunately, there are dozens of possible examples.

In 2019, a series of cyberattacks struck Airbus, the European aerospace corporation. The target was the Virtual Private Network (VPN) connecting suppliers and sub-contractors, such as Rolls Royce and Assystem, to the Airbus network. By exploiting vulnerabilities in the network, the cyberthugs accessed sensitive information and confidential data, including data from military systems. Three years later, on 24 February 2022, one hour before the invasion of Ukraine, Russia launched a cyberattack on Viasat's satellite network, KA-SAT. Russia was able to access the management segment of KA-SAT and disconnect the Ukrainian government, armed forces and security services from Viasat's satellite services. By exploiting a misconfiguration of a VPN appliance, the targets were the internet modems of the system located in Ukraine. After the attack, with a tsunami of malicious traffic pushed into the network, the internet modems turned out to be unusable. The effects of the cyberattack reverberated throughout the digital ecosystem. The Global Village meant, in this case, thousands of ordinary people affected in France, Germany, Greece, Hungary, Italy and Poland. Around 9,000 subscribers of Orange, via NordNet, lost their satellite broadband service. The same thing occurred to 13,000 subscribers of Eutelsat via BigBlu. The remote monitoring and control access of the wind turbines of Enercon, a German energy company, were also knocked out.

By the end of February, SpaceX came in, sending hundreds of Starlink ground terminals to the Ukrainian government. As affirmed by Elon Musk and confirmed by the director of electronic warfare for the Office of the US Secretary of Defense, Russia attempted 'to jam the terminals for hours at a time, until SpaceX responded with a software update that restored normal operability'.[46] On 25 March 2022, Musk tweeted: 'Starlink, at least so far, has resisted all hacking & jamming attempts.'[47]

On 10 May 2022, the US and the EU publicly attributed the KA-SAT cyberattack to Russia. However, the legal consequences of this attack are unclear. As was noted in Chapter 1, a landmark agreement was opened for signature in 2001 – the Cybercrime Convention with its current 50 signatories – and yet the definition of several crucial notions, such as 'cyberattack', still remains open to discussion. Some authoritative definitions exist, such as the Tallinn Manual's distinction

[46] Byers and Boley (n 5) 367.
[47] ibid.

between 'space-enabled cyber operations' and 'cyber-enabled space operations'.[48] However, whether a cyberattack represents a 'breach of sovereignty' under current international law remains a tricky question. There is no institutional framework or international mechanism for attributing cyberattacks, while states have no obligation to disclose evidence of attribution. For example, France very rarely reports attacks that have targeted its systems and almost never denounces attacks publicly, at least when these come from other states. In such cases, France prefers the use of diplomatic channels. Other states, like the 'Five Eyes' countries – the English-speaking nations of the US, the UK, Canada, Australia and New Zealand – support a 'name and shame' approach to public attribution of cyberattacks.[49]

This legal uncertainty is often aggravated by the digital negligence of private companies. In the words of the FBI: 'There are only two types of companies: those that were hacked, and those that will be.'[50]

The digital negligence of satellite companies can be illustrated by the reports of IOActive, a computer security services firm headquartered in Seattle. In 2022, the US company scanned the SATCOM terminals of Inmarsat and Iridium, such as the Classic Aero Service system, Inmarsat C, the Broadband Global Area Networks, BGAN Machine-to-Machine, etc. The security firm warned five companies developing such terminals against their own vulnerability and risk of cyberattacks. According to the company, only one company was responsive.[51] Then, further vulnerabilities were found in the SATCOM terminals of Addvalue Technologies Ltd. for Inmarsat's iSatHub services. Such vulnerabilities were similar to those we noted in the Ukrainian case with KA-SAT. IOActive disclosed such information to the company in 2019. 'Despite contacting the company and providing security solutions and fixes, most of the vulnerabilities were still present when IOActive published its report' in 2022.[52]

Law makers are progressively tackling the negligence of satellite operators through provisions on the cybersecurity of commercial space systems and the obligations of private companies providing space services. The previous chapter noted that the EU Space Programme Regulation addresses the cybersecurity issues of flagship initiatives such as Galileo, Copernicus, GOVSATCOM, EGNOS and EU SST. Arguably, such principles and provisions are complemented in many jurisdictions by ad hoc provisions on the cybersecurity of commercial space systems and obligations of private companies. In EU law, there are at least 18 regulations that concern cybersecurity law, including the following: the

[48] M Schmitt, *Tallinn Manual 2.0 on the International Law Applicable to Cyber Operations* (NATO Cooperative Cyber Defence Centre of Excellence, 2017).

[49] F Egloff et al, *Public Attribution of Cyber Incidents: CSS Analyses in Security Studies* (Zurich, ETH, 2019).

[50] European Space Policy Institute (n 44) 11.

[51] IOActive, 'Missed Calls for SATCOM Cybersecurity: SATCOM Terminal Cyberattacks Open the War in Ukraine', 2022, https://ioactive.com/missed-calls-for-satcom-cybersecurity.

[52] European Space Policy Institute (n 44) 10.

European Cyber Resilience Act; the Digital Operational Resilience Act (DORA); the Critical Entities Resilience Directive (CER); the Strategic Compass of the European Union; the European Cyber Defence Policy; the EU Cyber Solidarity Act; and the EU Cyber Diplomacy Toolbox.[53]

Special attention should be paid to the Network and Information Systems (NIS) Directives of EU law establishing cybersecurity obligations for operators of critical infrastructures and essential services. Whereas the first 2016 NIS Directive applied to critical sectors such as health and water, energy and transport, banking and financial markets, and digital infrastructures, the NIS2 Directive adds space to the list of Annex 1 on 'sectors of high criticality'. All duties and obligations set up with NIS2 shall apply to 'operators of ground-based infrastructure, owned, managed and operated by Member States or by private parties, that support the provision of space-based services, excluding providers of public electronic communications'. Space digital infrastructures and satellite services are thus integrated into the network of provisions devoted to the safeguarding of the Global Village, at least as regards the regulatory powers of the EU.

Leaving aside implementation problems concerning the goals of the NIS2 Directive, it should be stressed that this 'normative integration' not only concerns the field of cybersecurity law, but has a further purpose, and not only in EU law. The normative integration of space-related activities and space-based services with cybersecurity safeguards for critical digital infrastructures also relates to the environmental law provisions discussed earlier in this chapter. The digital disruption of space activities clearly affects the sustainability of human activities in the Global Village. The focus of the next section will be on how far this integration between cybersecurity and environmental law goes in outer space.

V. A Twin Challenge

Integrating space activities with cybersecurity law provisions will be complemented by the environmental regulations governing space activities. Cyberattacks increase risks of collateral damage that regard both the 'Kessler syndrome' (see Chapter 7) and the functioning of many critical industries that depend on the functioning of satellites and space-related activities.[54] The Global Village hinges on this interconnection between the challenges of environmental space law and those of cybersecurity space law, in particular in relation to: (i) the whole sustainability of outer space activities and missions; (ii) the use of space-related digital technologies, such as AI systems, to help tackle the environmental issues of outer

[53] U Pagallo, 'The Politics of Data in EU Law: Will it Succeed?' (2022) 1 *DISO* 20.

[54] G Falco, 'The Vacuum of Space Cybersecurity', 2018 AIAA SPACE and Astronautics Forum and Exposition, 2018, https://doi.org/10.2514/6.2018-5275.

space and the climate crisis on Earth; and (iii) the resilience and security of space activities that depend on digital technologies against misuses of technology and attacks in cyberspace. As the European Commission stressed in the Explanatory Memorandum of the AIA of April 2021, the green and digital transformation of human societies should be viewed as a 'twin challenge'.[55]

This twin challenge entails global problems that mostly rely on national or regional regulations. International agreements and cooperation are at work in the field of environmental law – for example, collaboration between the UN, states and NGOs to achieve the SDGs of the 2030 Agenda[56] – and yet most regulatory powers lie with governments or regional powers (for example, EU law). The same is true in cybersecurity space law: there are international cybersecurity partnerships, like the one between the Five Eyes countries, and other long-term partnerships that include the Member States of the EU.[57] However, the role that international law plays in the governance of cybersecurity space law is limited and should be understood against the background of a complex set of national legislation and intergovernmental or bilateral agreements.

Advances in technology have thus increased the complexity of the field in a twofold way. First, technology triggers new fields of expertise that complement the traditional focus of space law experts – for example, cybersecurity space law reinforces trends of decentralisation and even fragmentation of international law that, years ago, were summed up as a form of 'governance without government'.[58] Second, rather than a unique legal framework for the governance of space activities, according to the tenets of legal monism, from Kant to Kelsen, the governance of space law appears as a patchwork of regulatory powers that includes those of national governments, regional institutions and the de facto powers of private companies.[59] The previous chapters of this book have illustrated the growing intricacy of the field with the challenges created by the privatisation of space law, the governance of AI systems and smart robots, the development of technological standards for next-generation colonies on the Moon, the enveloping effect of satellites as a thin ant nest around the world, and the new problems of environmental protection and cybersecurity space law that have been the subject of this chapter.

[55] European Commission, 'Proposal for a Regulation of the European Parliament and of the Council Laying Down Harmonized Rules on Artificial Intelligence (Artificial Intelligence Act) and Amending Certain Union Legislative Acts', COM (2021) 206 final, 2021/0106 (COD), 2021.

[56] D Gugunskiy and N Emelianova, 'Space Activities and Sustainable Development Goals' in EG Popkova and BS Sergi (eds), *Modern Global Economic System: Evolutional Development vs. Revolutionary Leap* (Cham, Springer, 2021).

[57] U Pagallo, *La tutela della privacy negli Stati Uniti d'America e in Europa: Modelli giuridici a confronto* (Milan, Giuffrè, 2008).

[58] JM Rosenau and EO Czempiel, *Governance without Government: Order and Change in World Politics* (Cambridge, Cambridge University Press, 1992).

[59] M Ricolfi, 'Regulating de Facto Powers: Shifting the Focus' in G Ghidini and V Falce (eds), *Reforming Intellectual Property* (Cheltenham, Edward Elgar, 2022).

The next chapter aims to illustrate what kind of governance without government may have emerged in the field of international space law. By considering the governance and regulatory issues that regard either specific programmes on the colonisation of celestial bodies or how tenets of satellite law evolve with new provisions of cybersecurity space law and environmental space law, we may wonder about the overall distribution of regulatory powers at the national and international levels. Some wonder who may 'own' outer space.[60] The following chapter examines who may still exert some kind of 'authority'.

[60] Byers and Boley (n 5).

9

Authority

The chapter examines the crisis of authority in international space law, which affects: (i) its 'constitution' with agreements and conventions from the 1960s and 1970s; (ii) the governance model with multiple international agencies and unions, such as the ITU; (iii) the traditional scope of regulation, since environmental law, cybersecurity law or AI law complement the traditional fields of space law; and (iv) its ethos. Several scholars recommend the amendment of this legal framework, but only a few have paid attention to the interaction between the regulatory systems of the law, ethics and social customs. The ethos of space law regards cooperation as much as the role that opinions play in this context, such as legal customs. By shedding light on the crisis of authority in international law with the governance of space missions and activities, the overall aim of the chapter is to stress which new laws, regulations or agreements should be reasonably expected.

I. Bohr's Paradox

Niels Bohr, a Danish physicist, is known as one of the founding fathers of quantum physics and the author of a mathematical planetary model to explain the behaviour of atoms. Initially, Bohr described the atom as a positively charged nucleus with a number of electrons revolving around it in a circular trajectory called an orbit. Years later, he regretted this metaphor.[1] Nonetheless, the core concept may be fruitfully applied to the complex governance of today's space activities. This is Bohr's paradox. Although confusing in the field of physics, the metaphor of the atom as a solar system clearly illustrates the troubles of the complex legal governance of space activities – a governance without government with a very intricate distribution of power and authority. Indeed, from a normative viewpoint, how powers, jurisdiction and authority should work in space law can be grasped through the image of a solar system with the sun, the planets and their satellites.

[1] N Bohr, 'On the Constitution of Atoms and Molecules' (1913) 26(151) *London, Edinburgh, and Dublin Philosophical Magazine and Journal of Science* 1.

First, the 'sun' of the metaphor represents the traditional corpus of international space law – in particular, its agreements and conventions from the 1960s and 1970s, as well as institutions, agencies, committees or unions (for example, the ITU or COPUOS). The 'planets' are the sovereign states that have signed such treaties and agreements. By restricting their powers, international treaties and conventions should make the movement and activities of states as 'regular' as possible. 'Satellites' represent private companies and individuals under Article VI of the Outer Space Treaty. In Chapter 2 it was noted that provisions and regulations of international treaties and conventions do not directly affect private companies or individuals, but rather the responsibilities of sovereign states. In the wording of Article VI, 'States Parties to the Treaty shall bear international responsibility for national activities in outer space'. In accordance with the metaphor of atoms as a solar system applied to the law, satellites or private companies are legally 'national', the sun of pacts and agreements under the UN auspices is 'international', while states, as planets, are both.

As happens with every solar system, particular attention must be paid to the gravitational force of the 'legal sun', namely, the binding force of principles and provisions of international space law around which the activities of states and private companies should revolve. The assumption is that this gravitational force or binding power of international space law has been questioned since its very inception. The 'weak gravitational force' of international space law, so to speak, does not depend only on the phrasing of treaties and conventions born in the Cold War era, which would leave it open to multiple and even opposite interpretations; technological developments in space activities are also fundamental, from remote sensing to cybersecurity issues, which have progressively fallen into the loopholes of the international regulatory framework. In light of Bohr's image of the atom as a solar system, the evidence is that the movement of the planets is not always determined by the sun's gravitational force. Instead, it is the other way round: the irregular and even unlawful orbits of the planets, or sovereign states, shape the contours of the 'nucleus' of international space law – a white dwarf star scenario for the legal field.

A well-established domain of space law (that is, remote sensing) clarifies the assumption on the troubles of international law with the advancement of third-order technologies. Remote sensing refers to technologies for gathering Earth data from outer space, including the lunar orbits, with uses that span from meteorology and disaster management, to environmental monitoring and policing of agreements. Since 2001, Google Earth has made these technologies popular by providing the digitisation of traditional photos through pixelled images – that is, superimposing satellite images with geographic information system (GIS) data and aerial photography onto a three-dimensional globe. From a legal viewpoint, the collection of Earth data through remote sensing soon fell within the regulatory loophole of powers and principles of international space law. Formally, activities related to gathering Earth data through remote sensing technologies had to follow some basic principles. Examples range from the freedom of scientific investigation under Article I, paragraph 3 of the Outer Space Treaty to abidance by the regulatory powers of the ITU using radio frequencies for remote sensing of Earth data. However, in 1968, the year after the Outer Space Treaty, regulating the collection and processing of Earth data through satellites passing over territories of states and countries was inserted into the agenda of COPUOS.

In 1978, the USSR proposed a Convention on the Transfer and Use of Data on the Remote Sensing of the Earth from Outer Space. The Convention failed because only eight States Parties signed it. In 1986, drawing on the preparatory work of COPUOS, the UN General Assembly adopted a resolution on Principles Relating to the Remote Sensing of the Earth from Outer Space. The 1986 Resolution drew on the previous corpus of space law, such as Articles I and III of the Outer Space Treaty, to further specify the duties and obligations of states in their activities. It is worth mentioning the new right to access the data by 'the sensed states'. In the words of Principle XII of the Resolution:

> As soon as the primary data and the processed data concerning the territory under its jurisdiction are produced, the sensed State shall have access to them on a non-discriminatory basis and on reasonable cost terms. The sensed State shall also have access to the available analysed information concerning the territory under its jurisdiction in the possession of any State participating in remote sensing activities on the same basis and terms, taking particularly into account the needs and interests of the developing countries.

However, the principles and provisions of the Resolution are not binding, especially regarding the use of remote sensing for national security purposes and other political interests. At best, such principles and provisions should be deemed a form of soft law, which reflects previous national practices and regulations that have defined the legal boundaries of the field. Arguably, among such national practices and regulations of remote sensing, US law is one of the most relevant. The provisions are enshrined in Title 51 of the US Code on National and Commercial Programs. Such provisions are complemented with clauses on 'shutter control'.[2] The development and consolidation of the national commercial remote sensing system thus rests on the US national security interests. In 1984, Congress passed the Land Remote Sensing Commercialization Act (now 51 USC 601-605) and, in 1992, the Land Remote Sensing Policy Act (51 USC 601-603). In 2003, the Commercial Remote Sensing Policy Act was integrated with further provisions on the 'appropriate measures' that US companies should set up in order to protect the US national security. While the last word in such matters is up to the power of sovereign states, what is even more interesting is that such 'old practices' of remote sensing have been complemented by further trends in national security and technology, such as cybersecurity space law. This trend confirms that most regulatory powers on this side of space governance strictly remain at the national or regional level.

[2] F Lyall and PB Larsen, *Space Law: A Treatise* (Abingdon, Routledge, 2018) 385.

The evidence on advances in technology and their legal impact does not mean that international law is not relevant. In addition to the hard law of treaties and conventions, the focus should be on forms of soft law and collaboration, which are essential for the ethos of space law. Such an ethos, or moral grounds of the community, affects the functioning and resilience of every legal system. Regarding the use of remote sensing technologies, forms of international collaboration are particularly relevant: the Global Earth Observation System of Systems (GEOSS); the UN Platform for Space-Based Information for Disaster Management and Emergency Response (UN-SPIDER) or the initiatives of the World Meteorological Organization. These collaborations are fundamental because they evoke a formidable driver of human behaviour: customs. Customs certainly play a critical role in international law,[3] especially space law. The reasons why people and communities sometimes think it is right, or necessary, to behave in a certain way can be as binding as the regulatory powers of national, regional or international authorities. Such opinions on what is right or wrong are traditionally dubbed customary – as opposed to conventional law.

The following section explores the tenets of international customary space law that may exert some 'gravitational power' over the decisions and activities of states and private companies. Attention is drawn not only to the functioning of international law but also to its strength and resilience.

II. The Legal Cosmos

States' obligations under international law not only relate to treaties, agreements and conventions that ultimately depend on their will, but also international relations that rest on customs and their binding nature. According to the definition of ancient Roman jurists, the binding nature of a custom concerns the *opinio iuris ac necessitatis* – namely, the opinion of what is lawful or necessary in certain cases. People sometimes follow a norm of conduct because they reckon this is how people behaved throughout centuries or decades. However, this practice may entail a vicious circle. The collective behaviour of a group may emerge as a result of a given opinion about how things must be done. Still, such an opinion may also be the unintentional outcome of a group of individuals' material practice or behaviour. In legal theory, followers of legal positivism claim that material practice is a necessary and sufficient condition for binding customs.[4] By strictly distinguishing facts from moral assessments – for example, why humans follow certain rules of conduct – the assumption is similar to Kelsen's

[3] See J Kunz, 'The Nature of Customary International Law' (1953) 47(4) *American Journal of International Law* 662; RB Baker, 'Customary International Law in the 21st Century: Old Challenges and New Debates' (2010) 21(1) *European Journal of International Law* 173.

[4] R Guastini, 'Teoria e dogmatica delle fonti' in *Trattato Cicu-Messineo* (Milan, Giuffrè, 1998).

argument: there is no need to assess opinions on what is legally binding to flesh out valid customs.[5]

However, work on the emergence of unintentional orders and multi-agent systems has shown that the *opinio iuris* is relevant, in particular regarding the strength of the normative framework.[6] Whether agents, both humans and artificial, follow the rules – not just because it is what other agents do, but also because it is the proper way to behave – affects how resilient a legal system is and how well it tackles fragmentation problems. When dealing with the troubles and fragmentation of international space law governance, it is worth mentioning the self-reinforcing justification process that emerges in addition to the top-down rules of legislation and which is crystallised in customary norms. Such norms emerge from the ethos of the community and can be further incorporated into legislations that may trigger the formation of new customs.[7] For example, the *opinio iuris* can reinforce the normative acts of legislators through the 'subsequent practice' of the agents in the system, although 'opinions' can also trigger some binding norms of their own.

One of the most prominent advocates of the role that customs play in the governance of human societies is the Austrian economist Friedrich von Hayek. In his works on legal philosophy, Hayek stressed the importance of all the rules that 'spontaneously' emerge from large networks of individual components without central control.[8] Such spontaneous orders and customs can be as relevant as – if not more important than – the formal rules of legislation. Presenting himself as a follower of the natural law tradition and advocate of classical liberalism, Hayek summarised this part of the legal world as the 'cosmos' side of the law. Customs complement the 'taxis' or formal laws and provisions of political planning, such as the 'cosmos' approach of the USSR – also but not only – to the space race. In other words, according to Hayek, the USSR's cosmos is simply another form of *taxis* or constructivist rationalism. In the wording of *Law, Legislation, and Liberty*:

> Certain widely held scientific as well as political views are dependent on a particular conception of the formation of social institutions, which I shall call 'constructivist rationalism' – a conception which assumes that all social institutions are, and ought to be, the product of deliberate design. This intellectual tradition can be shown to be false both in its factual and in its normative conclusions, because the existing institutions are not all the product of design, neither would it be possible to make the social order wholly dependent on design without at the same time greatly restricting the utilization of available knowledge. That erroneous view is closely connected with the

[5] H Kelsen, *General Theory of the Law and the State*, A Wedberg (trans) (Cambridge, MA, Harvard University Press, 1945).

[6] U Pagallo, 'Robotrust and Legal Responsibility' (2010) 23 *Knowledge, Technology & Policy* 367.

[7] W Worster, 'The Transformation of Quantity into Quality: Critical Mass in the Formation of Customary International Law' (2013) 31(1) *Boston University International Law Journal* 1.

[8] FA Hayek, *Law, Legislation and Liberty: A New Statement of the Liberal Principles of Justice and Political Economy* (Chicago, University of Chicago Press, 1982).

> equally false conception of the human mind as an entity standing outside the cosmos of nature and society, rather than being itself the product of the same process of evolution to which the institutions of society are due.[9]

Cosmos and *taxis*, customs and legislation may diverge and even clash. This scenario is a variable of the competition among the regulatory systems of ethics, law, technology and market forces introduced in Chapter 1. History provides myriads of examples from ancient to modern times. For instance, the English Civil War in the 1640s illustrates the clash between the British tradition and customs of common law vis-a-vis the normative acts of the king – that is, between the 'spirit' and the 'letter' of the English royal institutions.[10] While in the case of Hayek, the clash concerned the cosmos of the market and the socialist planification of the economy, in international space law, the conflict often relates to the behaviour of states that may not only divert from principles and provisions of treaties and agreements, but also create some principles and customs of their own. This was discussed in Chapter 6 when dealing with the opinion of some scholars, according to which the 'safety zones' envisioned in the Artemis Accords may infringe upon the basic principles of the law.[11] Further concerns have been raised by some projects of the US Defense Advanced Research Projects Agency (DARPA): the Novel Orbital and Moon Manufacturing, Materials and Mass-Efficient Design (NOM4D) and the Demonstration Rocket for Agile Cislunar Operations (DRACO) programme. These initiatives can develop a new generation of standards and customs for outer space activities. Yet, aiming to develop pioneer technologies for adaptive, off-earth manufacturing to produce large space and lunar structures should be understood in accordance with the aim of the US military to protect NASA's Artemis programme with the governance of its cislunar space. To some, 'the NOM4D programme is inconsistent with the United States' legal commitments'.[12]

However, cosmos and *taxis* may not only clash but also reinforce each other. Formal conventions and agreements often incorporate customary law, as the Geneva Conventions from 1949 did with the 1907 Hague Convention on 'the Laws and Customs of War on Land'. Moreover, formal conventions and international law agreements can trigger the formation of new customs, which means that such principles and provisions of international law become binding regardless

[9] ibid 5.

[10] CH McIlwain, *Constitutionalism: Ancient and Modern* (Clark, NJ, Lawbook Exchange Ltd, 2005).

[11] See A Boley and M Byers, 'US Policy Puts the Safe Development of Space at Risk' (2020) 370(6513) *Science* 174; D O'Brien, The Artemis Accords: Repeating the Mistakes of the Age of Exploration, *Space Review*, 29 June 2020, https://www.thespacereview.com/article/3975/1; JW Nelson, 'The Artemis Accords and the Future of International Space Law' (2020) 24(31) *American Society of International Law*, available at: https://www.asil.org/insights/volume/24/issue/31/artemis-accords-and-future-international-space-law.

[12] M Byers and A Boley, *Who Owns Outer Space? International Law, Astrophysics, and the Sustainable Development of Space* (Cambridge, Cambridge University Press, 2023) 296.

of whether a state has signed the corresponding conventions and agreements. The Golden Age of space law and the subsequent behaviour of national states confirm this view: for example, Article I of the Outer Space Treaty on freedom of scientific research. A similar transformation of conventional law into customary law is likely occurring with the prohibition of intentionally creating dangerous debris in outer space under Article III of the Outer Space Treaty and Article 35(3) and 55 of Additional Protocol I of IHL. As stressed in Chapter 7, the embarrassment of the Chinese government after its 2007 ASAT test – as well as the reaction of the international community following India's 2019 test and Russia's 2021 test – suggests that an international consensus is emerging on why the intentional creation of dangerous debris in outer space is intolerable. The *opinio iuris* is supported by the *necessitatis* under scrutiny with Kessler's syndrome – that is, the collisional chain reaction that may trigger the unstoppable runaway proliferation of space debris.

Cosmos and *taxis*, customs and legal acts, material practices and formal declarations may converge and sometimes clash. Because of this, the gist of this dynamic can be reformulated with Bohr's paradox on the metaphor of the solar system and its 'nucleus' applied to the legal domain. By weighing the ups and downs of how international law agreements and customs interplay with the behaviour of sovereigns and private companies, we may wonder whether and to what extent the 'gravitational force' of international space law may still prevail over the centrifugal forces of the field. The previous sections of this chapter have mentioned four pillars of this 'gravitational power' of international space law: (i) the binding rules of the treaties and conventions from the 1960s and 1970s; (ii) the binding rules of customary international space law; (iii) the principles of soft law, such as the 1986 Remote Sensing Resolution; and (iv) international collaboration. Such 'gravitational power' of international space law is further supported by the constraints of another set of laws – that is, the laws of physics. Chapter 2 mentioned the regulation of radio frequencies and the assignment of orbits under the powers of the International Communications Union. The question that follows is thus whether these 'gravitational forces' of international space law are still strong enough to prevent the fragmentation of the system – that is, to guarantee, in the jargon of Bohr's metaphor, the 'regularity' of movements and activities of the planets, the states.

The short answer to this is no: the traditional 'weak gravitational forces' of international law are getting weaker and weaker. This is a problem because the crisis affects not only the enforcement of principles and provisions of legal regulation, but also the moral grounds on which such principles and rules lie. In his masterpiece from 1921–22, *Economy and Society*, Max Weber famously distinguished three kinds of legitimate domination or political authority.[13] His distinction of

[13] M Weber, *Economy and Society*, 2 vols, G Roth and C Wittich (eds) (Berkeley, University of California Press, 1978).

tradition, legal rationality, and charisma aimed to flesh out three ideal types of legal and political power with the corresponding social traditions: common law (traditional power), legal positivism (rational power) and individual power with its own charisma (which includes populism). In this context, Weber's distinction helps illustrate three different kinds of problems that international law faces in exercising power and political authority as regards the governance of space activities. The fact that international space law simultaneously raises concerns about traditional power, rationality and ethos tells us a lot about the current state of the art.

III. The Problems with Authority

The manifold open issues of international space law can be grasped following three sets of problems corresponding to Weber's famous tripartition of the political authority: traditional, rational and charismatic power. First, the 'traditional authority' of outer space rests on the regulatory powers of international authorities together with practices and customs that revolve around the agreements of the Golden Age (the 1967 Treaty, the 1972 and 1976 Conventions etc). In the previous section, we noted that the 'subsequent practice' of the international community may transform parts of such agreements into binding customs. However, such behaviour works both ways. This book has illustrated how the traditional authority of international space law has been declining over the decades. Four points have been examined: (i) the failure of the Moon Agreement in the 1980s; (ii) the privatisation of space activities since the 1990s; (iii) the development of intergovernmental or bilateral agreements rather than forms of international cooperation since the late 1990s and the early 2000s; and (iv) new issues of space law in the 2010s and early 2020s, triggered by advances in technology that fall outside the design of the original legal framework, such as AI systems, cybersecurity and the environmental sustainability of the sector both in space and on Earth. It seems fair to concede that there is a problem of obsolescence in terms of the powers of the traditional international authorities of space activities. Several attempts and proposals to amend the international legal framework confirm this obsolescence.[14]

The second partition, Weber's 'formal rationality' of space law, is another source for concern. The formula suggests a Kelsenian legal system: 'if A, then it ought to be B'.[15] The principle of legal certainty claims that clear provisions on conditions of legal responsibility, 'A', should trigger predetermined outcomes, for example, negative (prison and fines) or positive sanctions. The proliferation of space activities with thousands of satellites, rather than a few space objects launched in orbit every year, illustrates the formidable problems of legal rationality, efficiency

[14] We will return to these amendment proposals below.

[15] Weber (n 13); Kelsen (n 5).

and fairness that must be addressed: scale matters. The traditional problems of space law with issues of jurisdiction and definition of basic notions of the field – for example, fault, negligence or damages to be covered – persist. Nonetheless, they are exacerbated by the proliferation of space activities, such as Rwanda's 2021 filing for 327,320 satellites on behalf of Marvel Space Communications. The ITU is mulling over the revision of its traditional policies on the assignment of orbits and frequencies for the launch of mega-constellations of satellites.[16] Further problems of 'formal rationality' concern the registration system of human-created space objects. We noted earlier that, according to a NASA report,[17] there are over 20,000 human-created space objects larger than 10 cm^3, but only 7,949 space objects are present in the UN registry.[18] Moreover, the current registration system has been designed according to orbital objects and hardly fits, for example, with the use of objects on the lunar surface that entails duties in relation to useful information.[19]

The third and final power of Weber's tripartition – the 'charismatic authority' – should not be underestimated. It is not by chance that, under the rule of law, the agreements and conventions of the Golden Age in space law are not associated with a particular legislator or policy maker. Instead, the ethos of space missions has been traditionally associated with the face of astronauts. The third kind of authority is therefore connected to the extraordinary personal qualities of individuals and people who follow them because of such qualities. Weber's 'charismatic authority' stresses that the formation of communities and constitutions, their *nomos* and *politeia*, crucially depend on the ethos of such institutions. No charisma exists without ethos. Regardless of how far Musk's charisma goes, such issues, which were relevant during Russia's invasion of Ukraine in 2022, cover only a tiny fraction of the problems that the militarisation and commercialisation of space have raised vis-a-vis the ideals of the Golden Age, such as freedom in space as the 'province of mankind' (Article I of the 1967 Outer Space Treaty), repudiation of every claim of sovereignty under Article II, international peace, security and promotion of cooperation and understanding according to Article III, astronauts as 'envoys of mankind' in Article V etc. These principles set up not only the duties and obligations of sovereign states, but also the prestige of the institutions.[20] Such principles represented a model for the world.[21]

[16] R Pritchard-Kelly, 'WRC-23 on the Horizon: Large Satellite Constellations, ITU Issues, and Industry Perspective' (2023) 48 *Air and Space Law* 179.

[17] AL Allison, 'Requirements for Obtaining Spectrum and of Orbital Approvals for Small Satellite Constellations' in *Handbook of Small Satellites: Technology, Design, Manufacture, Applications, Economics and Regulation* (Dordrecht, Springer, 2020).

[18] The ESA updated the figures in December 2023, so that space debris objects now include 36,500 objects larger than 10 cm and 130 million fragments up to 1 cm. See ESA, 'Space Debris by the Numbers', 2023, https://www.esa.int/Space_Safety/Space_Debris/Space_debris_by_the_numbers.

[19] H Khera and H Vertadier (eds.), *Lunar Policy Handbook* (Moon Dialogs, 2023).

[20] R Sacco, 'Legal Formants: A Dynamic Approach to Comparative Law (Installment I of II)' (1991), 39(1) *American Journal of Comparative Law* 1.

[21] G Ajani, 'By Chance and Prestige: Legal Transplants in Russia and Eastern Europe' (1995) 43(1) *American Journal of Comparative Law* 93.

The problems of space law with the exercise of political authority have triggered multiple hard cases. Disagreement in the legal community may relate to the meaning of the terms framing the legal question, the way in which such terms relate to each other in legal reasoning, or the role of the principles that may be at stake in the case. 'Matters of principle' arguably provide some of the trickiest legal hard cases.[22] They concern all three kinds of authority under scrutiny in this section and the governance of international space law. Such hard cases range from legal issues such as the basis of the appropriability of space resources (Chapter 3); the challenges of autonomous AI systems and smart robots displayed in outer space (Chapter 5); the establishment of celestial colonies through lunar stations (Chapter 6); the interplay between space law and other fields of international law such as IHL (Chapter 7); and the applicability of principles and provisions of international law to private companies, such as environmental space law (Chapter 8). What all these hard cases of space law have in common is the fact that the authority of international law – its binding force or 'gravitational power' – has been increasingly stressed either because of its traditional legal powers, the overall rationality of the normative system or its moral grounds. To understand the cumulative effect of this threefold crisis, the deadlock of international space law can be illustrated with current projects of 'space colonisation' and the first 'permanent stations' on the Moon. In the wording of the US National Academies of Sciences, Engineering, and Medicine:

> Industrial processes are being developed for space, and NASA is headed back to the Moon with the Artemis program, and then on to Mars. All of this exists because the United States has invested in the science and technology to further develop space-based research and applications … For the United States to continue to lead among the pioneering nations that embrace space exploration for both national security and global sustainability interests, it is necessary to resolve several scientific challenges that leverage or require the space environment in the coming decade.[23]

As stressed in Chapter 6, projects involving human colonies, such as those envisioned in the Artemis Accords, have divided experts' opinions. Some think that such agreements and bilateral commitments violate the basic tenets of international space law; others claim that these agreements do not infringe per se on such pillars.[24] However, the focus in the next section is different. Regardless of the *opinio iuris* for this hard case, the assumption is that the authority of international space law can only suffer in terms of prestige, efficiency and binding forces of the tradition. Either international space law is violated by the Artemis Accords or the legitimacy of national law and bilateral agreements to govern

[22] R Dworkin, *A Matter of Principle* (Oxford, Oxford University Press, 1985).

[23] National Academies of Sciences, Engineering, and Medicine, *Thriving in Space: Ensuring the Future of Biological and Physical Sciences Research: A Decadal Survey for 2023–2032* (Washington DC: National Academies Press, 2023) 1.

[24] M Elvis et al, 'Concentrated Lunar Resources: Imminent Implications for Governance and Justice', *Philosophical Transactions of The Royal Society: A Mathematical Physical and Engineering Sciences*, 2021, 379.

next-generation space projects and their activities lawfully weakens the role of international authorities. Is there any feasible third way?

IV. The Deadlock of International Space Law

Chapter 6 examined how the establishment of 'permanent colonies' on the Moon or Mars – with the corresponding *politeia* (traditional power of space law), *nomos* (rational power) and *ethos* (customs and charisma) – has arguably triggered one of the hardest cases among the hard cases of space law. To be fair, the problem relates to not only Western but also Russian and Chinese attempts to build permanent colonies on the Moon. In particular, China has multiple endeavours in process: the Tiangong space station; the Chinese Chang'e Project; or the ILRS, which was launched in 2021 by China's National Space Administration in collaboration with Russia's Roscosmos. The ILRS was presented under the auspices of the Global Space Exploration Conference (GLEX 2021) in June of the same year. The station is expected to explore and use lunar resources, conduct scientific experiments and set up long-term autonomous operations from 2036 onwards. The ILRS will likely be both in orbit and on the lunar surface. However, this plan raises the same problem of international law under scrutiny with the Artemis Accords. Not only has China been a full member of the UN Committee on Peaceful Uses of Outer Space since 1980, but it ratified the Outer Space Treaty three years later, and the Rescue Agreement in 1988, together with the Liability and Registration Conventions. Therefore, the many legal questions posed by the ILRS are the same as those of the Artemis Accords: for example, the legal basis of the establishment of the ILRS on the lunar surface in the absence of an international agreement is unclear.

Going back to the wording of Article II of the Outer Space Treaty, the Moon 'is not subject to national appropriation by means of use or occupation'. Both the US administration and Chinese authorities claim that the use and occupation of the lunar surface – and the corresponding orbits – would be instrumental to pursue the peaceful purposes and scopes of their projects. Still, the risks are the corresponding of the 'orphan' oil wells or abandoned mine tailings that have plagued the Earth. Moreover, the occupation of the lunar surface entails adopting safety measures to avoid, for example, the harmful interferences that often occur alongside military plans. In the case of the 'safety zones' envisioned in section 11 of the Artemis Accords, we have already noted that the protection of such 'keep out' zones overlaps with further projects of DARPA – that is, the DRACO programme and the NOM4D programme. In the case of China, it is hard to draw a line between civil and military powers.[25] The powers of the CNSA must be

[25] N Goswami, 'China in Space: Ambitions and Possible Conflict' (2018) 12(1) *Strategic Studies Quarterly* 74.

complemented with those of China's State Administration of Science, Technology and Industry for National Defense (SASTIND). Western scholars have extensively discussed whether the militarisation and commercialisation of space could represent the two sides of the same coin – in China, they are:

> It can be seen that in the war under the conditions of informatization and intelligence, the role of space forces has become increasingly prominent. The use and counter-utilization, destruction and counter-sabotage of space systems will have a major impact on the process and outcome of the war.[26]

From the stance of international space law, the legitimate basis of lunar occupation entails the further legal hard case on conditions of appropriability under Article II of the 1967 Outer Space Treaty. Since the US Space Resource Exploration and Utilization Act of 2015 and the Luxembourg Law on the Exploration and Use of Space Resources of 2017, the legitimacy of national exploitation of space resources and lunar orbits has rested on a strict interpretation of Article II, so that if 'national appropriation by claims of sovereignty' is prohibited, private appropriation is deemed fair. The principle of this *opinio iuris* is similar to what occurs in criminal law. According to a basic tenet of the rule of law, whatever action or behaviour that is not strictly prohibited is permitted. In the wording of section 10, paragraph 2 of the Artemis Accords, this interpretation of 'contracts and other legal instruments' of the bilateral agreements 'should be consistent' with the Outer Space Treaty.

The book has argued that the appropriability of outer space resources, or the exploitation of lunar orbits, is not a Dworkinian matter of principle: space resources can be appropriated. After all, the Moon Agreement contemplated an international regime for exploiting celestial resources. The fact that such an international regime, under the auspices of the UN, has never materialised should not prevent sovereign states of the international community from developing their own plans for space exploration and commercialisation. Although scholars are still mulling over the legal basis of celestial national occupations, the appropriability of space resources and their exploitation is taken for granted in several jurisdictions. Following the US and Luxembourg, other states are adopting this view. In 2019, the United Arab Emirates (UAE) passed a regulation on space mining: the UAE is not only a partner of the Artemis Accords, but also a member of the ILRS, together with China, Russia, Venezuela and Pakistan. In 2021, Japan adopted the Law Concerning the Promotion of Business Activities Related to the Exploration and Development of Space Resources, according to which the authority to allow Japanese companies to extract and use space resources is up to the Japanese government.

Such trends on national occupation and private appropriation of space surfaces and resources are still not 'subsequent practice' in international law. Yet, according

[26] X Tianliang, L Yaoliang, K Wuchao and C Renzhao, *Science of Military Strategy* (Beijing, National Defense University Press, 2020) 129.

to the two opposing and popular opinions of scholars, they show the deadlock in the field. Some scholars claim that occupation and appropriation repudiate the spirit, if not the letter, of international space law treaties and conventions, while others claim that national programmes and bilateral agreements on how to govern the next-generation commercialisation of space resources may legitimately and increasingly fall outside the orbit of the regulatory powers of the international authorities.[27] A similar 'lack of gravitational force' was noted in other fields of international space law, such as environmental space law, cybersecurity space law, remote sensing space law and specific aspects of satellite law.[28] Although the problems of space law in terms of the exercise of power and authority in the international arena do not trigger any sort of Hobbesian state of nature, most scholars and organisations are keen to admit that the 1960s and 1970s international agreements are becoming out of date. The only way forward for both supporters and detractors of national or bilateral agreements on lunar programmes would be to amend the international legal framework.

As time passes, many attempts have been devoted to strengthening the current framework of international space law and its 'gravitational power'. There is hardly any book or paper that lacks its own list of recommendations. If truth be told, the previous chapters of this book also fall within this cluster, having collated – together with the open problems and hard cases of the discipline – several proposals and recommendations of scholars and organisations. Among other things, we have seen suggestions on how to improve the regulatory powers of the ITU, the appropriability regime of space resources, the environmental assessment of the rocket launches and satellite activities, the disposal, re-use or recovery of space objects in orbit or on the lunar surface, or the duties of information sharing that, although enshrined in Article XI of the Outer Space Treaty, should include new forms of active orbital data sharing in the colonisation of the Moon.[29] Further amendment proposals relate to the prevention of any arms race in space under several resolutions of the UN General Assembly on No First Placement of Weapons in Outer Space since 2014, or the Prevention of an Arms Race in Outer Space (PAROS). More recently, in 2023, the UN Working Group on the Legal Aspects of Space Resources Activities started formal discussions on principles, guidelines and recommendations for a peaceful, rational, safe and sustainable conduct of space resource activities. The best-case scenario is that such discussions will end with a new Resolution by 2025.

The following section explores what lessons can be learned from these next-generation resolutions and current academic recommendations. Most proposals to amend international space law address issues of governance, legislation and

[27] T Masson-Zwaan and MJ Sundahl, 'The Lunar Legal Landscape: Challenges and Opportunities' (2021) 46(1) *Air and Space Law* 29.

[28] FG von der Dunk, 'Legal Aspects of Satellite Constellations' in FG von der Dunk (ed), *Handbook of Space Law* (Cheltenham, Edward Elgar, 2015).

[29] Khera and Vertadier (n 19).

ethics of space missions and activities, aiming to reinforce the 'gravitational force' of the international legal framework regarding problems of obsolescence, efficiency and lack of prestige. Going back to Bohr's metaphor and its paradox, the aim of such proposals and recommendations of experts, think tanks and institutions is to prevent the formation of a white dwarf star – that is, the destiny which awaits our sun, once exhausted the store of its nuclear fuel five billion years from now. Admittedly, the problems of international space law appear more urgent.

V. Gravitational Powers

There have been many attempts to strengthen the 'gravitational power' of international space law. In *The Space Law Stalemate*, Anja Nakarada Pučujlić, for example, proposes the following:

> 1. Taking existing legal obligations seriously, resuming the process of strengthening the rule of law; and 2. Institutional innovations, by empowering the UN and the body (COPUOS) in charge of regulating the space issues, redefining its relevance and authority, and/or building new, inclusive institutions.[30]

Pučujlić examines several international governance systems that may inspire the re-engineering of the international space law institutions, including the ITU, the ICAO, UNCLOS, the Antarctic Treaty System and both European space agencies (EUSPA and the ESA). The problem with this kind of theoretical exercise is not only that we should not expect any grand legal agreement in the next few years, for example, a new Outer Space Treaty with the creation of an International Space Agency. Also, such discussions on how to redesign the international governance of space law should not overlook what could be done without the harsh task of shaping a new space treaty. For instance, the *Policy Lunar Handbook* of the Open Lunar Foundation recommends several strategies and policies on formal and effective institutional management of lunar resources that would not require any amendment to conventional law.[31] These recommendations often draw on the ethos of space law and include the sharing of fundamental information on the nature, location, conduct and results of space resource activities, appropriate restraint in the establishment of licensing conditions for the commercial recovery and use of lunar resources, and coordination among operators and policy makers involved in lunar resource activities to prevent or mitigate against any potential harmful interference among their activities.

It remains an open issue whether and to what extent these and further recommendations will be adopted in a formal legal act or by the material practice of the international community. One of the lessons learned in this chapter from

[30] AN Pučujlić, *The Space Law Stalemate: Legal Mechanisms for Developing New Norms* (Abingdon, Routledge, 2023).

[31] Khera and Vertadier (n 19).

Hayek's 'cosmos' side of the law – that is, the forces of customs and the decentralised powers of the legal community – is that the 'gravitational power' of international space law not only hinges on principles and provisions of legal acts and agreements, but also, on the moral grounds of the community, the ethos of the field. Although current proposals on how to ameliorate the provisions of international space law can arguably help foster this ethos, they cannot create it. The previous chapters of this book scrutinised this side of the law with numerous examples of sound international collaboration, open science and open access policies to satellite data adopted by many jurisdictions through their services,[32] alongside the emotions that the adventures of astronauts still evoke for many groups of followers and aficionados.[33] Scholars have correspondingly drawn attention to the role that ethos plays in outer space,[34] and yet, even the 'face of space programmes' – the astronauts – may evoke a sense of national spirit.[35]

The old and new problems of international space law should not overlook the further issues in the field relating to the governance of technology. Most recommendations and proposals on how to improve the current legal framework of space law at the international level do not consider challenges like cybersecurity, data protection, consumer law or AI governance. Such legal sectors fall outside the traditional focus of space law experts, but they are increasingly becoming crucial for the governance of space activities. As noted earlier, most of these fields relating to the regulation of space activities depend on the regulatory powers of national or regional authorities. The increasing complexity of the field was illustrated in Chapter 8 with the provisions of EU space law, such as Regulation (EU) 2023/588. The traditional rules of space law will be understood in accordance with further principles and provisions of cybersecurity law, data protection law, trustworthy AI systems, environmental protection, consumer law and liability for defective products. Remarkably, in the 2022 proposal of the European Commission for a new product liability directive (PLD) regime, the aim was to cover the functioning of both space-related services, such as navigation systems and AI products. In the wording of Recital 15:

> It is becoming increasingly common for digital services to be integrated in or interconnected with a product in such a way that the absence of the service would prevent the product from performing one of its functions, for example the continuous supply of traffic data in a navigation system. While this Directive should not apply to services as such, it is necessary to extend no-fault liability to such digital services as they determine the safety of the product just as much as physical or digital components.[36]

[32] NASA and other federal agencies, together with the White House, declared 2023 'a year of open science'. See https://www.earthdata.nasa.gov/news/year-of-open-science.

[33] Here it is worth mentioning *The Wonderful: Stories from the Space Station*, a documentary directed by Clare Lewine and released in April 2021.

[34] Z Norman and M J Reiss, 'The Emergence of an Environmental Ethos on Luna' in *The Human Factor in the Settlement of the Moon: An Interdisciplinary Approach* (Cham, Springer, 2021).

[35] JM Determann, *Space Science and the Arab World: Astronauts, Observatories and Nationalism in the Middle East* (London, Bloomsbury, 2019).

[36] See European Commission, 2022/0302 (COD), 2022.

The interconnection and integration of AI systems and space activities in complex digital ecosystems show that proposals and recommendations on how to amend international space law cover only a part of the crucial regulatory issues of the field. The fragmentation resulting from these trends adds a further layer of intricacy to the crisis of authority in international space law. This fragmentation not only refers to the proliferation of relevant national or regional legislations and regulators, but also the specialisation of such national or regional regulations in cybersecurity space law, environmental space law, space data governance etc. Whereas EU law alone has more than a dozen regulations, acts and directives in cybersecurity that potentially affect every outer space activity, further regulations on cybersecurity, surveillance and data governance are under the regulatory powers of states and regional authorities, such as the US Space Surveillance Network (SSN), the Russian Military Space Surveillance Network, the ESA Space Surveillance and Tracking Segment or China's networks of ground-and space-based assets on sensors.

Against this backdrop, the regulation and governance of AI systems and smart robots (see Chapters 4 and 5) arguably represent the most challenging field of governance and regulation of space-related activities and missions. This assumption rests on several national and international declarations warning against possible misuses and overuses of AI,[37] together with the disruptive nature of AI in outer space that has been stressed by the ESA since the mid-2010s[38] or the green and digital transformation of human societies that will result in the overall sustainability of outer space activities.[39] In addition to the impact of AI systems on fields of law like contractual obligations, tortious liability and the laws of war, the focus should be on how AI systems may affect the very notion of (human) authority. Most space law experts are silent in this regard, although the authority of AI systems and the meaningful human control over their decision-making processes are crucial elements of all elements of governance of space activities. Current proposals and recommendations for amendment in international space law should be assessed against this broader technological framework.

VI. Human Authority and Artificial Agents

The crisis of authority in international space law has been illustrated by four cumulative causes: (i) the failure of the Moon Agreement in the 1980s; (ii) the privatisation of space activities since the 1990s; (iii) the intergovernmental

[37] L Floridi et al, 'AI4People: An Ethical Framework for a Good AI Society: Opportunities, Risks, Principles, and Recommendations' (2018) 28(4) *Minds and Machines* 689.

[38] European Space Agency, 'What is Space 4.0?', 2016, https://www.esa.int/About_Us/Ministerial_Council_2016/What_is_space_4.0.

[39] European Commission, 'Communication from the Commission to the European Parliament, the European Council, the Council, the European Economic and Social Committee and the Committee of the regions, The European Green Deal' COM (2019) 640 final.

agreements increasingly complementing the international conventions in the late 1990s; and (iv) the disruption of digital technologies in the 2000s and the increasing use of AI systems since the mid-2010s. As the latest wave of disruption in outer space activities and regulations, AI and smart robots have changed the game by avoiding celestial collisions, helping humans solve critical problems on Earth or managing space missions, lunar stations or their rovers. Most next-generation colonies and lunar stations will be inhabited by such AI systems. Some reasons for this trend have been stressed by the US National Academies of Sciences, Engineering, and Medicine:

> Artificial intelligence (AI) algorithms allow processing of large streams of data and can enable decision making in situ with reduced communications to Earth. AI-based approaches can extract and transmit only the valuable information from a large data stream, reducing the demand on limited or delayed communications. These are valuable capabilities as distance from Earth increases and crew availability decreases.[40]

However, the legal regulation of AI systems raises formidable problems of its own. Previous chapters focused on the legal impact of AI, according to a short- and mid-term analysis of issues of space liability and responsibility in tort law, contracts and some aspects of criminal law (for example, IHL) as well as cybersecurity and environmental concerns relating to the overall sustainability of space activities. The analysis of how AI systems may affect space-related activities and missions should not, in any case, overlook the mid- and long-term impact of technology. 'Mid-term' refers to the time by which current projects, such as the ILRS or the Artemis Accords, aim to be at full speed, namely, by the mid-2030s, while 'long-term' refers to the almost zero possibility of attaining a new international general agreement of outer space in the foreseeable future. Some believe that, by that time, autonomous AI entities will have reached and surpassed humans in terms of intelligence, making our species irrelevant.[41]

The short- and mid-term legal challenges of AI and smart robots will determine and shape the long-term issues raised by the use of autonomous and intelligent systems in outer space. Such short- and mid-term issues will be considered to be legal precedents and conceptual building blocks for the future law of outer space and its authority. AI systems and robotics raise unique legal issues by making the establishment of lunar colonies with routine flights towards the colonies of Mars real. Many celestial stations will be populated only by AI robots, autonomous spacecraft, 3D bio-printers and smart rovers – that is, the new Argonauts of this book. Some missions and spacecrafts of the new Argonauts will likely visit the boundaries of the solar system, and it is even possible that AI systems could replicate themselves beyond such boundaries. Which rules or principles will be valid laws in such communities and deep-space missions remains controversial. The issue not only revolves around troubles of international space

[40] National Academies of Sciences, Engineering, and Medicine (n 23) 47.
[41] R Kurzweil, *The Singularity is Near: When Humans Transcend Biology* (New York, Penguin, 2016).

law with notions of appropriation and occupation; it also rests on the increasing autonomy of AI systems and robots, so far 'only' 239,000 million miles away from the nearest government office, while setting up their own station on the lunar surface.

The autonomy of AI systems may affect the meaning of 'authority' in next-generation space missions and activities. The conjecture rests on how AI may end up with new forms of legal status.[42] In the field of work-related regulations, for example, it is worth mentioning that experts discuss the real-life problems of robots as 'legal employers' with powers of command or recommendation over human employees.[43] Likewise, it is not science fiction to imagine that, by the mid-twenty-first century, some autonomous artificial colonies, spacecrafts, AI agents and smart robots could interact on their own legal terms between Saturn, Uranus and Neptune. This scenario is suggested by the fact that, in some jurisdictions, this eventuality has been considered reasonable in corporate law,[44] where several smart robots have been appointed board members of corporations.[45] Indeed, authorities can be 'artificial' and humans can legitimately trust their own AI robots. While scholars discuss how some AI robots may exert legal powers over humans, this earthly possibility will likely affect outer space anytime soon.[46] As argued in Chapter 4, some AI systems and smart robots can meet the FAA's issue order on the eligibility criteria for astronauts.[47] The scenario does not entail any science-fiction vision of smart robots exerting power and command over the human members of the crew; on the contrary, it shows how the increasing capabilities of autonomous and intelligent systems may impact matters of trust, decision making and empathy in the delicate teamwork with humans aboard deep-space missions or dealing with the human settlers of the first celestial colonies.

This is not the first time that work regarding space law has dealt with matters of non-human intelligence; at least one chapter in most manuals, treatises or handbooks is traditionally devoted to initiatives of detection of extra-terrestrial intelligence in outer space. However, the final chapter of this book deals with another kind of intelligence: the legal challenges that AI systems raise in outer

[42] DJ Gunkel, *Person, Thing, Robot: A Moral and Legal Ontology for the 21st Century and Beyond* (Cambridge, MA, MIT Press, 2023).

[43] I Wildhaber, 'Artificial Intelligence and Robotics, the Workplace, and Workplace-Related Law' in W Barfield and U Pagallo (eds), *Research Handbook on the Law of Artificial Intelligence* (Cheltenham, Edward Elgar, 2018).

[44] S Bayern, 'The Implications of Modern Business–Entity Law for the Regulation of Autonomous Systems' (2016) 7(2) *European Journal of Risk Regulation* 297.

[45] U Pagallo, 'Vital, Sophia, and Co: The Quest for the Legal Personhood of Robots' (2018) 9(9) *Information* 230.

[46] HLEG, *Liability for Artificial Intelligence and Other Emerging Technologies*, Report from the European Commission's Group of Experts on Liability and New Technologies, Brussels, 2019, available at: https://ec.europa.eu/transparency/regexpert/index.cfm?do=groupDetail.groupMeetingDoc&docid=36608.

[47] Federal Aviation Administration, *Commercial Space Astronaut Wings Program*, order 8800.2, 2021, https://www.faa.gov/documentLibrary/media/Order/FAA_Order_8800.2.pdf.

space. The previous chapters of this volume have tackled the issues posed by AI systems, both on Earth and in space-related activities, but the following chapter will focus on the set of challenges to space law regulations, both national and international, that follow as a result of this twofold uniqueness of AI and of outer space. Such challenges complement current discussions on how to amend today's regulatory framework. Even assuming the ideal scenario in which all problems of international law tackled in this chapter would be solved, a further set of issues relating to the behaviour and decision making of autonomous and intelligent systems will be taken into account. Although mostly ignored by scholars, the challenges that AI raises when employed in an outer space context will play a crucial role in how the field will be governed over the next few decades, waiting for a new overall agreement at the international level.

10

Celestial Standards

The chapter scrutinises the twofold uniqueness of outer space and of the legal issues that AI systems pose only when displayed in outer space. These problems demand the development of new standards, namely, thresholds of evaluation that, adopted as the basis of a legal decision, should allow policy makers and courts to assess the benefits and risks of technology. Current discussions on principles and norms of space law, and how to ameliorate them, shall be supplemented with a new generation of *sui generis* standards of space law, as well as stricter or more flexible standards for AI in outer space, including norms for HRI in deep-space missions. Such new standards for HRI and AI hinge on the 'principle of equality' between human and robotic standards. The aim is not to suggest some sort of legal personhood for our new artificial assistants and autonomous agents; instead, the principle of equality aims to prevent supererogatory solutions to extreme challenges in outer space vis-a-vis the use of AI robots as a part of today's crews in routine space missions and tomorrow's colonisation of celestial bodies.

I. The Development of *Sui Generis* Standards

So far, the new laws of outer space have been discussed in connection with recommendations and proposals to improve the legal framework through new international agreements or policies that would not require any amendment to conventional law. These recommendations must be complemented with further discussions on moral and legal standards. Even in the ideal scenario of clear rules, shared principles and law-abiding space actors, the uniqueness of the environment and the technologies that make the next-generation missions and colonies feasible – that is, AI systems and autonomous and intelligent robots – raises a further set of issues on thresholds of moral and legal evaluation. Standards regard, first of all, the constraints of the laws of physics. The unique challenges of a hostile and faraway environment, such as outer space, have recommended adopting specific standards, like security and safety, for every mission since the inception of space law in the late 1950s. Such standards include the European Cooperation for Space Standardization (ECSS) and the system of the ESA for the specification, qualification, and procurement of the electrical, electronic and electro-mechanical components for use in space programmes (ESA/SCC).

The granularity of these fields illustrates the complexity of the task. At the time of writing, there are 139 active standards in the ECSS system alone. These standards regard the specification of the components, which includes resistors and thermistors, fuses and inductors, capacitors, wires and cables, connectors, relays and switches, crystal and surface acoustic wave (SAW) devices, oscillators and discrete semiconductors, integrated circuits, cable assembly and optoelectronics. The qualification of such components also relates to capacitors, connectors and crystal oscillators, diodes, filters, thermostats, relays, transistors, resistors etc.[1] In addition, the qualification process concerns 'flow qualified manufacturers' that hold ECSS technology flow qualifications, such as Norway's Kongsberg Space Electronic, Denmark's FLUX A/S or several French companies, such as Microchip-Atmel, Exxelia and Vishay.

Recent technological advances and the speed of technological innovation require the continuous expansion of such standards. These developments relate to standards for cyber-risk analysis in extreme environments, such as the colonisation of Mars;[2] standards for new types of enterprises opened up by technology, such as suborbital flights for scientific missions and human transportation;[3] cybersecurity standards;[4] standards for space traffic management;[5] and the new standards that will be developed under section 5 of the Artemis Accords. Such standards complement traditional efforts of national and international authorities like the GNSS signals and services – the 1999 UNISPACE III Resolution 54/68 – and the International Organization for Standardization (ISO) standards on Space Debris Mitigation Requirements for all satellites and spacecrafts. The ISO standards were first adopted by the European Cooperation for Space Standardization in 2015, then by the European Commission, and were later applied to all ESA projects under EU law.[6]

Such standardisation efforts also include AI systems. In the US, for example, NASA has made progress in establishing an AI agenda through the development of its *Framework for the Ethical Use of Artificial Intelligence (AI)* of April 2021, the *Responsible AI Plan* in September 2022 and the 'Artificial Intelligence Machine

[1] ECSS, *Active Standards*, 2023, https://ecss.nl/standards/active-standards.

[2] P Radanliev et al, 'Design of a Dynamic and Self-Adapting System, Supported with Artificial Intelligence, Machine Learning and Real-Time Intelligence for Predictive Cyber Risk Analytics in Extreme Environments – Cyber Risk in the Colonisation of Mars' (2020) 2 *Safety in Extreme Environments* 219.

[3] SM Pekkanen, 'Governing the New Space Race' (2019) 113 *American Journal of International Law* 92.

[4] G Falco and NG Gordon, 'Cybersecurity and Human Spaceflight Safety' in *2023 IEEE Aerospace Conference*, IEEE, 2023, 1–7.

[5] See P Larsen, 'Space Traffic Management Standards' (2018) 83(2) *Journal of Air Law and Commerce* 359; H Osborn, 'Agreeing on the Rules-of-the-Road: Distilling Building Blocks from Proposed Space Traffic Management Treaties, Guidelines and Standards', *72nd International Astronautical Congress (IAC)*, Dubai, United Arab Emirates, 2021.

[6] European Space Agency, 'Mitigating Space Debris Generation', 2022, www.esa.int/Safety_Security/Space_Debris/Mitigating_space_debris_generation.

Learning SharePoint' website. The overall aim is to meet the implementation requirements of US Executive Order 13960 of December 2020 to promote the transparency and trustworthiness of technology. However, in May 2023, the Office of the Inspector General stressed that, notwithstanding NASA's progress, most work still had to be done, starting with 'a standardised definition of AI'.[7] So far, three 'separate' notions of AI have been adopted in the Framework for the Ethical Use of AI, the Responsible AI Plan and the SharePoint website. A standardised definition should allow for the identification, update and maintenance of NASA's 'AI use case inventory' as well as the identification of a 'classification mechanism' for cybersecurity controls and monitoring practices.[8]

NASA's troubles with the development of AI standards and the identification of a standardised definition of AI draw attention to different kinds of standards, particularly the very difference between technical and moral standards. On the one hand, technical standards refer to parameters – such as safety, security or cyber-resilience of AI systems – that must consider the environmental constraints of outer space as concerns, such as the functioning of storm prediction tools that use image recognition technology to identify atmospheric conditions. The aim is to provide timely warnings for destructive hailstorms that may affect (also but not only) the autonomous navigation system of space vehicles, such as the Mars Perseverance rover. On the other hand, moral standards concern human values and principles, such as the 'explicability' of the AI systems,[9] that should be embedded into the technology design. This embedding of values and principles can be illustrated with IEEE standard 7010-2020 on the use of autonomous and intelligent systems for the well-being of humans – as mentioned in Chapter 4 – or ISO standard 13482:2014 on specific requirements for the use of personal care robots, such as mobile servant robots, physical assistants or person carrier robots.[10] The distinction between technological and moral standards does not aim to suggest any sharp line between hard science and humanities. Instead, the assumption is that moral and legal issues related to the design of autonomous artificial agents supplement the role that technical standards play in this context. In addition to technical requirements on, for example, safety and cybersecurity, the focus should be on how autonomous and intelligent systems should behave in accordance with the 'human-centric approach' to AI discussed in Chapter 4.[11]

In the late 1960s, Herbert A Simon, a pioneer of design theory and organisational decision making, lamented the lack of research on 'the science of design', thus

[7] NASA, *NASA's Management of its Artificial Intelligence Capabilities*, Office of Inspector General, IG-23-012, 3 May 2023.

[8] ibid.

[9] L Floridi et al 'AI4People – An Ethical Framework for a Good AI Society: Opportunities, Risks, Principles, and Recommendations' (2018) 28(4) *Minds and Machines* 689.

[10] ISO, 'Robots and Robotic Devices – Safety Requirements for Personal Care Robots', 2020, https://www.iso.org/standard/53820.html.

[11] HLEG, *Ethics Guidelines for Trustworthy AI*, Brussels, European Commission, 2019, https://digital-strategy.ec.europa.eu/en/library/ethics-guidelines-trustworthy-ai.

affecting the curricula of both professional schools and universities.[12] Sixty years later, applying human-centric design principles has become a common approach to creating AI systems and robots that act ethically towards humans. Debates on 'value-sensitive design', 'ethically aligned design' and 'social system design' set the level of abstraction to appreciate the second way in which the behaviour of AI systems displayed in outer space may require the development of new standards. After the *sui generis* standards covered in this section – and technical standards on safety, cybersecurity and resilience of AI systems and robots that will take into account the constraints of outer space – the focus moves on to how safe, secure and resilient AI robots should be designed in accordance with moral principles and legal rules.

II. Designing Law-Abiding Robots

Design relates to how humans shape spaces and places, communication media and artefacts, including systems and components that determine autonomous and intelligent systems design. Such shaping can be instrumental, like design as a means to attain a specific end. Further design problems revolve around the aims of a certain design project. The goals can be as different: as (i) preventing human or artificial behaviour from occurring; (ii) reducing the impact of their harm-generating conducts; or (iii) nudging human or artificial behaviour.[13] These different design aims arguably impact human values and principles in different ways, just as precluding a particular agent from doing something is different from trying to change that agent's behaviour through self-imposed choices.

The 'science of design' relating to the development of standards also (but not only) in the field of space law should thus be grasped in connection with two different sets of issues. On the one hand, the focus must be on the means of design – techniques and methods to attain the final model of the project and, hence, its standardisation. According to Simon's thesis in *The Sciences of Artificial*,[14] work should be split into several tasks and then assigned to a different working team. Each project should start with smaller parts and sub-solutions and end up with global answers. A critical part of design is the evaluation phase, which consists of testing both the internal consistency of the project and what Herbert Simon used to dub the 'generator test-cycle', namely, the breaking down of the complete design into functional components. The test-cycle should generate alternatives and examine them against the set of requirements and constraints of the project. The expected outcome is summed up by Simon: 'Important indirect consequences will be noticed and weighed. Alternative decompositions correspond to different ways of dividing the responsibilities for the final design between generators and tests.'[15]

[12] H Simon, *The Sciences of Artificial* (Cambridge, MA, MIT Press, 1996 [1969]).
[13] U Pagallo, 'Designing Data Protection Safeguards Ethically' (2011) 2(2) *Information* 247.
[14] Simon (n 12).
[15] ibid 128.

On the other hand, specific design choices may result in conflicts between values, which may affect the design features. Such conflicts can make the standardisation of design projects extremely difficult. Since the early 2000s, scholars have stressed that 'some technical artefacts bear directly and systematically on the realisation, or suppression, of particular configurations of social, ethical, and political values'.[16] The disruption of AI and its possible bad uses as 'weapons of math destruction' have caused this impact to spread out.[17] Designers and developers of AI systems standards and multiple robotic applications face practical problems. Consider privacy and data protection: this field will arguably affect provisions of space law for space tourists or mass space explorers interacting with smart robots and AI systems in lunar hotels. So far, privacy issues of space law have mainly dealt with the use of space technologies, such as satellite remote sensing, that may impinge on the privacy of individuals down on Earth. However, the plethora of new Argonauts discussed in Chapter 4 – from CIMON to Robonaut – suggests further privacy and data protection issues that will progressively relate to the interaction between humans and artificial agents in celestial colonies and space missions. NASA's Callisto project illustrates this point:

> Callisto is a technology demonstration project that involves a customized version of Amazon's digital voice assistant Alexa to act as a virtual assistant to astronauts while onboard their spacecraft. This AI was incorporated into the Orion Multi-Purpose Crew Vehicle spacecraft in 2022 for the Artemis I unmanned mission to the Moon and is planned for inclusion on future Artemis missions. These types of AI projects and applications will be crucial for Artemis and other missions as NASA continues to explore low Earth orbit, our solar system, and beyond.[18]

In many jurisdictions, the panoply of artificial agents, such as CIMON, Robonaut and Callisto, should process personal data or personal identifying information according to a principle of data protection – that is, privacy 'by' design. The overall idea is that legal safeguards and normative constraints should be embedded into the design of a robotic system, or of an autonomous agent, before any single bit of personal information can be collected. The aim is that data protection safeguards should work in proactive rather than reactive terms – that is, making privacy (and data protection) by design preventive and not simply remedial, such as Article 25 of the GDPR in EU law.[19] However, the aim to design moral and law-abiding robots faces a twofold problem.[20] First, what should be embedded within the system may be ambiguous. This could be caused by the crucial

[16] M Flanagan, DC Howe, and M Nissenbaum, 'Embodying Values in Technology: Theory and Practice' in J van den Hoven and J Weckert (eds), *Information Technology and Moral Philosophy* (Cambridge, Cambridge University Press, 2008).

[17] C O'Neil, *Weapons of Math Destruction: How Big Data Increases Inequality and Threatens Democracy* (New York, Random House, 2016).

[18] NASA (n 7).

[19] A Cavoukian, *Privacy by Design: The 7 Foundational Principles* (Ontario, Information and Privacy Commissioner of 2009).

[20] W Wallach and C Allen, *Moral Machines: Teaching Robots Right from Wrong* (Oxford, Oxford University Press, 2008).

differences among jurisdictions which hold multiple conflicting values and legal traditions –for example, the idea that, in US constitutional law, privacy should be understood as secrecy. In the end, every project on privacy by design or data protection may acquire different features once grasped in terms of property rights or human dignity, total control or contextual integrity, restricted access or limited control over information in digital environments.[21] Therefore, should a robot be designed in accordance with the traditional European opt-in model for users of electronic communication systems or, vice versa, according to the American opt-out approach?

The second problem relates to the technical difficulty of embedding normative constraints into the design of autonomous and intelligent systems so that they can comprehend concepts traditionally employed by lawyers through the formalisation of norms, rights and duties.[22] A case study showed that the NAO robot falsely understood its human partners' consent to collect their personal data.[23] The approach to the protection of privacy and personal data 'by' design – and its counterpart in EU law 'by' default – often overlooks the complexity of multi-agent systems: the interplay between humans and their artificial companions should be understood 'through' rather than 'by' design.[24] The formula suggests that legal protection should encompass all elements of the regulatory governance and consider: (i) the nature or material in which the artificial agent or autonomous system manifests itself; (ii) its level of independence from external human control; (iii) the application or service provided by such autonomous and intelligent systems; (iv) the environment in which they operate and behave; and (v) the relationship established with human beings – that is, the design of HRI.[25] This complexity of designing law-abiding robots and moral AI systems explains why the standardisation process can be complex and controversial.

Such normative and technical hurdles do not mean that progress at the international level is not possible. Earlier we mentioned the IEEE 7010-2020 standard on 'contextual well-being metrics that facilitate the use of a Well-being Impact Assessment (WIA) process in order to proactively increase and help safeguard human well-being throughout the lifecycle of autonomous and intelligent systems'.[26] According to Simon's recommendations, such standards often rest on

[21] Pagallo (n 13).

[22] V Rodríguez-Doncel, M Palmirani, M Araszkiewicz, P Casanovas, U Pagallo and G Sartor, *AI Approaches to the Complexity of Legal Systems XI–XII* (Cham, Springer, 2021).

[23] Y-H. Weng, S Gulyaeva, J Winter, A Slavescu and Y Hirata, 'HRI for Legal Validation: On Embodiment and Data Protection', in *Proceedings of the 29th IEEE International Symposium on Robot and Human Interactive Communication (RO-MAN)*, 2020, 1387–94.

[24] M Hashmi, P Casanovas and L de Koker, 'Legal Compliance through Design: Preliminary Results of a Literature Survey', *TERECOM2018@ JURIX, Technologies for Regulatory Compliance*, https://ceur-ws.org/Vol-2309/06.pdf.

[25] R Leenes, E Palmerini, BJ Koops, A Bertolini, P Salvini and F Lucivero, 'Regulatory Challenges of Robotics: Some Guidelines for Addressing Legal and Ethical Issues' (2017) 9(1) *Law, Innovation and Technology* 1.

[26] IEEE, 'Recommended Practice for Assessing the Impact of Autonomous and Intelligent Systems on Human Well-Being', 7010-2020, 2020, 1–96.

the decomposability and scalability of the design project. In the field of Value-Sensitive Design (VSD), the aim to embed human values in the design process of autonomous technologies – to tackle further issues of non-discrimination, transparency or accountability – entails conceptual, empirical and technological phases that should allow designers to continuously improve their products via iterative processes.[27] The more such projects are decomposable and scalable, the better. Such an iteration process should tackle the risk of leaving behind certain values,[28] or specific unforeseen values or disvalues that may emerge after system development.[29] Likewise, in the field of legal ontologies – a sub-field of legal informatics devoted to the automation of legal reasoning – projects on AI systems and robots follow a similar methodology. In order to grasp legal classes, relations, properties or instances on a given domain problem, projects start from smaller parts and sub-solutions of the ontological requirements, such as taxonomies and the set of rules and restraints that belong to that problem domain (for example, ontological constraints), and end up with large-scale solutions.[30]

Designing moral and law-abiding robots is thus feasible, despite the time any attempt requires for its standardisation and implementation across the fields of HRI and legal regulation. However, the feasibility of law-abiding and trustworthy AI systems – in the wording of both NASA and European institutions – should not overlook a further problem of standardisation. We may concede an ideal scenario in which autonomous and intelligent systems behave in accordance with all regulations of data privacy law, consumer law, cybersecurity law or anti-discrimination law. Still, even in this case, the space-related uses of such autonomous and intelligent systems would trigger a further class of legal issues and moral problems. In Chapter 5, the analysis focused on the normative challenges that depend on the uniqueness of the technology and its impact, whether on Earth or in space. The following sections of this chapter will focus on the types of problems that AI robots only pose in outer space.

These kinds of problems entail the development of new standards that realign the terrestrial standards developed so far in the fields of HRI, social robotics, VSD or legal ontologies. Designers and developers of AI systems should pay attention to this re-adjustment of standards that the increasing use of smart robots and artificial companions in space activities triggers. Such increasing use may at times require lowering the standards adopted on Earth or at other times strengthening

[27] B Friedman and DG Hendry, *Value Sensitive Design: Shaping Technology with Moral Imagination* (Cambridge, MA, MIT Press, 2019).

[28] CA le Dantec, ES Poole and SP Wyche, 'Values as Lived Experience' in *Proceedings of the 27th International Conference on Human Factors in Computing Systems – CHI 09* (New York, ACM Press, 2009).

[29] I van de Poel, 'Embedding Values in Artificial Intelligence (AI) Systems' (2020) 30(3) *Minds and Machines* 385.

[30] See J Breuker et al (eds), *Law, Ontologies and the Semantic Web: Channelling the Legal Information Flood* (Amsterdam, IOS Press, 2009); U Pagallo, 'As Law Goes By: Topology, Ontology, Evolution' in P Casanovas et al (eds), *AI Approaches to the Complexity of Legal Systems: Complex Systems, the Semantic Web, Ontologies, Argumentation, and Dialogue. AICOL 2009* (Berlin, Springer, 2010).

them. The focus of the next section is on what happens from a normative viewpoint when the uniqueness of AI systems meets the uniqueness of a harsh and faraway environment such as outer space.

III. The Re-alignment of Terrestrial Standards

Long space flights already require professional astronauts to face the emotional challenges of deep space missions through the support of AI and smart robots. A consistent amount of empirical evidence on the pros of humanoid AI robots for human well-being was discussed in Chapter 4. Work on HRI suggests that benefits can be even more vital during an extended space mission. Artificial agents, such as smart robots equipped with AI systems, constructively develop in a machine the illusion of human traits that can either help manage a need for a degree of social interaction or extend human sensing and action through more immersive telepresence robotics.[31] Because the aim is to create robots capable of engaging 'in meaningful social interaction with people',[32] such engagement should be tested with all specificities of space missions, namely, the kind of aid that robots may provide to older adults,[33] children,[34] dependent people[35] or in relation to any social background and gender of the HRI observer.[36]

The social acceptability of AI robots and human preference for their anthropomorphic features[37] suggest that HRI and social robotics standards will be adapted to the extreme circumstances of space missions. Furthermore, such standards may lower the bar of moral and legal assessment. Indeed, personal choices play a prominent role when humans modulate different levels of access to and control

[31] K Zawieska and BR Duffy, 'Human-Robot Exploration', *23rd IEEE International Symposium on Robot and Human Interactive Communication*, 2014, 808–13.

[32] BR Duffy, 'Anthropomorphism and the Social Robot' (2003) 42 *Robotics and Autonomous Systems* 177.

[33] S Pedell, K Constantin, D Muñoz and L Sterling, 'Designing Meaningful, Beneficial and Positive Human Robot Interactions with Older Adults for Increased Wellbeing During Care Activities' in CP Lin et al (eds), *Handbook of Artificial Intelligence in Healthcare* (Cham, Springer, 2022).

[34] A Alabdulkareem, N Alhakbani and A Al-Nafjan, 'A Systematic Review of Research on Robot-Assisted Therapy for Children with Autism' (2022) 22(3) *Sensors* 944.

[35] A Chandani, O Prakash, P Prakash, S Wagholikar and M Mehta, 'Robots and Artificial Intelligence: An Aid to Dependent People' in A Joshi et al (eds), *Information and Communication Technology for Competitive Strategies* (Singapore, Springer, 2022).

[36] J Zlotowski et al, 'Anthropomorphism: Opportunities and Challenges in Human-Robot Interaction' (2015) 7 *International Journal of Social Robotics* 347.

[37] See W Barfield, Y-H Weng and U Pagallo (eds), *The Cambridge Handbook of the Law, Policy, and Regulation for Human–Robot Interaction* (Cambridge, Cambridge University Press, 2024); CU Krägeloh, J Bharatharaj, S Kutty, PR Irmala and L Huang, 'Questionnaires to Measure Acceptability of Social Robots: A Critical Review' (2019) 8(4) *Robotics* 88; K Klüber and L Onnasch, 'Appearance is Not Everything: Preferred Feature Combinations for Care Robots' (2022) 128 *Computers in Human Behavior* 107128; and, K Liu and D Tao, 'The Roles of Trust, Personalization, Loss of Privacy, and Anthropomorphism in Public Acceptance of Smart Healthcare Services' (2022) 127 *Computers in Human Behavior* 107026.

over data and information depending on the context and circumstances.[38] In the jargon of US constitutional privacy law, it makes sense to say that scientists or space explorers can 'reasonably' expect a sphere of privacy in outer space missions when dealing with their new artificial companions. Such a 'reasonable expectation' matches the sphere or level of privacy that scientists and space explorers would presume when interacting with the other human members of the crew. We can even suppose that such reasonable expectation, meaning the confidentiality between humans and smart robots in a spacecraft or a colony, may be even stronger than the trust among humans of that same spacecraft or colony. Personal data sharing with humanoid robots for healthcare and entertainment in outer space may thus require softer standards than those at work on Earth. This is because anthropomorphism, trust, personalisation, HRI privacy and increasing social acceptance show that society at large would consider the opinion that a certain situation or interaction with AI robots must be kept private in outer space to be reasonable.

New, softer standards for outer space activities do not prevent or contradict the adoption of stricter standards. Privacy and data protection are once again instructive in this regard. Contrary to the tenets of US federal privacy law, privacy should not be considered as an equivalent of secrecy.[39] People reveal a great deal of information about themselves to third parties in their daily lives. Still, they do not expect their personal life – and sensitive data – to fall into the public domain. In other words, privacy and data protection do not trigger any zero-sum game between softer or stricter standards for HRI in outer space because they entail both. The expectation that a particular HRI interaction is private concerns the extent to which end users of smart robots exert meaningful control over their own artificial systems and companions – for example, making the degree of confidentiality and intimacy between humans and artificial agents personal. This meaningful control entails that third parties, such as private companies or the government, should be excluded from that data flow. This critical point must be considered against promises of space tourism, mass exploration or settlers of new celestial colonies. Space law is no exception to the rules and principles of data privacy which apply on Earth.

Before the disruption of AI in outer space in the mid-2010s and into the 2020s, the availability of all personal data activities in outer space missions was conceived of as the rule for professional astronauts with few exceptions. The convergence between technological innovation and trends in the privatisation of space makes it likely that the current exception will turn into a default rule. Privacy rights should be taken as seriously as the integrity and safety of the whole space mission with the next-generation scientists and space explorers, mass tourists and dwellers of colonies. Correspondingly, some scholars claim that, as a general norm, the uses

[38] H Nissenbaum, 'Privacy as Contextual Integrity' (2004) 79(1) *Washington Law Review* 119.

[39] W Barfield and U Pagallo, *Advanced Introduction to the Law and Artificial Intelligence* (Cheltenham, Edward Elgar, 2020).

of AI systems and robots may demand the adoption of stricter standards.[40] Indeed, in addition to the *sui generis* standards on safety and security, such as the standards of the ECSS system, previous chapters of this book have stressed the shortcomings of current regulations on contractual and tortious obligations that require the strengthening of legal standards – for example, duties of care and information for space missions and related activities, as well as stricter standards for AI systems in relation to environmental protection, machinery safety, consumer safeguards and cybersecurity measures. In the field of autonomous vehicles, some believe that the design and employment of the technology should hinge on standards that are stricter than human standards – that is, the traditional duties and obligations of human drivers.[41] Also, the approach applies to the fields of healthcare and medicine in accordance with the further principle of precaution and current rules on the use of AI systems as medical devices.[42] All these regulations support the view that privacy and data protection need stricter standards in outer space so that in celestial colonies or lunar hotels, third parties should not have access to HRI-sensitive data by default or through design.[43]

However, the claim that the use of autonomous and intelligent systems must be allowed if, and only if, they guarantee standards that are stricter than human or terrestrial standards is contradicted by the HRI scenarios of privacy, trust and confidentiality in outer space that rest on softer standards for the behaviour of AI systems and smart robots. Scholars have advanced even more thought-provoking cases, such as the issues raised by the possibility of having sex with robots on a very long space mission.[44] AI standards must not always be stricter than human standards in outer space, just as standards of HRI in outer space should not always be stricter than standards of traditional HRI on Earth. Bars of legal standards and corresponding lowering, or strengthening, of moral and legal thresholds for assessing AI behaviour should be understood as more than just conceiving stricter standards as the general rule and softer standards as the exception. The golden rule for the re-alignment of terrestrial standards must be found elsewhere.

The following section claims that such a golden rule can be found in a new 'principle of equality' in space missions.[45] The exercising of applied ethics must

[40] R Sparrow and M Howard, 'When Human Beings are Like Drunk Robots: Driverless Vehicles, Ethics, and the Future of Transport' (2017) 80 *Transportation Research Part C: Emerging Technologies* 206.

[41] R Jenkins, D Cerný and T Hríbek (eds), *Autonomous Vehicle Ethics: The Trolley Problem and beyond* (Oxford, Oxford University Press, 2022).

[42] See H Kempt, JC Heilinger and SK Nagel, 'Relative Explainability and Double Standards in Medical Decision-Making' (2022) 24 *Ethics and Information Technologies* 20; U Pagallo, *Il dovere alla salute. Sul rischio di sottoutilizzo dell'intelligenza artificiale in ambito sanitario* (Milan, Mimesis, 2022).

[43] In EU law, see L Keogh, 'EU Data Protection Considerations for the Space Sector' in PJ Blount and M Hofmann (eds), *Space Law in a Networked World* (Brill, Nijhoff, 2023).

[44] M Scheutz and T Arnold, 'Are We Ready for Sex Robots?', *2016 11th ACM/IEEE International Conference on Human-Robot Interaction (HRI)*, 2016, 351–58.

[45] U Pagallo, E Bassi and M Durante, 'The Normative Challenges of AI in Outer Space: Law, Ethics, and the Realignment of Terrestrial Standards' (2023) 36(2) *Philosophy & Technology* 23.

shed light on the set of moral dilemmas created by technology with the potential proliferation of new legal hard cases. After *sui generis* standards, and stricter or softer standards that may follow the use of AI systems and smart robots in space activities, the focus will be on how to discern cases of applied ethics and tackle further disagreement in the legal community.

IV. The Principle of Equality

The 'principle of equality' is often associated with the claims of the Robot Liberation Front. The overall idea is that the more we admit the existence of an artificial mind in a machine that affords autonomy and intentional actions, the more likely it is that a new generation of ethical issues concerning the legal personhood of AI robots will follow.[46] Such issues include debates on the 'moral rights' of robots and a new 'legal status' for artificial agents with their own constitutional rights (and duties). The most common objections against AI systems' moral and legal status – namely, that they are not humans or that they miss some key feature to attain any moral or legal status – were arguably dismantled in a seminal paper from the early 1990s entitled 'Legal Personhood for Artificial Intelligences'. In the words of Lawrence Solum: 'One cannot, on conceptual grounds, rule out in advance the possibility that AIs should be given the rights of constitutional personhood.'[47]

However, in this section, we can set aside this kind of problem and focus on autonomous and intelligent systems understood as the object, rather than the subject, of moral standards and legal regulations. The 'principle of equality' under scrutiny in this context relates to how the behaviour of AI systems and robots should abide by standards of conduct, such as the safety and integrity of space missions. While such standards can sometimes soften terrestrial standards or, vice versa, strengthen them, the claim is that the 'principle of equality' offers the golden rule to tackle the hard cases of applied ethics and the law. The principle of equality embraces a non-discriminatory approach between human and artificial behaviour with equivalent effects – that is, that which EU law makers often present as a principle of 'functional equivalence'.[48]

The principle of equality, or functional equivalence, can be endorsed as the purpose of all legislation, as is the case with the principle of non-discrimination between technologies with equivalent effects.[49] The principle entails the equalisation

[46] U Pagallo, *The Laws of Robots: Crimes, Contracts, and Torts* (Dordrecht, Springer, 2013).

[47] LB Solum, 'Legal Personhood for Artificial Intelligence' (1992) 70 *North Carolina Law Review* 1231.

[48] BJ Koops, 'Should ICT Regulation be Technology-Neutral?' in BJ Koops et al (eds), *Starting Points for ICT Regulation: Deconstructing Prevalent Policy One-Liners* (The Hague, TMC Asser Press, 2006).

[49] U Pagallo, 'LegalAIze: Tackling the Normative Challenges of Artificial Intelligence and Robotics through the Secondary Rules of Law' in M Corrales, M Fenwick and N Forgó (eds), *New Technology, Big Data and the Law: Perspectives in Law, Business and Innovation* (Singapore, Springer, 2017).

of different kinds or sources of activity: between online and offline activities, or between human and artificial behaviour, meaning that AI robots should not guarantee standards higher than human standards by default, but rather the same standards of due diligence, care and rates of success following the further principle of equal protection under the law.[50] Equal procedural and substantive safeguards of the law must, in fact, be 'ensured for all those who are the receivers of the effects of AI systems or the performance of emerging digital technologies'.[51] By drawing attention to patients or receivers of the effects of someone else's behaviour, the aim is to prevent unnecessary or unfair different levels of protection, depending on the source of such behaviour, whether human or artificial.

How the principle of equality works in practice can be illustrated by next-generation AI systems, medical robots and personal assistants that will accompany projects of colonisation and deep-space missions with humans aboard. Consider the use of AI robots for diagnostics and prevention,[52] precision medicine and medical research,[53] clinical decision making and mobile health[54] or healthcare management and service delivery[55] – such AI assistants, or at least most of them, will increasingly be an essential part of all crews in space missions regarding the well-being of humans. It is not unrealistic to imagine the urgency of a human tourist with fever and nausea, diffuse abdominal rigidity and sinus tachycardia. What would the standards for diagnosing and treating human peritonitis through the X-rays and robotic arms of the humanoid AI system be during an emergency between Mars and the Moon?

This question is not entirely new. Ethical dilemmas concerning the use of technologies in harsh, extreme environments are the bread and butter of scholars working on the design and deployment of humanoid robot surgeons on the battlefield.[56] A balance should be struck between the risks (and also the

[50] M Durante and L Floridi, 'A Legal Principles-Based Framework for AI Liability Regulation' in J Mokander and M Ziosi (eds), *The 2021 Yearbook of the Digital Ethics Lab* (Dordrecht, Springer, 2022).

[51] ibid.

[52] See M Alsharqi, W Woodward, J Mumith, D Markham, R Upton and P Leeson, 'Artificial Intelligence and Echocardiography' (2018) 5(4) *Echo Research and Practice* R115; P Rajkomar, J Dean and I Kohane, 'Machine Learning in Medicine' (2019) 380(14) *New England Journal of Medicine* 1347; and D Wang, A Khosla, R Gargeya, H Irshad and AH Beck, 'Deep Learning for Identifying Metastatic Breast Cancer', *arXiv preprint arXiv:160605718*, 2016.

[53] See SI Lee et al, 'A Machine Learning Approach to Integrate Big Data for Precision Medicine in Acute Myeloid Leukaemia' (2018) 9 *Nature Communications* 42; K Liu and D Tao, 'The Roles of Trust, Personalization, Loss of Privacy, and Anthropomorphism in Public Acceptance of Smart Healthcare Services' (2022) 127 *Computers in Human Behavior* 107026.

[54] See SS Jamal, A Goyal, A Shanker and T Grover, 'Predicting Neurological Adverse Drug Reactions Based on Biological, Chemical and Phenotypic Properties of Drugs Using Machine Learning Models' (2017) 7(1) *Scientific Reports* 872; JP Higgins, 'Smartphone Applications for Patients' Health and Fitness' (2016) 129(1) *American Journal of Medicine* 11.

[55] C Davenport and R Kalakota, 'The Potential for Artificial Intelligence in Healthcare' (2019) 6(2) *Future healthcare Journal* 94.

[56] S O'Sullivan et al, 'Legal, Regulatory, and Ethical Frameworks for Development of Standards in Artificial Intelligence (AI) and Autonomous Robotic Surgery' (2019) 15(1) *International Journal of Medical Robotics and Computer Assisted Surgery* e1968.

impossibility) of humans intervening in and operating on the battlefield, and the standards of safety and security provided by such robot surgeons. Such a balance suggests that under these extreme circumstances, AI robots should not guarantee higher standards compared to those of human doctors, but rather the same standards of diligence and rates of success in accordance with the 'principle of equality'. The alternative to this conclusion – that is, stricter robot standards by default – would be counterintuitive and flawed.[57] According to this stance, we would have to let soldiers die without attempting to save them, or fail to provide assistance for space patients suffering from a fulminant peritonitis – that is, up until they can return from their lunar hotels holidays and be assisted by human doctors on Earth.

The 'principle of equality' between robot and human standards presupposes that human standards should already be sufficiently satisfactory to be adopted as the golden rule of outer space. It seems reasonable that our humanoid doctor should not need to provide higher standards than the best human doctor on Earth, especially when travelling towards Mars during an emergency. Therefore, the principle of equality should guarantee procedural and substantive safeguards for all humans interacting with autonomous and intelligent systems. In relation to procedural safeguards, the equivalence of human and robotic standards rests on the fundamental control humans have over their decision making – for example, the success rate and risks posed by manifold applications of AI systems and robotics for medicine and healthcare in outer space. Analyses of the probabilities of events, consequences and costs determine the speed at which AI systems can be implemented and adopted in laboratories and hospitals, both on Earth and in outer space stations, colonies and missions.[58] As regards the substantial safeguards of the law, the principle of equality offers the golden rule to address the hard cases that we may expect with the advances of technology and HRI in outer space, namely, disagreement about different values and principles on whether robots should treat a case of peritonitis, keep personal data private or provide comfort to humans. If in doubt, the overall idea is that AI standards should only be as strict as human standards because the aim is to prevent supererogatory solutions – for example, the peritonitis crisis of a space tourist that would have to wait until return to Earth or, vice versa, the default rule that all space tourists must have their appendix removed before any launch or mission.

The equalisation of robotic and human standards as the golden rule of outer space does not entail any equalisation of moral and legal statuses for AI systems and humans. Artificial agents and 'systems of systems' can exert authority, be trusted or make decisions by themselves. Still, they represent the object rather than the subject of the new laws of outer space. Therefore, the equalisation of robotic and human standards does not hinge on any claim of the Robot Liberation Front, but rather on: (i) current research on safety and integrity management of missions

[57] Sparrow and Howard (n 40).
[58] Davenport and Kalakota (n 55).

and operations in harsh environments; (ii) trust and data protection in HRI; (iii) liability safeguards for autonomous technologies; and (iv) legal methods of technological regulation. What remains to be seen is whether a further set of standards should follow as a result of smart robots and AI systems being understood as moral and legal agents with rights (and duties) of their own. Since next-generation colonies and stations will mostly concern such AI systems, shouldn't we take this hypothetical of AI's moral agency and legal personhood seriously?

V. Time Horizons

Over the past few decades, scholars have discussed the concept of AI systems and robots either as 'moral persons',[59] 'legal persons'[60] or with the same citizenship rights as humans.[61] The analysis in this chapter on 'celestial standards' has discarded these views for two reasons. On the one hand, it seems fair to admit that robots and AI systems are 'capable of a measure of empathy' and 'a type of autonomy that affords intentional actions' so that 'the emergence of such entities will probably require us to rethink notions of consciousness, self-consciousness and moral agency'.[62] However, we are far from designing and creating autonomous and intelligent systems with human-like properties like suffering or experiencing emotions. This does not mean that it is not possible to set up AI systems and robots that act ethically towards humans, or that AI systems and robots should not be considered 'moral patients' that deserve respect and protection as such.[63] An incident in Japan, in which a drunk human attacked the humanoid robot Pepper in a SoftBank store, is interesting in this regard. Lawyers and ordinary people vividly discussed whether the attack should have been interpreted as an obstruction of business by damaging a computer, harm to property, or unjust damages in tort law.[64] Regardless of how we should interpret the norms of Japanese law, the case of poor robot Pepper is instructive because it sheds light on why, for the foreseeable future, such artificial agents should be considered moral patients rather than subjects of legal protection with rights and claims of their own. At the risk of being lambasted for reactionary anthropocentrism, the new stricter or softer standards for HRI in outer space discussed in the previous sections of this chapter

[59] SJ Hall, *Beyond AI: Creating the Conscience of the Machine* (New York, Prometheus, 2007).

[60] S Chopra and LF White, *A Legal Theory for Autonomous Artificial Agents* (Ann Arbor, University of Michigan Press, 2011).

[61] UK Office of Science and Innovation's Horizon Scanning Centre, *The Sigma and Delta Scans*, Foresight Annual Review, 2007.

[62] M Hildebrandt, 'Criminal Liability and "Smart" Environments', *Conference on the Philosophical Foundations of Criminal Law at Rutgers-Newark*, August 2010.

[63] L Floridi, *Information Ethics* (Oxford, Oxford University Press, 2013).

[64] JJ Roberts, 'Drunk Man Arrested in Latest Outburst of Anti-robot Violence', *Fortune*, 8 September 2015, https://fortune.com/2015/09/08/robot-assault.

concerned the protection of human rights and interests rather than those of the AI system or smart robot.

On the other hand, we noted that AI robots may exert legal power and authority in fields such as corporate law, labour law or space law. The argument is that either the law does not exclude such legal powers and authority, or it could address its own loopholes in cases of complex legal causation or distributed legal responsibility.[65] Although such legal status is still controversial among scholars,[66] it draws attention to a crucial distinction between the agency and the personhood of those autonomous and intelligent systems. Several examples of legal history – from the status of slaves in Ancient Roman law to the legal status of the EU for almost two decades – show that forms of dependent or restricted legal status, such as agents in contract law, are not related to forms of independent legal personhood.[67] In other words, different types of AI robotic agenthood can be examined irrespective of whether such artificial agents are conscious, capable of suffering or experiencing emotions, desires, pleasure or pain. The approach is, and should be, pragmatic because rather than AI robotic dignity, what is at stake is potential loopholes in the law. Correspondingly, whether autonomous artificial colonies, spacecrafts, AI agents and smart robots will be interacting on their own legal terms by the end of this century – either between Saturn, Uranus and Neptune, or even beyond the solar system[68] – is a pragmatic issue that should be tackled as such; that is, moving from the pressing problems of today to the likely issues of tomorrow.

Scholars often jump to the long-term issues in the field. This stance is legitimate because it draws on the exponential growth of technological innovation, often providing food for thought. Such long-term issues relate to the human imagining of outer space,[69] the alternative of utopian versus dystopian futures, such as *Star Trek* versus *Star Wars* scenarios,[70] the harsh life humans should expect on their first cities on Mars,[71] the role and evolution of cyberhumans,[72] and new perspectives on 'generation ships' and 'reproductive ethics' that aim 'to look at how genetic enhancement interventions can and should be used not only to ensure that

[65] Pagallo (n 46).

[66] S Chesterman, *We, the Robots? Regulating Artificial Intelligence and the Limits of the Law* (Cambridge, Cambridge University Press, 2021).

[67] U Pagallo, 'Apples, Oranges, Robots: Four Misunderstandings in Today's Debate on the Legal Status of AI Systems' (2018) 376(2133) *Philosophical Transactions of the Royal Society A: Mathematical, Physical and Engineering Sciences* 20180168.

[68] NASA (n 7).

[69] See R Tutton, 'Sociotechnical Imaginaries and Techno-optimism: Examining Outer Space Utopias of Silicon Valley' (2021) 30(3) *Science as Culture* 416; JF Salazar and A Gorman (eds), *The Routledge Handbook of Social Studies of Outer Space* (Abingdon, Taylor & Francis, 2023).

[70] E Nesvold, *Off-Earth: Ethical Questions and Quandaries for Living in Outer Space* (Cambridge, MIT Press, 2023).

[71] K Weinersmith and Z Weinersmith, *A City on Mars: Can We Settle Space, Should We Settle Space, and Have We Really Thought this Through?* (Toronto, Penguin, 2023).

[72] W Barfield, *Cyber-Humans: Our Future with Machines* (Cham, Springer, 2015).

future generations of offspring on the ships, and eventual exoplanet colonies, live a minimally good life but that their births are contingent on them living genuinely good and fulfilling lives'.[73]

These views fall outside the timeframe of this book. The reason for this is not a lack of imagination; instead, following the methodological approach of the volume, the aim has been to get things right in the short term and mid-term because decisions in this timeframe will determine the long-term issues of the field. This is why the previous chapters of the book examined the most urgent hard cases of space law that advances of technology will multiply in the mid-term. From the establishment of celestial colonies and the appropriation of space resources to the direct applicability of international law to private companies, the new laws of outer space – that can be expected as a result of these hard cases – will likely define such long-term issues of the field, as imagining a right to self-determination and secession for the next-generation colonies on the Moon.[74]

Along the same lines, this chapter complemented the analysis of these hard cases with the moral and legal challenges that relate to a next generation of standards for robots and AI systems because the development of such standards and principles of applied ethics, like equality, will define the governance of outer space activities in the short term and mid-term. By the end of the 2030s, both the China-led ILRS and the US Artemis Accords should be operating at full speed. The same is true for the exploration and exploitation of rare elements on Mars by the 2040s. The speed of technological innovation, together with current efforts of standardisation of AI at the national, regional and international levels, support this view on new permanent colonies on the Moon and commuting missions on Mars. Space law experts should be attentive to the regulatory work in progress on how technology affects the epistemic and normative dimensions of human life and race to space. The challenges pretend *sui generis* standards and ad hoc standards. The more Mother Earth depends on space-related activities and space-based services progressively hinging on the behaviour and decision making of autonomous and intelligent systems, the more we should be attentive to what is unique to AI in outer space. Let's get the short- and mid-term challenges of AI agenthood right.

[73] S Umbrello and M Balistreri, 'Human Enhancement and Reproductive Ethics on Generation Ships' (2023) *Argumenta* 1.

[74] M Byers, 'Elon Musk, President of Mars?', *Washington Post*, 22 January 2016, www.washingtonpost.com/opinions/elon-musk.

Conclusions

There are three different kinds of novelty in this book's quest for 'the new laws of outer space'. The first reason why new laws should be expected relates to the obsolescence of the previous laws, in particular, the principles and provisions of the Golden Age of outer space in the 1960s and 1970s. Both the vague notions of these agreements and the structural problems of international law – such as coordination and potential clashes between public international law and national space law – have been exacerbated by: (i) the failure of the Moon Agreement in the 1980s; (ii) the privatisation of space since the 1990s; and (iii) the development of intergovernmental or bilateral agreements rather than forms of international cooperation. As a result of these trends, a whole set of hard cases has followed. The questions that triggered such cases include: (i) the applicability of principles and provisions of international law to private companies; (ii) the interplay between space law and other fields of international law, such as international humanitarian law; (iii) the moral and legal issues on the appropriability of space resources; and (iv) the establishment of celestial colonies and lunar stations. In legal theory, such hard cases of the law have sparked further disagreement among scholars.[1] Some, following Ronald Dworkin's ideas on a 'uniquely right answer', think that jurists can identify the principles of the system that fit the established law so as to apply such principles in a way that interprets the case in the best possible light.[2] Others claim that 'there is no possibility of treating the question raised by the various cases as if there were one uniquely correct answer to be found, as distinct from an answer which is a reasonable compromise between many conflicting interests'.[3] A third option concerns the material practice of governments and sovereign states with their bilateral or multilateral agreements that either fill the gaps of the current legal framework or diverge from it. The alternative was illustrated with the US-led Artemis Accords and its Chinese counterpart, the ILRS programme. In both cases, the new laws of outer space revolve around gathering consensus in the international community and that which civil lawyers refer to as the material, rather than formal, sources of law.[4]

[1] See B Bix, 'HLA. Hart and the "Open Texture" of Language' (1991) 10(1) *Law and Philosophy* 51; SJ Shapiro, 'The "Hart-Dworkin" Debate: A Short Guide for the Perplexed', Public Law and Legal Theory Working Paper Series, no 77, Michigan Law School, 2007.

[2] R. Dworkin, *A Matter of Principle* (Oxford, Oxford University Press, 1985).

[3] HLA Hart, *The Concept of Law* (Oxford, Oxford University Press, 1961) 128.

[4] U Pagallo, 'The Realignment of the Sources of the Law and their Meaning in an Information Society' (2015) 28 *Philosophy & Technology* 57.

The second set of reasons why new laws of outer space will likely come to life concerns the disruption of AI and other emerging technologies, such as anthropomorphic robots. In addition to the regulation of traditional actors in the field – that is, public organisations, governments and sovereign states in international space law, as well as private corporations and individuals in national space law – the next generation of regulatory efforts will increasingly concern a third type of actor: artificial agents and autonomous and intelligent systems. This book has discussed the myriad ways in which AI systems and robots help improve space-related activities and, moreover, materialise what a generation ago was only science fiction: the establishment of permanent celestial colonies. However, such progress entails significant risks caused by the unique features of the technology and its particular amount of opacity and unpredictability. Several law makers are currently at work to refine their rules: Canada presented its AI and Data Act in 2022; the UK released the principles that were designed to underpin its AI regulatory approach in 2023; the White House issued the Executive Order on the Safe, Secure, and Trustworthy Development and Use of Artificial Intelligence in October 2023; China adopted strict top-down regulations for algorithmic recommendation systems in 2022 and interim measures for generative AI in 2023; and the EU passed the AI Act in 2024. Although such a regulatory race to AI is impressive, it only partly covers the use of AI in space-related activities. It has been noted in this book that AI systems and smart robots pose unique moral and legal challenges when displayed in outer space. Therefore, a new generation of provisions and regulations concerning the use of AI systems and robots in space-related activities should be expected. Such provisions and regulations will further be complemented with the development of new standards. Even in the ideal scenario of clear rules, shared principles and law-abiding space actors, the uniqueness of the environment and the technologies that make next-generation missions and colonies feasible raises a further set of moral and legal dilemmas. Such problems regard either stricter or more flexible standards for AI in outer space, including norms and rules for HRI in deep-space missions. The book offered some guidance for this kind of investigation, drawing on previous work and current research on the safety and integrity management of missions and operations in harsh environments, trust and data protection in HRI, liability safeguards for autonomous systems and legal methods of technological regulation. The book has also discussed the benefits of the principle of functional equivalence for the use of AI under the extreme conditions of outer space.

The third set of reasons why we should expect new laws for outer space is the increasing interdependence between outer space and Mother Earth. Since the first chapter of this book, such interdependence has been illustrated with the 'enveloping effect' of third-order technologies providing the environment in which further technologies interact. Around 12,000 satellites placed into Earth's orbit – whilst such figures keep growing vertiginously – highlight this enveloping effect both because of the environmental sustainability of the space sector and the integration of outer space activities with the protection of critical digital infrastructures on Earth. Although outer space is a unique environment with proper laws – both astrophysical and prudential – such laws should be grasped in close connection with Earth's environment and therefore more as a single interconnected ecosystem. New fields of legal regulation follow as a result. They complement the traditional focus of experts in space law with a new generation of specialists in environmental space law, cybersecurity space law, space data protection and privacy law, machinery safety for smart robots, or consumer law. Some legal systems, such as EU law, have undertaken considerable efforts in this regard. Still, it seems fair to concede that most of the work remains to be done. The problem revolves not only around the need for new regulations in cybersecurity space law, environmental space law etc, but also new models of space governance that will establish and implement policies, procedures and standards for the integration of space-related activities with the protection of critical digital infrastructures and the interdependence between space and Earth environments.

The three sets of reasons making the new laws of outer space likely to be set are not mutually exclusive, but rather interdependent. Advancements in technology can accelerate the obsolescence of traditional provisions of space law, just as environmental and cybersecurity concerns can shape the regulation and governance of AI systems. Accordingly, this book has illustrated what the new laws of outer space may look like in terms of the legal regulation of AI systems and smart robots (Chapters 5 and 10), the establishment of celestial colonies (Chapters 6 and 9), the environmental sustainability of satellite activities (Chapters 7 and 8), the integration of cybersecurity space law with the protection of critical digital infrastructures on Earth (Chapter 8) and the further development of standards (Chapter 10). It has examined both the military and civilian sides of these legal problems.

However, the search for the new laws of outer space must not be viewed in strictly legal terms. Since the Introduction to this book, drawing on the warnings of Aristotle's work on ethics and politics, principles and rules of the law, its very constitution and regulations, were further referred to the ethical dimension of the political community – that is, its ethos. It is the role of politics to shape the constitution of a state and its norms, according to the moral grounds on which the public dimension of civic life lies. This book has discussed the manifold features of this side of the law with examples of soft law, customary law, international collaboration and open access policies. The moral grounds of the community are essential not only to determine the principles and rules that should be established, but also the ways in which such principles and rules can be preserved. The risk is as old as Aristotle's sarcastic remarks in the sixth book of *Politics*:

> But it is not the greatest or only task of the legislator or of those who desire to construct a constitution of this kind merely to set it up, but rather to ensure its preservation; for it is not difficult for any form of constitution to last for one or two or three days.[5]

In the quest for the new laws of outer space, scholars and institutions will thus pay attention to how amendments and new agreements, legislation and governance of

[5] Aristotle, *Politics*, by J Barnes (ed and trans) (Princeton, Princeton University Press, 2017) 1319 B.

space activities and missions must strengthen the ethos. Law makers of the Golden Age admirably envisioned some of these principles, such as space as the 'province of mankind' or 'astronauts as envoys of mankind'. The new ethos of outer space will complement these principles and provisions by acknowledging three novelties of our age: (i) the interdependence between the Earth and space environments; (ii) the increasing dependence of our planet on space-related activities; and (iii) the new partnership between human actors and artificial agents that can well represent the 'new face' of space missions. None of these goals on sustainability, safety and security, and sound technological innovation represents an easy task. However, it must be clear that the resilience of the body politic – namely, of its governance and multiple laws, norms, rules and acts – rests on whether both the constitution and the laws will 'make the citizens good by forming habits in them'.[6]

Aristotle's reflection has guided this quest for the laws of new spaces despite his misguided views on technology and the laws of physics. The classic question of how to govern a new space or territory concerns moral values, economic interests and legal principles that will be complemented by both the regulatory claims of technology and the laws of physics. This book has focused on this interplay of *nomos* and *ethos*, *poiesis* and *politeia*, discussing multiple efforts to amend or to set up new laws for outer space. Since such efforts will likely multiply over the next couple of decades, it has provided some guidance for what laws should be expected in the 2030s and even the 2040s. The view did not rest on any prophetic powers, but rather on Aristotle's warnings relating to the establishment and resilience of the body politic. This book has examined a list of things to get right in the short term and mid-term because such decisions will determine the long-term issues of the field, with increasingly autonomous and intelligent systems creating their own colonies even beyond our solar system.

This scenario entails a final Aristotelian warning. Aristotle deemed humans to be a 'political species', a social animal, or *zoon politikón*, but freely admitted that all humans aim to get rich, love themselves above all else and are ruled by their own habits.[7] Human nature suggests that creating legal systems is easier than ensuring their conservation. The success of projects, such as China's-led ILRS and the US's Artemis Accords, will critically depend on the ethos of next-generation colonies in the mid-2030s. In *The Nichomachean Ethics*, Aristotle distinguishes four forms of political and economic organisations: (i) 'fathers and sons' (monarchy); (ii) 'masters and slaves' (tyranny); (iii) 'husbands and wives' (aristocracies and republics); and (iv) 'between brothers' (democracy).[8] The interdependence between Earth and space environments, the increasing dependence of our planet on space-related activities, and the new partnership between human actors and artificial agents can reinforce this 'brotherhood'. The ISS has been a model of

[6] Aristotle, *The Nichomachean Ethics*, R Crisp (ed and trans) (Cambridge, Cambridge University Press, 2000) 1103 B.
[7] ibid 1150 a 1.
[8] ibid s VIII.12.

international collaboration, but alas it will be terminated and sent spiralling into the Pacific Ocean in 2031. China and the US intend to establish lunar colonies and stations soon after. According to Aristotle, the risk of political and economic organisations between brothers is a state of anarchy.

This book has explained why this state of anarchy is unlikely and, yet, why we should be concerned about the current fragmentation of the international legal framework. These worries comprise public habits and individual attitudes of economic aristocracies. The aim of the 'true law maker' should be to take care of virtue, 'for he wishes to make his fellow citizens good and obedient to the laws'.[9] This book has noted that trust is not a virtue, that values can be inserted into the state-transition system of AI smart robots and that it is still a valid truth that the opinion of what is lawful or necessary strengthens the resilience of the body politic, whether through the behaviour of human beings (Aristotle) or of artificial agents (our age). The wonders of technology will require a robust dose of ethos over the next few decades. AI systems and smart robots can help humans tackle this endeavour not only through the means and goals of environmental sustainability, cybersecurity or traffic management systems, but also through autonomous and intelligent artificial agents, which will play a critical role in the formation and strength of the new moral grounds of the body politic with its *nomos* and *politeia*. This critical role emphasises the uniqueness of AI and the novelties of our age. While waiting for the next grand international agreement in the long term, we should get the short- and mid-term issues of the new laws of outer space right. The exponential pace of technological innovation will test the traditional linear approach of politics and legislation. The law should be ready.

[9] ibid 1102 a 8.

BIBLIOGRAPHY

Abbasi, M and El Hanandeh, A (2016) Forecasting Municipal Solid Waste Generation using Artificial Intelligence Modelling Approaches, *Waste Management*, 56: 13–22.

Ajani, G (1995) By Chance and Prestige: Legal Transplants in Russia and Eastern Europe, *American Journal of Comparative Law*, 43(1): 93–117.

Alabdulkareem A, Alhakbani N and Al-Nafjan, A (2022) A Systematic Review of Research on Robot-Assisted Therapy for Children with Autism, *Sensors*, 22(3): 944.

Albert, C (2014) Liability in International Law and the Ramifications on Commercial Space Launches and Space Tourism, *Loyola of Los Angeles International and Comparative Law Review*, 36: 233–61.

Allison, AL (2020) Requirements for Obtaining Spectrum and of Orbital Approvals for Small Satellite Constellations. In: *Handbook of Small Satellites: Technology, Design, Manufacture, Applications, Economics and Regulation*, Dordrecht, Springer.

Alonso, E et al (2012) Evaluating Rare-Earth Element Availability: A Case with Revolutionary Demand from Clean Technologies, *Environmental Science and Technology*, 46(6): 3406–14.

Alsharqi, M, Woodward, W, Mumith, J, Markham, D, Upton, R and Leeson, P (2018) Artificial Intelligence and Echocardiography, *Echo Research and Practice*, 5(4): R115–R125.

Alvarado, SC (2023) The Regulation of the 'Open Data' Policy and Its Elements: The Legal Perspective of the EU Copernicus Programme. In: *Space Law in a Networked World*, Brill, Nijhoff.

Apollonius (2014) *The Argonautica*, L Norfolk (ed), London, The Folio Society.

Aristotle (2000) *The Nichomachean Ethics*, Robert Crisp (ed and trans), Cambridge, Cambridge University Press.

——. (2017) *Politics*, J Barnes (ed and trans), Princeton, Princeton University Press.

Arkin, RC (2007) *Governing Lethal Behaviour: Embedding Ethics in a Hybrid Deliberative/Hybrid Robot Architecture*, Report GIT-GVU-07-11, Georgia Institute of Technology's GVU Center, Atlanta, GA.

Aylett, R, Vargas, PA and Sharkey, N (2021) 10 Emotions: Could Robots Have Feelings? In: *The Living with Robots: What Every Anxious Human Needs to Know*, Cambridge, MA, MIT Press.

Baker, RB (2010) Customary International Law in the 21st Century: Old Challenges and New Debates, *European Journal of International Law*, 21(1): 173–204.

Balistreri, M and Umbrello, S (2023) Modifying the Environment or Human Nature? What is the Right Choice for Space Travel and Mars Colonisation?, *NanoEthics*, 17(1): 1–13.

Barfield, W (2015) *Cyber-humans: Our Future with Machines*, Cham, Springer.

Barfield, W and Pagallo, U (eds) (2018) *Research Handbook on the Law of Artificial Intelligence*, Cheltenham, Edward Elgar.

Barfield, W and Pagallo, U (2020) *Advanced Introduction to the Law and Artificial Intelligence*, Cheltenham, Edward Elgar.

Barfield, W, Weng, Y-H and Pagallo, U (eds) (2024) *The Cambridge Handbook of the Law, Policy, and Regulation for Human–Robot Interaction*, Cambridge, Cambridge University Press.

Barlow, JP (1996) 'A Declaration of the Independence of Cyberspace', available at https://www.eff.org/it/cyberspace-independence.

Bassi, E (2020) From Here to 2023: Civil Drones Operations and the Setting of New Legal Rules for the European Single Sky, *Journal of Intelligent Robotic Systems*, 100, 493–503.

Bassi, E and Pagallo, U (2024) The Democratization of Outer Space: On Law, Ethics, and Technology. In: M Arias-Oliva et al (eds), *Smart Ethics in the Digital World – Ethicomp*, Madrid, Dialnet.

Bayern, S (2016) The Implications of Modern Business–Entity Law for the Regulation of Autonomous Systems, *European Journal of Risk Regulation*, 7(2): 297–309.

Bekey, GA (2005) *Autonomous Robots: From Biological Inspiration to Implementation and Control*, Cambridge, MA, MIT Press.

Benkö, M (1985) *Space Law in the United Nations*, Leiden, Martinus Nijhoff.

Berge JV and L Odgaard (2023) NATO in the Global Commons: Defending Outer Space against Threats from China, *International Journal*, 78(4). DOI: 10.1177/00207020231217119.

Bertolini, A and Episcopo, F (2021) The Expert Group's Report on Liability for Artificial Intelligence and Other Emerging Digital Technologies: A Critical Assessment, *European Journal of Risk Regulation*, 12(3): 644–59.

Blount, PJ (2017) Satellites are Just Things on the Internet of Things, *Air and Space Law*, 3: 273–93.

Blount, PP and Robinson, CJ (2016) One Small Step: The Impact of the US Commercial Space Launch Competitiveness Act of 2015 on the Exploitation of Resources in Outer Space, *North Carolina Journal of Law & Technology*, 18(2): 160–86.

Blumenstock, J (2018) Don't Forget People in the Use of Big Data for Development, *Nature*, 561(7722): 170–72.

Bohr, N (1913) On the Constitution of Atoms and Molecules, *London, Edinburgh, and Dublin Philosophical Magazine and Journal of Science*, 26(151): 1–25.

Boley, A and Byers, M (2020) US Policy Puts the Safe Development of Space at Risk, *Science*, 370(6513): 174–75.

Bolton, M, Raven, R and Mintrom, M (2019) Can AI Transform Public Decision-Making for Sustainable Development? An Exploration of Critical Earth System Governance Questions, *Earth System Governance*, 9: 100116.

Boone, N and Bettinger, R (2023) Simulation of Debris Events in Selected Low Lunar Orbits. *Journal of the Astronautical Sciences*, 70(3): 16.

Bowen, BE (2022) *Original Sin: Power, Technology and War in Outer Space*, London, Hurst.

Bradford, A (2012) The Brussels Effect, *Northwestern University Law Review*, 107(1): 1–68.

——. (2020) *The Brussels Effect: How the European Union Rules the World*, Oxford, Oxford University Press.

Bratu, I (2021) Blaming Galileo: Liability for Damage Caused by Artificial Intelligence Operating Based on GNSS, *Proceedings of the International Institute of Space Law*, 64(6), December.

Bratu I, Lodder AR and van der Linden, T (2021) Autonomous Space Objects and International Space Law: Navigating the Liability Gap, *Indonesian Journal of International Law*, 18(3): 423–46.

Breuker, J et al (eds) (2009) *Law, Ontologies and the Semantic Web: Channelling the Legal Information Flood*, Amsterdam, IOS Press.

Bix, B (1991) HLA Hart and the 'open texture' of language, *Law and Philosophy*, 10(1): 51–72.

Brzezinski, M (2007) *Red Moon Rising: Sputnik and the Hidden Rivalries That Ignited the Space Age*, New York, Henry Holt & Co.

Byers, M (2016) Elon Musk, President of Mars?, *Washington Post*, 22 January, available at www.washingtonpost.com/opinions/elon-musk.

Byers, M and Boley, A (2023) *Who Owns Outer Space? International Law, Astrophysics, and the Sustainable Development of Space*, Cambridge, Cambridge University Press.

Caley, A (2014) Liability in International Law and the Ramifications on Commercial Space Launches and Space Tourism, *Loyola of Los Angeles International and Comparative Law Review*, 36: 233–61.

Calo, R and Citron, DK (2020) The Automated Administrative State: A Crisis of Legitimacy, *Emory Law Journal*, 70: 797–846.

Camporeale, E (2023) Artificial Intelligence for Space Weather Forecasting. In M Madiand and O Sokolova (eds), *Artificial Intelligence for Space: Trends, Applications, and Perspectives*, Boca Raton, FL, CRC Press.

Castelfranchi, C and Falcone, R (1998) Principles of Trust for MAS: Cognitive Anatomy, Social Importance, and Quantification, *Third International Conference on Multi-agent Systems*, Paris, France: IEEE Computer Society.

Cavoukian, A (2009) 'Privacy by Design: The 7 Foundational Principles', Information and privacy Commissioner of Ontario, Canada, available at https://privacy.ucsc.edu/resources/privacy-by-design---foundational-principles.pdf.

Chandani, A, Prakash, O, Prakash, P, Wagholikar, S and Mehta, M (2022). Robots and Artificial Intelligence: An Aid to Dependent People. In: A Joshi, M Mahmud, RG Ragel and NV Thakur (eds), *Information and Communication Technology for Competitive Strategies*, Springer, Singapore.

Chen, H and Breazeal, C (2021) Toward Designing Social Human–Robot Interactions for Deep Space Exploration, *arXiv*, 2105.08631, available at https://arxiv.org/abs/2105.08631.

Chesterman, S (2021) *We, the Robots? Regulating Artificial Intelligence and the Limits of the Law*, Cambridge, Cambridge University Press.

Chopra, S and White, LF (2011) *A Legal Theory for Autonomous Artificial Agents*, Ann Arbor, University of Michigan Press.

Christol, CQ (1980) International Liability for Damage Caused by Space Objects, *American Journal of International Law*, 74(2): 346–71.

——. (1982) *The Modern International Law of Outer Space*, New York, Pergamon Press.

Cobbe, J, Veale, M and Singh, J (2023) Understanding Accountability in Algorithmic Supply Chains, *Proceedings Association for Computing Machinery*, New York.

Colavito, J (2014) *Jason and the Argonauts through the Ages*, Jefferson, NC, MacFarland.

Collis, C (2017) Territories beyond Possession? Antarctica and Outer Space, *Polar Journal*, 7(2): 287–302.

Committee on the Peaceful Uses of Outer Space (2020) *Report on the United Nations/Austria World Space Forum 'Access to Space4All'*, Scientific and Technical Subcommittee, Fifty-Seventh Session of COPUOUS, Vienna, February, available at https://www.unoosa.org/res/oosadoc/data/documents/2020/aac_105c_12020crp/aac_105c_12020crp_11_0_html/AC105_C1_2020_CRP11E.pdf.

Cooper, F (2005) *Colonialism in Question: Theory, Knowledge History*, Berkeley, University of California Press.

Council of the European Union (2023) *Draft Council conclusions on "Fair and Sustainable Use of Space"*, 8962/23, available at https://data.consilium.europa.eu/doc/document/ST-8962-2023-INIT/en/pdf#:~:text=The%20conclusions%20recall%20that%20space,and%20sustainable%20use%20of%20space.

Dallas, JA, Raval, S, Gaitan, JA, Saydam, S and Dempster, AG (2020) The Environmental Impact of Emissions from Space Launches: A Comprehensive Review, *Journal of Cleaner Production*, 255: 120209.

Davenport, C and Kalakota, R (2019) The Potential for Artificial Intelligence in Healthcare, *Future Healthcare Journal*, 6(2): 94–98.

Davis, C and Sundahl, MJ (2017) The Hague Working Group on Space Resources: Creating the Legal Building Blocks for a New Industry, *Law Faculty Articles and Essays*, Cleveland State University, no. 1044.

De Man, P (2017) State Practice, Domestic Legislation and the Interpretation of Fundamental Principles of International Space Law, *Space Policy*, 42: 92–102.

De Zwart, M (2021) To the Moon and beyond: The Artemis Accords and the Evolution of Space Law. In: M de Zwart and S Henderson (eds), *Commercial and Military Uses of Outer Space. Issues in Space*, Singapore, Springer.

Deem, CL (1983) Liability of Private Space Transportation Companies to Their Customers, *International In-House Counsel Journal*, 51: 340–75.

Demidov O and Persi Paoli, G (2020) *Supply Chain Security in the Cyber Age: Sector Trends, Current Threats and Multi-stakeholder Responses*, UNIDIR, United Nations.

Dempsey, PS (2016) National Laws Governing Commercial Space Activities: Legislation, Regulation, & Enforcement, *Northwestern Journal of International Law and Business*, 36(1): 1–44.

Dennerley, JA (2018) State Liability for Space Object Collisions: The Proper Interpretation of 'Fault' for the Purposes of International Space Law, *European Journal of International Law*, 29(1): 281–301.

Deplano, R (2021) The Artemis Accords: Evolution or Revolution in International Space Law?, *International & Comparative Law Quarterly*, 70(3): 799–819.

Determann, JM (2019) *Space Science and the Arab World: Astronauts, Observatories and Nationalism in the Middle East*, London, Bloomsbury.

D'Olimpio, L (2018) Trust as a Virtue in Education, *Educational Philosophy and Theory*, 50(2): 193–202.

Duffy, BR (2003) Anthropomorphism and the Social Robot, *Robotics and Autonomous Systems*, 42: 177–90.
Dunnett, O (2023) The Spaces of Outer Space. In: *The Routledge Handbook of Social Studies of Outer Space*, Abingdon, Routledge.
Durante, M (2010) What is the Model of Trust for Multi-agent Systems? Whether or Not E-Trust Applies to Autonomous Agents, *Knowledge, Technology and Policy*, 23(3–4): 347–66.
Durante, M (2021) *Computational Power: The Impact of ICT on Law, Society and Knowledge*, Abingdon: Routledge.
Durante, M and Floridi, L (2022) A Legal Principles-Based Framework for AI Liability Regulation. In: J Mökander and M Ziosi (eds), *The 2021 Yearbook of the Digital Ethics Lab. Digital Ethics Lab Yearbook*, Cham, Springer.
Dworkin, R (1985) *A Matter of Principle*, Oxford, Oxford University Press.
Easterbrook, FH (1996) Cyberspace and the Law of the Horse, *University of Chicago Legal Forum*, 207, Article 7.
ECSS (2023) 'Active Standards', available at https://ecss.nl/standards/active-standards.
Egloff, F et al (2019) *Public Attribution of Cyber Incidents. CSS Analyses in Security Studies*, ETH Zurich.
Ellis, JJ (2016) *The Quartet: Orchestrating the Second American Revolution*, New York, Vintage.
Elvis, M et al (2021) Concentrated Lunar Resources: Imminent Implications for Governance and Justice, *Philosophical Transactions of the Royal Society: A Mathematical Physical and Engineering Sciences*, 379.
Engstrom, DE, Ho, DE, Sharkey, CM and Cuéllar, MF (2020) Government by Algorithm: AI in Federal Administrative Agencies. *NYU School of Law, Public Law Research Paper No 20-54.*
Ernest, VC (1990) Third Party Liability of the Private Space Industry: To Pay What No One Has Paid before, *Case Western Reserve Law Review*, 41: 503–41.
ESPI (2022) Report 84 – The war in Ukraine from a space cybersecurity perspective, European Space Policy Institute, Vienna.
European Council (2019) *Conclusions of 12 December 2019*, Brussels, EUCO 10/11, available at https://data.consilium.europa.eu/doc/document/ST-10-2011-INIT/en/pdf.
European Space Policy Institute (ESPI) (2022) *Rising Opportunities in the Satellite Connectivity Market: Eutalsat and One Web Combination*, ESPI Brief No 60.
——. (2022) *The War in Ukraine from a Space Cybersecurity Perspective*, Report 84, Vienna.
European Commission (2019) 'Communication from the Commission to the European Parliament, the European Council, the Council, the European Economic and Social Committee and the Committee of the Regions, the European Green Deal, COM (2019) 640 final.
——. (2021) Proposal for a Regulation of the European Parliament and of the Council Laying down Harmonized Rules on Artificial Intelligence (Artificial Intelligence Act) and Amending Certain Union Legislative Acts, COM (2021) 206 final 2021/0106.
——. (2022) Joint Communication to the European Parliament and the Council: An EU Approach for Space Traffic Management, JOIN (2022) 4.
——. (2023) EU Space Programme, Defense Industry and Space, Brussels, available at https://defence-industry-space.ec.europa.eu/eu-space-policy/eu-space-programme_en.
European Space Agency (ESA 2016) What's Space 4.0?, available at https://www.esa.int/About_Us/Ministerial_Council_2016/What_is_space_4.0.
European Space Agency (ESA) (2022) Mitigating Space Debris Generation, available at www.esa.int/Safety_Security/Space_Debris/Mitigating_space_debris_generation.
——. (2023) ESA Moves Ahead with In-Orbit Servicing Missions, available at https://www.esa.int/Enabling_Support/Preparing_for_the_Future/Discovery_and_Preparation/ESA_moves_ahead_with_In-Orbit_Servicing_missions2.
——. (2023) Space Debris by the Numbers, available at https://www.esa.int/Space_Safety/Space_Debris/Space_debris_by_the_numbers.
Falco, G (2018) *The Vacuum of Space Cybersecurity*, 2018 AIAA SPACE and Astronautics Forum and Exposition.

Falco, G and Gordon, NG (2023) Cybersecurity and Human Spaceflight Safety, *2023 IEEE Aerospace Conference*, 1–7.

Federal Aviation Administration (FAA) (2021) *Commercial Space Astronaut Wings Program*, order 8800.2, July 20, available at https://www.faa.gov/documentLibrary/media/Order/FAA_Order_8800.2.pdf.

Feichtner, I (2019), Mining for Humanity in the Deep Sea and Outer Space: The Role of Small States and International Law in the Extraterritorial Expansion of Extraction, *Leiden Journal of International Law*, 32(2): 255–74.

Field, AJ (2014) Schelling, von Neumann, and the Event that Didn't Occur, *Games*, 5(1): 53–89.

Filthaut, L (2023) Cosmic Troubleshooting: Designing Supervised Autonomy for Astronaut–Robot Coaction in Space, Doctoral dissertation, Delft University of Technology.

Flanagan, M, Howe, DC and Nissenbaum, M (2008) Embodying Values in Technology: Theory and Practice. In: J van den Hoven and J Weckert (eds), *Information Technology and Moral Philosophy*, Cambridge, Cambridge University Press.

Floridi, L (2013) *Information Ethics*, Oxford, Oxford University Press.

——. (2013) Technology's In-Betweenness, *Philosophy & Technology*, 26: 111–15.

——. (2016) Faultless Responsibility: On the Nature and Allocation of Moral Responsibility for Distributed Moral Actions, *Philosophical Transactions of the Royal Society A*, 374: 201601122.

——. (ed) (2015) *The Onlife Manifesto*, Dordrecht: Springer.

Floridi, L and Sanders, J (2004) On the Morality of Artificial Agents, *Minds and Machines*, 14(3): 349–79.

Floridi, L et al (2018) AI4People – An Ethical Framework for a Good AI Society: Opportunities, Risks, Principles, and Recommendations, *Minds and Machines*, 28(4): 689–707.

Foster, C (2016) Excuse Me, You're Mining My Asteroid: Space Property Rights and the US Space Resource Exploration and Utilization Act of 2015, *University of Illinois Journal of Law, Technology & Policy*, 2: 407–30.

Foust J (2020) NASA Offers to Buy Lunar Samples to Set Space Resources Precedent, *Space News*, 10 September, spacenews.com/nasa-offers-to-buy-lunar-samples-to-setspace-resources-precedent.

Franssen, M, Lokhorst, G-J and van de Poel, I (2023) Philosophy of Technology. In: EN Zalta and U Nodelman (eds), *The Stanford Encyclopedia of Philosophy*, available at https://plato.stanford.edu/archives/spr2023/entries/technology.

Freeland, S (2010) Matching Detail with Practice: The Essential Elements of National Space Legislation. In: CM Jorgensen (ed), *Proceedings of International Institute of Space Law*, The Hague, Eleven International Publishing.

Freeland, S (2020) Legal Issues Related to the Future Advent of Small Satellite Constellations. In: *Handbook of Small Satellites: Technology, Design, Manufacture, Applications, Economics and Regulation*, Dordrecht, Springer.

Freeland, S and Jakhu, R (2014) What's Human Rights Got to Do with Outer Space? Everything! In: R Moro-Aguilar, PJ Blount and T Masson-Zwaan, *Proceedings of the International Institute of Space Law*, The Hague, Eleven International Publishing.

Freeland, S and Ireland-Piper, D (2022). Space Law, Human Rights and Corporate Accountability, *UCLA Journal of International Law and Foreign Affairs*, 26(1): 1–34.

Friedman, B and Hendry, DG (2019) *Value Sensitive Design: Shaping Technology with Moral Imagination*, Boston, MIT Press.

Froehlich, A (ed) (2020) *Outer Space and Cyberspace*, Dordrecht: Springer.

Frohloff, J (2019) Arbitration in Space Disputes, *Arbitration International*, 35(3): 309–29.

Gabrynowicz, JI (2010) One Half Century and Counting: The Evolution of US National Space Law and Three Long-Term Emerging Issues, *Harvard Law and Policy Review*, 4: 405–26.

Gailhofer, P et al (2021) *The Role of Artificial Intelligence in the European Green Deal*, Study for the Special Committee on Artificial Intelligence in a Digital Age (AIDA), Policy Department for Economic, Scientific and Quality of Life Policies, European Parliament, Luxembourg.

Gao, Q, Liu, J and Ju, Z (2020) Robust Real-Time Hand Detection and Localization for Space Human–Robot Interaction Based on Deep Learning, *Neurocomputing*, 390: 198–206.

Ghidini, T (2018). Regenerative Medicine and 3D Bioprinting for Human Space Exploration and Planet Colonisation, *Journal of Thoracic Disease*, 10(Suppl 20): S2363.
Goguichvili, S, Linenberger, A, Gillette, A and Novak, A (2021) The Global Legal Landscape of Space: Who Writes the Rules on the Final Frontier?, *Wilson Center*, 1 October, available at https://www.wilsoncenter.org/article/global-legal-landscape-space-who-writes-rules-final-frontier.
Goswami, N (2018). China in Space: Ambitions and Possible Conflict, *Strategic Studies Quarterly*, 12(1): 74–97.
Gragl, P (2018), *Legal Monism: Law, Philosophy, and Politics*, Oxford: Oxford University Press.
Graves, R (1990 [1955]) *The Greek Myths*, Baltimore: Penguin.
Greg, P (1880) *Across the Zodiac*, London, Trübner.
Guastini, R (1998) Teoria e dogmatica delle fonti. In: *Trattato Cicu-Messineo*, Milan, Giuffrè.
Gugunskiy, D and Emelianova, N (2021) Space Activities and Sustainable Development Goals. In: EG Popkova and BS Sergi (eds), *Modern Global Economic System: Evolutional Development vs Revolutionary Leap*. Cham, Springer.
Gunkel, DJ (2023) *Person, Thing, Robot: A Moral and Legal Ontology for the 21st Century and Beyond*, Cambridge, MA, MIT Press.
Guyot, J, Akhil, R and Rouillon, S (2023) Oligopoly Competition between Satellite Constellations Will Reduce Economic Welfare from Orbit Use, *Proceedings of the National Academy of Sciences*, 120(43): e2221343120.
Habuka, H (2023) Japan's Approach to AI Regulation and its Impact on the 2023 G7 Presidency, *Center for Strategic & International Studies*, February.
Hall, SJ (2007) *Beyond AI: Creating the Conscience of the Machine*, New York, Prometheus.
Hallevy, G (2015) *Liability for Crimes Involving Artificial Intelligence Systems*, Dordrecht, Springer.
Hart, HLA (1961) *The Concept of Law*, Oxford, Oxford University Press.
Hashmi, M, Casanovas, P and de Koker, L (2018) Legal Compliance through Design: Preliminary Results of a Literature Survey, *TERECOM2018@ JURIX, Technologies for Regulatory Compliance*, https://ceur-ws.org/Vol-2309/06.pdf.
Hastings, A and Wysham, DB (2010) Regime Shifts in Ecological Systems Can Occur with No Warning, *Ecology Letters*, 13(4): 464–72.
Hayek, FA (1982) *Law, Legislation and Liberty: A New Statement of the Liberal Principles of Justice and Political Economy*, Chicago, University of Chicago Press.
Hechler, D (ed) (2023) Cybersecurity in Outer Space Unprepared?, *Tag CYBER Security Annual*, 9(3).
Hersh, MH (2012), *Inventing the American Astronaut*, London, Palgrave Macmillan.
Hertzfeld, HR (2021) Unsolved Issues of Compliance with the Registration Convention, *Journal of Space Safety Engineering*, 8(3): 238–44.
Higgins JP (2016) Smartphone Applications for Patients' Health and Fitness, *American Journal of Medicine*, 129(1): 11–19.
Hildebrandt, M (2010) Criminal Liability and 'Smart' Environments, *Conference on the Philosophical Foundations of Criminal Law at Rutgers-Newark*, August.
Hildebrandt, M (2015) *Smart Technologies and the End(s) of Law: Novel Entanglements of Law and Technology*, Cheltenham, Edward Elgar.
High-Level Expert Group (HLEG) (2019) Ethics Guidelines for Trustworthy AI, Brussels: European Commission, online at https://digital-strategy.ec.europa.eu/en/library/ethics-guidelines-trustworthy-ai.
——. (2019) *Liability for Artificial Intelligence and Other Emerging Technologies*, Report from the European Commission's Group of Experts on Liability and New Technologies, available at https://op.europa.eu/en/publication-detail/-/publication/1c5e30be-1197-11ea-8c1f-01aa75ed71a1/language-en.
Hobbes, T (2011 [1651]) *Leviathan*, Seattle, Pacific Publishing Studio.
Hoffmann, M and Bergamasco, F (2020) Space Resources from the Perspective of Sustainability: Legal Aspects, *Global Sustainability*, 3: E4. DOI: 10.1017/sus.2019.27.
International Astronomical Union (IAU) and UN Office for Outer Space Affairs (UNOOSA) (2021) *Dark and Quiet Skies for Science and Society – Report and Recommendations*, International Astronomical Union and UNOOSA, C Walker and S Di Pippo (eds), available at www.iau.org/static/publications/dqskies-book-29-12-20.pdf.

——. (2022), *Dark and Quiet Skies II for Science and Society – Working Group Reports*, C Walker and P Benvenuti (eds), available at https://zenodo.org/records/5874725.

IEEE Standard Association (2020) IEEE Recommended Practice for Assessing the Impact of Autonomous and Intelligent Systems on Human Well-Being, *IEEE 7010-2020*, *16*, 1–96, available at https://ieeexplore.ieee.org/document/9084219.

Ihde, D (2004) Philosophy of Technology. In: P Kemp (ed), *Philosophical Problems Today*, Dordrecht, Springer.

International Telecommunication Union (ITU) (2014) *Characteristics, Definitions and Spectrum Requirement of Nanosatellites and Picosatellites, as Well as Systems Composed of Such Satellites*, ITU-R SA.2312-0.

——. (2019) ITU World Radiocommunication Conference Adopts New Regulatory Procedures for Non-geostationary Satellites, press release, 20 November, available at www.itu.int/en/mediacentre/Pages/2019-PR23.aspx.

IOActive (2022) Missed Calls for SATCOM Cybersecurity: SATCOM Terminal Cyberattacks Open the War in Ukraine, available at https://ioactive.com/missed-calls-for-satcom-cybersecurity/#_ftn14.

Ireland-Piper, D (2021) Extraterritoriality in East Asia: Jurisdiction and Criminal Law in China, Japan, and South Korea. In: D Ireland-Piper (ed), *Recapping Principles of Jurisdiction at International Law*, Cheltenham, Edward Elgar.

ISO (2020) *Robots and Robotic Devices – Safety Requirements for Personal Care Robots*, available at https://www.iso.org/standard/53820.html.

Jamal, SS, Goyal, A, Shanker, A and Grover, T (2017) Predicting Neurological Adverse Drug Reactions Based on Biological, Chemical and Phenotypic Properties of Drugs Using Machine Learning Models, *Scientific Reports*, 7(1): 872.

Jans, JH (2010) Stop the Integration Principle?, *Fordham International Law Journal*, 33: 1533–47.

Jenkins, R, Cerný, D and Hríbek, T (eds) (2022) *Autonomous Vehicle Ethics: The Trolley Problem and Beyond*, Oxford, Oxford University Press.

Jobin, A, Ienca, M and Vayena, E (2019) The Global Landscape of AI Ethics Guidelines, *Nature Machine Intelligence*, 1: 389–99.

Jones, N (2018) How to Stop Data Centres from Gobbling up the World's Electricity, *Nature*, 561: 163–66.

Johnson, C (2020) SpaceWatchGL Feature: The Space Law Context of the Artemis Accords: Part II, *Space Watch Global*, available at https://spacewatch.global/2020/05/spacewatchgl-feature-the-spacelaw-context-of-the-artemis-accords-part-2.

Kant, I (1903) *Perpetual Peace: A Philosophical Essay*, MC Smith (trans), Crows Nest, Allen & Unwin.

Karnow, CEA (1996) Liability for Distributed Artificial Intelligence, *Berkeley Technology Law Journal*, 11: 147–83.

Kelsen, H (1945) *General Theory of the Law and the State*, A Wedberg (trans), Cambridge, MA, Harvard University Press.

Kempt, H, Heilinger, JC and Nagel, SK (2022) Relative Explainability and Double Standards in Medical Decision-Making, *Ethics and Information Technology*, 24: 20.

Keogh, L (2023) EU Data Protection Considerations for the Space Sector. In: P J Blount and M Hofmann (eds), *Space Law in a Networked World*, Leiden, Brill Nijhoff.

Kessler, DJ and Cour-Palais, BG (1978) Collision Frequency of Artificial Satellites: The Creation of a Debris Belt, *Journal of Geophysical Research: Space Physics*, 83(A6): 2637–46.

Khera, H and Vertadier, H (eds) (2023) *Lunar Policy Handbook*, Moon Dialogs.

Kingston, S (2012) *Greening EU Competition Law and Policy*, Cambridge, Cambridge University Press.

Klüber, K and Onnasch, L (2022) Appearance is Not Everything: Preferred Feature Combinations for Care Robots, *Computers in Human Behavior*, 128: 107128.

Kong, D (2017) Shaping a Legal Framework for China's BeiDou Navigation Satellite System, *Space Policy*, 42: 26–30.

Koops, B-J (2006) Should ICT Regulation be Technology-Neutral? In: BJ Koops et al (eds), *Starting Points for ICT Regulation: Deconstructing Prevalent Policy One-Liners*, The Hague, TMC Asser.

Krägeloh, CU, Bharatharaj, J, Kutty, SKS, Irmala, PR and Huang, L (2019) Questionnaires to Measure Acceptability of Social Robots: A Critical Review, *Robotics*, 8(4): 88.

Krakat, MB (2018) Genuine Links beyond State and Market Control: The Sale of Citizenship by Investment in International and Supranational Legal Perspective, *Bond Law Review*, 30(1): 145–84.

Kunz, J (1953) The Nature of Customary International Law, *American Journal of International Law*, 47(4): 662–69.

Kurzweil, R (2006) *The Singularity is Near: When Humans Transcend Biology*, New York, Penguin.

Lamsal, R and Kumar, TVV (2020) Artificial Intelligence and Early Warning Systems. In: TVV Kumar and K Sud (eds), *AI and Robotics in Disaster Studies. Disaster Research and Management Series on the Global South*, Singapore, Palgrave Macmillan.

Lapenta, G, Califano, F, Dupuis, R, Innocenti, ME and Pedrazzi, G (2023) Using Unsupervised ML to Make New Discoveries in Space Data. In: M Madi and O Sokolova (eds), *Artificial Intelligence for Space: Trends, Applications, and Perspectives*, Boca Raton, FL, CRC Press.

Larsen, P (2018) Space Traffic Management Standards, *Journal of Air Law and Commerce*, 83(2): 359–87.

——. (2019). Commercial Operator Liability in the New Space Era, *AJIL Unbound*, 113: 109–13.

Larson, EJL et al (2017) Global Atmospheric Response to Emissions from a Proposed Reusable Space Launch System, *Earth's Future*, 5(1): 37–48.

Larsson, S, Anneroth, M, Felländer, A, Heintz, F and Ångström, RC (2019) *Sustainable AI: An Inventory of the State of Knowledge of Ethical, Social, and Legal Challenges Related to Artificial Intelligence*, Stockholm, AI Sustainability Center.

Le Dantec, CA, Poole, ES and Wyche, SP (2009) Values as Lived Experience, *Proceedings of the 27th International Conference on Human Factors in Computing Systems CHI 09*, New York, ACM Press.

Lee, SI, Celik, S, Logsdon, BA et al (2018) A Machine Learning Approach to Integrate Big Data for Precision Medicine in Acute Myeloid Leukaemia, *Nature Communications*, 9: 42.

Leenes, R, Palmerini, E, Koops, BJ, Bertolini, A, Salvini, P and Lucivero, F (2017) Regulatory Challenges of Robotics: Some Guidelines for Addressing Legal and Ethical Issues, *Law, Innovation and Technology*, 9(1): 1–44.

Lessig, L (1999) *Code and Other Laws of Cyberspace*, New York, Basic Books.

Lessig, L (2004) *Free Culture: The Nature and Future of Creativity*, New York, Penguin Press.

Lim, J (2020) Charting a Human Rights Framework for Outer Space Settlements, *71st International Astronautical Congress (IAC) – The CyberSpace Edition*, October, available at https://www.jusadastra.org/assets/files/IAC-20,E7,2,11,x60311(1).pdf.

Lin, P, Bekey, G and Abney, K (2008) *Autonomous Military Robotics: Risk, Ethics, and Design*, Report for US Department of Navy, Office of Naval Research Ethics + Emerging Sciences Group at California Polytechnic State University, San Luis Obispo, CA.

Liu, K and D Tao (2022) The Roles of Trust, Personalization, Loss of Privacy, and Anthropomorphism in Public Acceptance of Smart Healthcare Services, *Computers in Human Behavior*, 127: 107026.

Litschewski Paulson, B and Paulson, SL (eds) (1997) *Introduction to the Problems of Legal Theory: A Translation of the First Edition of the Reine Rechtslehre or Pure Theory of Law*, Oxford, Oxford University Press.

Lo, SY et al (2022) Robots and Sustainability: Robots as Persuaders to Promote Recycling, *International Journal of Social Robotics*, 14: 1261–72.

Locke, J (2013 [1689]) *Two Treatises of Government*, P Laslett (ed), Cambridge, Cambridge University Press.

Loder, RE (2018) Asteroid Mining: Ecological Jurisprudence beyond Earth, *Virginia Environmental Law Journal*, 36(3): 275–317.

Lohani, S and Joshi, R (2020) Satellite Network Security, *2020 International Conference on Emerging Trends in Communication, Control and Computing (ICONC3)*, Lakshmangarh, India, 1–5.

Luhmann, N (2000) Familiarity, Confidence, Trust: Problems and Alternative. In: D Gambetta (ed), *Trust: Making and Breaking Cooperative Relations*, Department of Sociology, University of Oxford.

Lyall, F and Larsen, PB (2018) *Space Law: A Treatise*, Abingdon, Routledge.

Madi, M and Sokolova, O (eds) (2023) *Artificial Intelligence for Space: Trends, Applications, and Perspectives*, Boca Raton, FL, CRC Press.

Manzione, LL (2002) Multinational Investment in the Space Station: An Outer Space Model for International Cooperation, *American University International Law Review*, 18(2): 507–36.

Martin, A-S and Freeland, S (2021) The Advent of Artificial Intelligence in Space Activities: New Legal Challenges, *Space Policy*, 55: 101408.

Martinez, P (2021) UN COPUOS Guidelines for the Long-Term Sustainability of Outer Space Activities, *Journal of Space Safety Engineering*, 8(1): 98–107.

Masson-Zwaan, T and Sundahl, MJ (2021) The Lunar Legal Landscape: Challenges and Opportunities, *Air and Space Law*, 46(1): 29–56.

Maury, T, Loubet, P, Serrano, SM, Gallice, A and Sonnemann, G (2020) Application of Environmental Life Cycle Assessment (LCA) within the Space Sector: A State of the Art, *Acta Astronautica*, 170: 122–35.

McIlwain, CH (2005) *Constitutionalism: Ancient and Modern*, Clark, NJ, Lawbook Exchange Ltd.

McIntyre, O (2013) The Principles of Integration and Interrelationships in International Law related to Sustainable Development: Sobering Lessons from EU Law. In: L Westra, P Taylor and A Michelot (eds), *Confronting Ecological and Economic Collapse: Ecological Integrity for Law*, Abingdon, Routledge.

McLuhan, M (1994) *Understanding Media: The Extensions of Man*, Boston, MA, MIT Press.

Millwood, S (2023) *The Urgent Need for Regulation of Satellite Mega-constellations in Outer Space*, Cham, Springer.

Mittelstadt, B, Allo, P, Taddeo, M, Wachter, S and Floridi, L (2016) The Ethics of Algorithms: Mapping the Debate, *Big Data & Society*, July–December: 1–21.

Moor, H (1985) What is Computer Ethics?, *Metaphilosophy*, 16: 266–75.

Nader AB, Gavrilov, A and Khalaf, W (2020) Artificial Intelligence Based Methods for Accuracy Improvement of Integrated Navigation Systems during GNSS Signal Outages: An Analytical Overview, *Gyroscopy and Navigation*, 11: 41–58.

NASA (2018) *Systems Engineering Handbook*, US Government Printing Office, NASA/SP-2016-6105 Rev2, 2018.

——. (2020) NASA Selects Companies to Collect Lunar Resources for Artemis Demonstrations, press release 20-118, 3 December, available at www.nasa.gov/press-release/nasaselects-companies-to-collect-lunar-resources-for-artemis-demonstrations.

——. (2023) *NASA's Management of its Artificial Intelligence Capabilities*, Office of Inspector General, IG-23-012, 3 May.

——. (2023) Why We are Going to the Moon, available at https://www.nasa.gov/specials/artemis/#why.

NASA Autonomous Systems – Systems Capability Leadership Team (2018) Autonomous Systems Taxonomy, NASA Technical Reports Server, Document ID 20180003082.

National Academies of Sciences, Engineering, and Medicine (2023) *Thriving in Space: Ensuring the Future of Biological and Physical Sciences Research: A Decadal Survey for 2023-2032*, Washington DC: National Academies Press.

Nelson, JW (2020) The Artemis Accords and the Future of International Space Law, *American Society of International Law*, 24(31), available at https://www.asil.org/insights/volume/24/issue/31/artemis-accords-and-future-international-space-law.

Nesnas, IA, Fesq, LM and Volpe, RA (2021) Autonomy for Space Robots: Past, Present, and Future, *Current Robotics Reports*, 2: 251–63.

Nesvold, E (2023) *Off-Earth: Ethical Questions and Quandaries for Living in Outer Space*, Cambridge, MA, MIT Press.

Neto, O (2021) Outer Space as a Global Commons and the Role of Space Law. In: K-U Schrogl, C Giannopapa and N Antoni (eds), *A Research Agenda for Space Policy*, Cheltenham, Edward Elgar.

Nissenbaum, H (2004) Privacy as Contextual Integrity, *Washington Law Review*, 79(1): 119–58.

Norman, Z and Reiss, MJ (2021) The Emergence of an Environmental Ethos on Luna. In: *The Human Factor in the Settlement of the Moon: An Interdisciplinary Approach*, Cham, Springer International.

O'Brien, D (2020) The Artemis Accords: Repeating the Mistakes of the Age of Exploration, *Space Review*, available at https://www.thespacereview.com/article/3975/1.

O'Neil, C (2016), *Weapons of Math Destruction: How Big Data Increases Inequality and Threatens Democracy*, New York, Random House.

O'Sullivan S et al (2019), Legal, Regulatory, and Ethical Frameworks for Development of Standards in Artificial Intelligence (AI) and Autonomous Robotic Surgery, *International Journal of Medical Robotics and Computer Assisted Surgery*, 15(1): e1968.
Oduntan, G (2016) Aspects of the International Legal Regime concerning Privatization and Commercialization of Space Activities, *Georgetown Journal of International Affairs*, 17(1): 79–90.
——. (2017) Imagine There are No Possessions: Legal and Moral Basis of the Common Heritage Principle in Space Law. In: K de Feyter (ed), *Globalization and Common Responsibilities of States*, Abingdon, Routledge.
Osborn, H (2021) Agreeing on the Rules-of-the-Road: Distilling Building Blocks from Proposed Space Traffic Management Treaties, Guidelines and Standards, *72nd International Astronautical Congress (IAC)*, Dubai, United Arab Emirates.
Pagallo, U (2008) *La tutela della privacy negli Stati Uniti d'America e in Europa: modelli giuridici a confronto*, Milan, Giuffrè.
——. (2010) As Law Goes by: Topology, Ontology, Evolution. In: *AI Approaches to the Complexity of Legal Systems. Complex Systems, the Semantic Web, Ontologies, Argumentation, and Dialogue. AICOL 2009*, Berlin, Springer.
——. (2010) Robotrust and Legal Responsibility, *Knowledge Technology & Policy*, 23: 367–79.
——. (2011) Designing Data Protection Safeguards Ethically, *Information*, 2(2): 247–65.
——. (2011) Robots of Just War: A Legal Perspective, *Philosophy and Technology*, 24: 307–23.
——. (2013) *The Laws of Robots: Crimes, Contracts, and Torts*, Dordrecht, Springer.
——. (2013) Online Security and the Protection of Civil Rights: A Legal Overview, *Philosophy and Technology*, 26: 381–95.
——. (2015) Good Onlife Governance: On Law, Spontaneous Orders, and Design. In: L Floridi (ed), *The Onlife Manifesto: Being Human in a Hyperconnected Era*, Springer, Dordrecht.
——. (2015) The Realignment of the Sources of the Law and their Meaning in an Information Society, *Philosophy & Technology*, 28: 57–73.
——. (2017) From Automation to Autonomous Systems: A Legal Phenomenology with Problems of Accountability, *IJCAI International Joint Conference on Artificial Intelligence*, 17–23.
——. (2017) LegalAIze: Tackling the Normative Challenges of Artificial Intelligence and Robotics through the Secondary Rules of Law. In: M Corrales, M Fenwick and N Forgó (eds), *New Technology, Big Data and the Law: Perspectives in Law, Business and Innovation*, Singapore, Springer.
——. (2018) Algo-rhythms and the Beat of the Legal Drum. *Philosophy and Technology*, 31: 507–24.
——. (2018) Apples, Oranges, Robots: Four Misunderstandings in Today's Debate on the Legal Status of AI Systems, *Philosophical Transactions of the Royal Society A: Mathematical, Physical and Engineering Sciences*, 376(2133): 20180168.
——. (2018) Vital, Sophia, and Co: The Quest for the Legal Personhood of Robots, *Information*, 9(9): 230.
——. (2021) The Governance of AI and its Legal Context-Dependency. In: J Cowls and J Morley (eds), *The 2020 Yearbook of the Digital Ethics Lab. Digital Ethics Lab Yearbook*, Cham, Springer.
——. (2022) The Politics of Data in EU Law: Will it Succeed?, *DISO*, 1: 20.
——. (2022), *Il dovere alla salute. Sul rischio di sottoutilizzo dell'intelligenza artificiale in ambito sanitario*, Milan, Mimesis.
Pagallo, U and Bassi, E (2020) E The Governance of Unmanned Aircraft Systems (UAS): Aviation Law, Human Rights, and the Free Movement of Data in the EU, *Minds & Machines*, 30: 439–55.
Pagallo, U and Durante, M (2016) The Pros and Cons of Legal Automation and its Governance, *European Journal of Risk Regulation*, 7(2): 323–34.
Pagallo, U, Bassi, E and Durante, M (2023) The Normative Challenges of AI in Outer Space: Law, Ethics, and the Realignment of Terrestrial Standards. *Philosophy & Technolology*, 36: 23.
Pagallo, U, Ciani Sciolla, J and Durante, M (2022) The environmental challenges of AI in EU Law: Lessons Learned from the Artificial Intelligence Act (AIA) with its Drawbacks, *Transforming Government: People, Process and Policy*, 16(3): 359–76.
Pagallo U and Durante, M (2022) The Good, the Bad, and the Invisible with its Opportunity Costs:, *J*, 5(1): 139–49.

Pal, S, Mukhopadhyay, S and Suryadeyara, N (2021) Development and Progress in Sensors and Technologies for Human Emotion Recognition, *Sensors*, 21(16): 5554.

Paliouras, Z (2014) The Non-appropriation Principle: The Grundnorm of International Space Law, *Leiden Journal of International*, 27(1): 37–54.

Paseri, L, Varrette, S and Bouvry, P (2021) Protection of Personal Data in High Performance Computing Platform for Scientific Research Purposes. In: N Gruschka, LFC Antunes, K Rannenberg and P Drogkaris (eds), *Privacy Technologies and Policy*, Cham, Springer.

Pavesi, G and Wouters, J (2023) The Final Frontier? The European Union and the Governance of Outer Space, *Journal of European Integration*, 45(8): 1199–217.

Pečujlić, AN (2023) *The Space Law Stalemate: Legal Mechanisms for Developing New Norms*, New York, Routledge.

Pedell, S, Constantin, K, Muñoz, D and L Sterling (2022) Designing Meaningful, Beneficial and Positive Human Robot Interactions with Older Adults for Increased Wellbeing During Care Activities. In: CP Lin et al (eds), *Handbook of Artificial Intelligence in Healthcare. Intelligent Systems Reference Library*, Cham, Springer.

Pekkanen, SM (2019) Governing the New Space Race, *American Journal of International Law*, 113: 92–97.

Pelton, JN and Madry, S (2023) Space Systems, Quantum Computers, Big Data and Sustainability. In: M Madi and O Sokolova (eds), *Artificial Intelligence for Space: Trends, Applications, and Perspectives*, Boca Raton, FL, CRC Press.

Petersen, T (2020) Deep Learning Algorithms Helping to Clear Space Junk from Our Skies, *EPFL*, October, available at https://actu.epfl.ch/news/deep-learning-algorithms-helping-to-clear-space-ju/.

Plato (1945) *The Republic*, Francis MacDonald Cornford (ed), Oxford, Oxford University Press.

Plutarch (1967) *Plutarch's Lives*, B Perrin (trans), Cambridge, MA, Harvard University Press.

Pocar, F (2012) An Introduction to the PCA's Optional Rules for Arbitration of Disputes Relating to Outer Space Activities, *Journal of Space Law*, 38: 171–78.

Posner, R (1988) The Jurisprudence of Skepticism, *Michigan Law Review*, 86(5): 827–91.

Potter, NN (2002) *How Can I Be Trusted? A Virtue Theory of Trustworthiness*, Lanham, MD: Rowman & Littlefield.

Pritchard-Kelly, R (2023) WRC-23 on the Horizon: Large Satellite Constellations, ITU Issues, and Industry Perspective, *Air and Space Law*, 48: 179–90.

Pučujlić, AN (2023) *The Space Law Stalemate: Legal Mechanisms for Developing New Norms*, New York, Routledge.

Radanliev, P et al (2020) Design of a Dynamic and Self-Adapting System, Supported with Artificial Intelligence, Machine Learning and Real-Time Intelligence for Predictive Cyber Risk Analytics in Extreme Environments, *Safety in Extreme Environments*, 2: 219–30.

Rajkomar P, Dean, J and Kohane, I (2019) Machine Learning in Medicine, *New England Journal of Medicine*, 380(14): 1347–58.

Reinert, AP (2020) Updating the Liability Regime in Outer Space: Why Spacefaring Companies Should Be Internationally Liable for Their Space Objects, *William & Mary Law Review*, 62(1): 324–56.

Ricolfi, M (2022) Regulating de Facto Powers: Shifting the Focus. In: G Ghidini and V Falce (eds), *Reforming Intellectual Property*, Cheltenham, Edward Elgar.

Roberts, JJ (2015) Drunk Man Arrested in Latest Outburst of Anti-robot Violence, *Fortune*, 8 September, available at https://fortune.com/2015/09/08/robot-assault/.

Roberts, TG (2023) Cislunar Space Situational Awareness. In: H Khera and H Vertadier (eds), *Lunar Policy Handbook*, Moon Dialogs.

Rodríguez-Doncel, V, Palmirani, M, Araszkiewicz, M, Casanovas, P, Pagallo, U and Sartor, G (eds) (2021) *AI Approaches to the Complexity of Legal Systems XI–XII*, Cham, Springer.

Rohde, F, Gossen, M, Wagner, J and Santarius, T (2021) Sustainability Challenges of Artificial Intelligence and Policy Implications, *Ökologisches Wirtschaften – Fachzeitschrift*, 36: 36–40.

Rosenau, JM and Czempiel, EO (1992) *Governance without Government: Order and Change in World Politics*, Cambridge, Cambridge University Press.

Russell, B (1972) *The Philosophy of Logical Atomism*, New York, Routledge.
Russell, S and Norvig, P (2014) *Artificial Intelligence: A Modern Approach*, New Delhi, Pearson.
Sacco, R (1991) Legal Formants: A Dynamic Approach to Comparative Law, *American Journal of Comparative Law*, 39(1): 1–34.
Salazar, JF and Gorman, A (eds) (2023) *The Routledge Handbook of Social Studies of Outer Space*, Abingdon, Taylor & Francis.
Salkind, NJ (2010) *Encyclopedia of Research Design*. London, SAGE Publications.
Salmeri, A (2023) Infrastructure Activities. In: H Khera and H Vertadier (eds), *Lunar Policy Handbook*, Moon Dialogs.
Sandoz, Y, Swinarski, C and Zimmermann, B (eds) (1987) *Commentary on the Additional Protocols of 8 June 1977 to the Geneva Conventions of 12 August 1949*, International Committee of the Red Cross, Geneva, Martinus Nijholf.
Santoni de Sio, FS et al (2022) Realising Meaningful Human Control over Automated Driving Systems: A Multidisciplinary Approach, *Minds & Machines*, DOI: 10.1007/s11023-022-09608-8.
Sanyal, J and Hashwani, K (2022) Changing Landscape of Satellite Communication Laws in India, *International Bar Association*, London, available at https://www.ibanet.org/changing-landscape-of-satellite-communication-laws#:~:text=%5B1%5D%20The%20Satcom%20Policy%20was,operating%20an%20Indian%20satellite%20system.
Sartor, G (2009) Cognitive Automata and the Law: Electronic Contracting and the Intentionality of Software Agents, *Artificial Intelligence and Law*, 17(4): 253–90.
Saunders, PC and Lutes, CD (2007) China's ASAT Test: Motivations and Implications, *Joint Force Quarterly*, 46(3), available at apps.dtic.mil/sti/pdfs/ADA517485.pdf.
Schaefer, M (2015) The Need for Federal Preemption and International Negotiations Regarding Liability Caps and Waivers of Liability in the US Commercial Space Industry, *Berkeley Journal of International Law*, 33(1): 223–73.
Shapiro, SJ (2007) The 'Hart-Dworkin' Debate: A Short Guide for the Perplexed, *Public Law and Legal Theory Working Paper Series*, 77, Michigan Law School.
Scheutz, M and Arnold, T (2016) Are We Ready for Sex Robots?, *2016 11th ACM/IEEE International Conference on Human-Robot Interaction (HRI)*, 351–58.
Schingler, JK (2020) Imagining Safety Zones: Implications and Open Questions, *Space Review*, available at https://www.thespacereview.com/article/3962/1.
Schmaus, P et al (2023). Extending the Knowledge Driven Approach for Scalable Autonomy Teleoperation of a Robotic Avatar, *2023 IEEE Aerospace Conference*.
Schmitt, M (2017) *Tallinn Manual 2.0 on the International Law Applicable to Cyber Operations. NATO Cooperative Cyber Defence Centre of Excellence*, Cambridge, Cambridge University Press.
Schulz, L and Glassmeier, KH (2021) On the Anthropogenic and Natural Injection of Matter into Earth's Atmosphere, *Advances in Space Research*, 67(3), 1002–25.
Seneca (2014) *Medea*, AJ Boyle (ed), Oxford, Oxford University Press.
Shaw, MN (2021) *International Law*, 9th edn, Cambridge, Cambridge University Press.
Shionoya, Y (2001). Trust as a Virtue. In: Y Shionoya and K Yagi (eds), *Competition, Trust, and Cooperation*, Berlin, Springer.
Siemuri, A, Kuusniemi, H, Elmusrati, MS, Välisuo, P and Shamsuzzoha, A (2021) Machine Learning Utilization in GNSS: Use Cases, Challenges and Future Applications, *2021 International Conference on Localization and GNSS (ICL-GNSS)*, Tampere, Finland, 1–6.
Sills, J, Gilbert, A, Bazilian, M and Sowers, G (2020) US Space Policy: Multilateral Mining, *Science*, 370(6520): 1045–46.
Silverstein, B (2023) China's Space Dream is a Legal Nightmare, *Foreign Policy*, April, available at https://foreignpolicy.com/2023/04/21/china-space-law-treaty-djibouti-obock-launch-facility-ost.
Simon, H (1996 [1969]) *The Sciences of Artificial*, Cambridge, MA, MIT Press.
Singer, P (2009) *Wired for War: The Robotics Revolution and Conflict in the 21st Century*, London, Penguin.

Smith, M (2015) International Institute of Space Law OK with US Asteroid Mining Law, *Spacepolicyonline*, 24 December, available at https://spacepolicyonline.com/news/international-institute-of-space-law-ok-with-u-s-asteroid-mining-law.

Smith, WA (2021) Using the Artemis Accords to Build Customary International Law: A Vision for a US-Centric Good Governance Regime in Outer Space, *Journal of Air Law and Commerce*, 86(4), available at https://scholar.smu.edu/cgi/viewcontent.cgi?article=4189&context=jalc.

Smith, M, and Miller, S (2022) The Ethical Application of Biometric Facial Recognition Technology, *AI & Society*, 37: 167–75.

Solum, LB (1992) Legal Personhood for Artificial Intelligence, *North Carolina Law Review*, 70: 1231–87.

SpaceTech Analytics (2022) *SpaceTech Industry Year 2021*, available at https://www.spacetech.global/spacetech-industry-year-overview-2021.

Sparrow, R and Howard, M (2017) When Human Beings are Like Drunk Robots: Driverless Vehicles, Ethics, and the Future of Transport, *Transportation Research Part C: Emerging Technologies*, 80: 206–15.

St John, D (2012) The Trouble with Westphalia in Space: The State-Centric Liability Regime, *Denver Journal International Law & Policy*, 40: 686–713.

Starke, JG (1999) Monism and Dualism in the Theory of International Law. In: SL Paulson (ed), *Normativity and Norms: Critical Perspectives on Kelsenian Themes*, Oxford, Oxford Academic.

Steele, J (2021) Luxembourg and the Exploitation of Outer Space, *Nottingham Law Journal*, 29(1): 32–42.

Steer, C and Stephens, D (2021) International Humanitarian Law and its Application in Outer Space. In: C Steer and M Hersch (eds), *War and Peace in Outer Space*, Oxford, Oxford University Press.

Stessens, G (2000) *Money-Laundering: A New International Law Enforcement Model*, Cambridge, Cambridge University Press.

Stirn, A (2020) Do NASA's Lunar Exploration Rules Violate Space Law?, *Scientific American*, 12 November, available at https://www.scientificamerican.com/article/do-nasas-lunar-exploration-rules-violate-space-law.

Stimers, P (2020) The President's Space Resources Executive Order: A Step in the Right Direction, *Space Review*, available at https://www.thespacereview.com/article/3925/1.

Stimers, P and James, A (2021) The Artemis Accords after One Year of International Progress, *Space Review*, available at https://www.thespacereview.com/article/4267/1. Accessed on 28 June 2023.

Su, J (2017) Legality of Unilateral Exploitation of Space Resources under International Law, *International and Comparative Law Quarterly*, 66(4): 991–1008.

Sullins, JP (2020) Trust in Robots. In: J Simon (ed), *The Routledge Handbook of Trust and Philosophy*, New York, Routledge.

Taddeo, M (2010) Modelling Trust in Artificial Agents, A First Step toward the Analysis of e-Trust, *Minds & Machines*, 20: 243–57.

Taddeo, M and Blanchard, AA (2022) Comparative Analysis of the Definitions of Autonomous Weapons Systems, *Science and Engineering Ethics*, 28: 37.

Taghdiri, A (2014) Flags of Convenience and the Commercial Space Flight Industry: The Inadequacy of Current International Law to Address the Opportune Registration of Space Vehicles in Flag States, *Boston University Journal of Science & Technology Law*, 19: 405–32.

Tan, D (2000) Towards New Regime for the Protection of Outer Space as the Province of All Mankind, *Yale Journal of International Law*, 25(1): 145–94.

Tepper, E (2018) Structuring the Discourse on the Exploitation of Space Resources: Between Economic and Legal Commons, *Space Policy*, 49: 1–12.

Tianliang, X, Yaoliang, L, Wuchao, K and Renzhao, C (2020) *Science of Military Strategy*, Beijing, National Defense University Press.

Tricco, G (2023) The Upcoming of Iris2: Bridging the Digital Divide and Strengthening the Role of the EU in International Space Law, *Journal of Law, Market & Innovation*, 2(2): 17–42.

Tronchetti, F (2008) The Non-appropriation Principle as a Structural Norm of International Law: A New Way of Interpreting Article II of the Outer Space Treaty, *Air and Space Law*, 33(3): 277–305.
——. (2013) The PCA Rules for Dispute Settlement in Outer Space: A Significant Step Forward, *Space Policy*, 29(3): 181–89.
——. (2015) The Space Resource Exploration and Utilization Act: A Move Forward or a Step Back?, *Space Policy*, 34: 6–10.
Tsetskhladze, GR (ed) (2018) *Greek Colonisation*, Leiden, Brill.
Tutton, R (2021). Sociotechnical Imaginaries and Techno-optimism: Examining Outer Space Utopias of Silicon Valley, *Science as Culture*, 30(3): 416–39.
Umbrello, S and Balistreri, M (2023) Human Enhancement and Reproductive Ethics on Generation Ships, *Argumenta*: 1–15.
UNIDIR (2014) *The Weaponization of Increasingly Autonomous Technologies: Considering How Meaningful Human Control Might Move the Discussion Forward*, Geneva, UN.
UNGA (1992) *Principles Relevant to the Use of Nuclear Power Sources in Outer Space*, Resolution 47/68 of the UN General Assembly, available at https://digitallibrary.un.org/record/159141?ln=en.
UN Office for Outer Space Affairs (UNOOSA) (2019) *Annual Report 2018*, United Nations, June, available at https://www.unoosa.org/documents/pdf/annualreport/UNOOSA_Annual_Report_2018.pdf.
——. (2023) Online Index of Objects Launched into Outer Space, available at https://www.unoosa.org/oosa/osoindex/search-ng.jspx?lf_id=.
US Government (2023) *National Low Earth Orbit Research and Development Strategy*, available at https://www.whitehouse.gov/wp-content/uploads/2023/03/NATIONAL-LEO-RD-STRATEGY-033123.pdf.
Van de Poel, I (2020) Embedding Values in Artificial Intelligence (AI) Systems, *Minds and Machines*, 30(3): 385–409.
Van Wynsberghe, A (2021) Sustainable AI: AI for Sustainability and the Sustainability of AI, *AI and Ethics*, 1: 213–18.
Vernile, A (2018) *The Rise of Private Actors in the Space Sector*, Dordrecht, Springer.
Viikari, L (2008) *The Environmental Element in Space Law: Assessing the Present and Charting the Future*, Leiden, Martinus Nijhoff.
Vinuesa, R et al (2020) The Role of Artificial Intelligence in Achieving the Sustainable Development Goals, *Nature Communications*, 11(233): 1–10.
Von der Dunk, FG (2013) Outer Space Law Principles and Privacy. In: D Leung and R Purdy (eds), *Evidence from Earth Observation Satellites: Emerging Legal Issues*, Leiden, Brill.
——. (2015) Legal Aspects of Satellite Constellations. In: FG von der Dunk (ed), *Handbook of Space Law*, Cheltenham, Edward Elgar.
Wallach, W and Allen, C (2008) *Moral Machines: Teaching Robots Right from Wrong*, Oxford, Oxford University Press.
Wang, D et al (2016) Deep Learning for Identifying Metastatic Breast Cancer, *arXiv preprint arXiv:160605718*.
Warf, B (2007) Geopolitics of the Satellite Industry, *Tijdschrift voor economische en sociale geografie*, 98(3): 385–97.
Weber, M (1978) *Economy and Society*, 2 vols, G Roth and C Wittich (eds), Berkeley, University of California Press.
Weinersmith, K and Weinersmith, Z (2023) *A City on Mars: Can We Settle Space, Should We Settle Space, and Have We Really Thought This Through?*, Toronto, Penguin Press.
Weng, YH, Gulyaeva, S, Winter, J, Slavescu, A and Hirata, Y (2020) HRI for Legal Validation: On Embodiment and Data Protection, *Proceedings of the 29th IEEE International Symposium on Robot and Human Interactive Communication (RO-MAN)*, 1387–94.
Werner, D (2020) Aerospace Corp Raises Questions about Pollutants Produced during Satellite and Rocket Re-entry, *Space News*, 11 December, available at https://spacenews.com/aerospace-agu-reentry-pollution.

White House (2020) *Encouraging International Support for the Recovery and Use of Space Resources*, Executive Order 13914, available at https://trumpwhitehouse.archives.gov/wp-content/uploads/2020/04/Fact-Sheet-on-EO-Encouraging-International-Support-for-the-Recovery-and-Use-of-Space-Resources.pdf.

Wildhaber, I (2008) Artificial Intelligence and Robotics, the Workplace, and Workplace-Related Law. In: W Barfield and U Pagallo (eds), *Research Handbook on the Law of Artificial Intelligence*, Cheltenham, Edward Elgar.

Wilson, C and van der Velden, M (2022) Sustainable AI: An Integrated Model to Guide Public Sector Decision-Making, *Technology in Society*, 68: 101926.

Wong, H (1998) The 'Paper Satellite' Chase: The ITU Prepares for its Final Exam in Resolution, *Journal of Air Law and Commerce*, 18: 849–79.

World Economic Forum (2018), *Harnessing Artificial Intelligence for the Earth*, available at https://www.pwc.com/gx/en/services/sustainability/publications/ai-for-the-earth.html.

Worster, W (2013) The Transformation of Quantity into Quality: Critical Mass in the Formation of Customary International Law, *Boston University International Law Journal*, 31(1): 1–74.

Young, R (2001) *Postcolonialism: An Historical Introduction*, Oxford, Blackwell.

Zannoni, D (2020) The Dilemma between the Freedom to Use and the Proscription against Appropriating Outer Space and Celestial Bodies, *Chinese Journal of International Law*, 19(2): 329–58.

Zawieska, K and Duffy, BR (2014) Human-Robot Exploration, *The 23rd IEEE International Symposium on Robot and Human Interactive Communication*, 808–13.

Zelnio, RJ (2007) Whose Jurisdiction over the US Commercial Satellite Industry? Factors Affecting International Security and Competition, *Space Policy*, 23(4): 221–33.

Ziemblicki, B and Oralova, Y (2021) Private Entities in Outer Space Activities: Liability Regime Reconsidered, *Space Policy*, 56: 101427.

Zlotowski, J et al (2015) Anthropomorphism: Opportunities and Challenges in Human-Robot Interaction, *International Journal of Social Robotics*, 7: 347–60.

Zubrin, R (1999) *Entering Space*, New York, Jeremy P Tarcher/Putnam.

Zuiderwijk, A, Chen, Y-C and Salem, F (2021) Implications of the Use of Artificial Intelligence in Public Governance: A Systematic Literature Review and a Research Agenda, *Government Information Quarterly*, 38: 101577.

INDEX

www.ingramcontent.com/pod-product-compliance
Ingram Content Group UK Ltd.
Pitfield, Milton Keynes, MK11 3LW, UK
UKHW020809290926
15470UKWH00003B/1050

9 781509 976188